No Way Through

Great Glen Railway Schemes

John McGregor

HIGHLAND RAILWAY SOCIETY

The Caledonian Canal, seen from high above Invergarry station, crosses the Great Glen's almost imperceptible watershed. Loch Lochy (far left) drains to Loch Linnhe and the Firth of Lorne; Loch Oich (right), fed by Loch Garry and Loch Quoich, drains to Loch Ness and ultimately the Beauly Firth. Invergarry village, at the mouth of Glen Garry, lies some distance away.   (LMS series)

Front Cover: The piers of the River Oich viaduct, relics of the Invergarry & Fort Augustus Railway, are a reminder that construction had its challenges; they contrast with spacious Fort Augustus station, now long demolished, in its North British years.

(John Gray and LGRP respectively)

Dedicated to Professor Ian Donnachie and Dr Alastair Durie, who guided me
towards Scotland's railway politics – they are both missed.

© John McGregor 2021
ISBN: 978-0-9927311-2-0

Published by the Highland Railway Society : www.hrsoc.org.uk.

Printed in the United Kingdom by Henry Ling Limited at the Dorset Press
Dorchester, DT1 1HD

CONTENTS

Acknowledgements

Neither my doctoral research nor the book based upon it (*The West Highland Railway: Plans, Politics and People*) dealt thoroughly with the Great Glen, and I am grateful to the Highland Railway Society for suggesting a complementary study, now some four years in the making.

I have attempted to set the story in the whole railway politics of the western Highlands, and the debts incurred along the way are many. Both Ewan Crawford of RailScot and Hege Hernæs, my colleague on Glenfinnan Station Museum Trust, have offered help and encouragement. My wife Christine has helped in the down-to-earth business of checking and organising. Special thanks are due to Professor Annie Tindley of Newcastle University for commenting on an early draft, chapter by chapter, and to Nick Jones, another Glenfinnan colleague, who has not only read but also re-read the entire text.

I have benefitted from the insights of others, not least Peter Fletcher and Neil Sinclair – over a dozen years and more, the former has unstintingly shared the results of his own wide-ranging investigations. Doug Watts of the Midland & Great Northern Joint Railway Society has enlarged my knowledge of the background to the Glasgow & North Western promotion, and I must put on record also the assistance of the late Alan Johnstone, who organised two expeditions to photograph a range of locations on that 160-mile, might-have-been, route. Donald Cattanach has shared the findings of his extensive research into the career of North British Railway chairman, George Wieland; and this has shaped my treatment of Wieland's relations with the Invergarry & Fort Augustus Company. Moreover, Donald has alerted me to several other sources of which I was unaware.

For photographs generously provided in the past and re-employed in this volume, I am grateful to Doug Carmichael, Alex Gillespie, John Gray, Tom Noble, John Sinclair, Hamish Stevenson and Douglas Yuill. Materials previously made available by the Scottish Railway Preservation Society, with the guidance of their then archivist Julia Stephen, have also seen another outing. Photographs are individually acknowledged. BRB material held by National Records of Scotland is used with permission from Department for Transport, under Open Government Licence.

I am bound to single out Keith Fenwick, who undertook to ready the book for publication in a form acceptable to the Highland Railway Society. Even as a mechanical task, this would have been a huge labour, entailing much patience; but I am also indebted to Keith for accessing a large proportion of the photographs and for finding, modifying or preparing all the maps. Moreover, he has corrected errors, provided additional information and kept a very necessary eye on style. Any remaining errors are mine alone.

John McGregor, November 2021

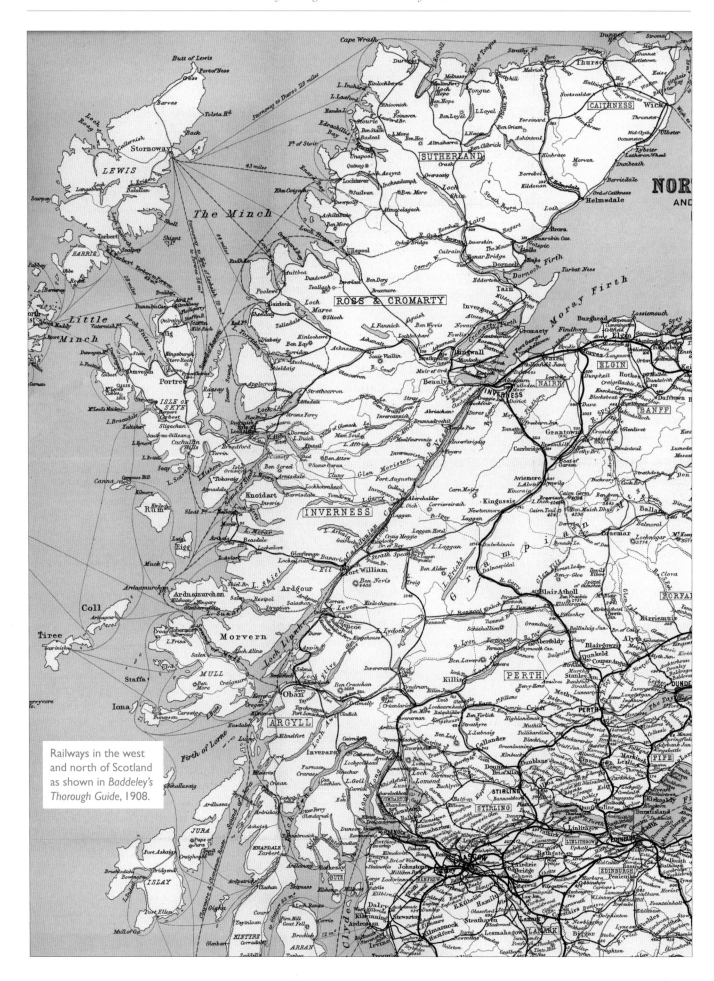

Railways in the west and north of Scotland as shown in *Baddeley's Thorough Guide*, 1908.

CHAPTER ONE

BACKGROUND: THE LATE-COMING WEST HIGHLAND RAILWAY C1840-89

The promoters of early railway schemes for the North of Scotland, over-optimistic, naïve or fraudulent, frequently downplayed the difficulties of construction. But a railway following the Caledonian Canal was at least plausible and, on of the face of things, the shortest line from the Central Belt to the North ran by Loch Lomond, Glen Coe and the Great Glen. In the 1880s and '90s protagonists of a new westerly railway to Inverness would assert that this "direct" and "natural" route had been lost in the troubled aftermath of the 1840s Mania, with the unfortunate result that the Tay-and-Spey line conceived by engineer Joseph Mitchell had prevailed instead.[1] The facts told otherwise. Too bold to win approval in 1846 but authorised with some alterations fifteen years later, Mitchell's Inverness & Perth Junction Railway for the most part followed the grain of the country. Despite long ascents to Druimuachdar summit and a testing up-and-over from Strathspey into Moray, it offered relatively easy building and would be completed with remarkable speed (1861-3). A comparable trunk route through the western Highlands could not have been achieved without much heavier works, while the seemingly easy conditions offered by the Great Glen were deceptive, as time would tell. Moreover, the Scottish Grand Junction Railway and the Caledonian Northern Direct Railway, the only westerly projects of real substance which the Mania produced, had Crianlarich as their primary goal, leaving the next steps uncertain (see panel below). The cruciform Scottish Grand Junction, if fully completed, would have conjoined an east-west, Stirling–to–Oban arm with a northward arm from Loch Lomond into Breadalbane by Bridge of Orchy, Rannoch and Loch Ericht, meeting Mitchell's route at Dalwhinnie. There was no declared intention to strike north-west for Glen Coe and the Great Glen, and it is likely that a connection into Strathtay via Killin would have been substituted for the Rannoch and Ericht line; this was redundant in any case once Parliament had rejected the Inverness & Perth Junction in its original form.

Popular histories rightly concentrate on the successful revival of Mitchell's project, which greatly improved on

Among the vaguer projects of the 1840s was the proposed Caledonian Canal and Great North West of Scotland Railway – perhaps the only Mania scheme to specify a Great Glen line in any detail. No serious survey can have taken place: north from Loch Lomond it followed the then parliamentary road to Kingshouse, drove (improbably) through the Mamores to Fort William (like the old military road), then exactly paralleled the waterway to Inverness.

the circuitous easterly route to Inverness via Aberdeen, in operation from 1858. In intimate association with the Inverness & Aberdeen Junction Company, which reached as far as Keith, the reinvented Inverness & Perth Junction was modified to turn south from Forres instead of Nairn. Thereby it tapped the traffic of Moray and Banffshire, outbidding the rival Morayshire & Perthshire Direct Junction Railway (Elgin to Strathmore via Rothes, Tomintoul, Glenshee and Strathisla). It subsumed the Perth & Dunkeld Railway (opened in 1856) and by this means obtained running powers, from Stanley Junction into Perth, over the Scottish North Eastern Railway. Aberdeen interests were inevitably hostile, arguing (though to no avail) that a 100-mile line across the Grampians was unnecessary – instead, through traffic by the existing easterly route could be expedited by better connections within the city or by an inland cut-off north of Stonehaven. No serious westerly alternative was in prospect. Reduced to an Ardlui–Oban scheme and reliant on the Loch Lomond steamers, the Scottish Grand Junction Railway had been abandoned for lack of funds in 1852; and subsequent efforts in this quarter would concentrate on finding a better line to Oban, with no water break.

Mitchell, whose original vision embraced Lochaber, had envisaged an eventual branch from the upper Spey, on his Perth–Inverness route, to Fort William and Ballachulish.[2] Something of the sort indeed appeared in 1862-3 in the shape of the proposed "Fort William Railway", surveyed by Thomas Bouch (later of first Tay Bridge notoriety). Diverging from the Inverness & Perth Junction at Etteridge or Newtonmore, the line would have run by Loch Laggan and Glen Spean. It might have continued through Corpach, at the southern end of the Caledonian Canal, to a harbour on the west coast. The aspiring promoters were for the most part Lochaber landowners. They sought the benevolent sympathy of all the companies in the South who stood to gain contributory traffic at Perth, and they looked above all to the Inverness companies for a substantial capital input and a working and maintenance agreement. But plans were already afoot for what became the Dingwall & Skye Railway, across Ross-shire to Loch Carron and Loch Alsh, which Mitchell had come to prefer.[3]

The Inverness & Perth Junction could give no immediate assistance, as chairman Thomas Bruce explained to Cameron of Lochiel, who represented the Lochaber proprietors:

[With] our line unfinished and ...a great many things to adjust we cannot undertake at present any further pecuniary liabilities [but] I have a great interest in your undertaking ...and I can only hope you will go on.[4]

Alexander Matheson, who chaired the Inverness & Aberdeen

Junction, had already replied in very cautious and on the whole discouraging tones (see also panel on right). Practical help for any new project was at least twelve months away, and that included the Dingwall & Skye:

> We are in debt and [cannot] borrow any more money... We shall be able in the course of another year to dispose of [all] our shares and [only] then it will be a question ...how far we could assist the Lochaber line beyond working it... There are parties in the Isle of Skye and on the west coast of Ross-shire who are very anxious for a railway ...to Kyleakin Ferry but they are in much the same position as regards funds and nothing will be done [for them] for the present.[5]

At the half-yearly meeting of the Inverness & Aberdeen shareholders on 27th October 1863, Matheson stated that to undertake more obligations might compromise the company's independence. As for the proposed Fort William Railway, Mitchell now held that Hebridean traffic was better channelled by Dingwall and Inverness than by Fort William, where one day another company might penetrate from the South and divert valuable business. His opinion, however, was not decisive. At the time it mattered more that the resources of Lochiel and his fellow landlords were insufficient to sustain a promotion – and they declined to look further. By seeking additional finance on the general money market, as Bouch urged them to do,[6] they might have kept their project alive, perhaps to be gathered into the united Highland Company (below).

* * *

Amalgamations became the keynote of the 1860s. The powerful Caledonian Railway and the more ramshackle North British both emerged much expanded;* and in 1865 the Inverness & Aberdeen Junction, which had already absorbed the Inverness & Nairn and Inverness & Ross-shire, joined formally with the Inverness & Perth Junction to create the Highland Railway. The Dingwall & Skye Railway (authorised in 1865) would open to Stromeferry on Loch Carron in 1870, some way short of the intended terminus at Kyle of Lochalsh; it merged with the Highland ten years later. The Far North route, extending the Inverness & Ross-shire Railway, would be completed to Wick and Thurso by 1874, though its ultimate components, the Sutherland Railway, the Duke of Sutherland's Railway and the Sutherland & Caithness Railway, were to keep their nominal independence into the 1880s. Meanwhile the Highland's Perth–Inverness main line had become the great artery of northern Scotland, by which Caledonian and North British alike, and their respective English partners, all sent through traffic. The Highland's advance and consolidation hasdbeen largely unimpeded, save that at Keith, Elgin and Boat of Garten they marched uncomfortably with the Great North of Scotland Company, whose original goal had been Inverness – and the disgruntled Great North still hoped for an independent line, or at least running powers, onwards from Elgin.

From 1866 the Highland's access to Perth from Stanley was controlled by the enlarged Caledonian Company, who

---

* The North British Company acquired the Edinburgh, Perth & Dundee in 1862 and the Edinburgh & Glasgow in 1865; the Caledonian acquired the Scottish Central in 1865 and the Scottish North Eastern in 1866.

> The Caithness people [want] a line to Wick; the people of Fort William want one to Kingussie; and the people of Skye are urging one from Dingwall to the West coast... My answer...has been, that if they subscribe the capital and make the lines, they will find us anxious to afford them all reasonable assistance and encouragement...to complete them, and [we shall] work them afterwards...
>
> *Alexander Matheson, chairman, Inverness & Aberdeen Junction Railway, 27th October 1863 reported in* Herepath's Railway Journal, *4th November 1863.*

waived their right to tolls in return for an assured and generous share of exchange traffic. The Caledonian thus became the Highland's strong (but sometimes overbearing) ally. Though disadvantaged, the North British might have retaliated – after 1865 their system bestrode the Central Belt, with outposts at Balloch, Helensburgh and (from 1882) Aberfoyle, and they had inherited the pretensions of the Edinburgh & Glasgow Railway to expand into the Highlands. Here, clearly, was an incentive for a westerly advance to Inverness; but the bits-and-pieces North British of the 1870s did not prove adventurous. Overcoming the water-breaks of Forth and Tay was a formidable task, not completed till 1890 and inhibiting other initiatives; much of the company's energy was devoted instead to consolidating their earlier heartlands in the Borders and Fife.

Nervous for their regional monopoly, the Highland chose to refine the otherwise outdated doctrine that railway acts were inviolable contracts, immune from further interference by the state.[7] Unlike the Caledonian and North British when first formed, the original Inverness companies had attracted little English capital.[8] Their principal subscribers were public-spirited landowners, who, as Highland Railway shareholders, continued to make sacrifices in order that the backward districts beyond Inverness might enjoy a year-round service of barely profitable trains. In short, the Highland Company, on their own valuation at least, thoroughly exemplified "private risk for public benefit" and had earned Parliament's protection against piratical invasion by any aggressor who looked to cream-off their hard-won profitable business. That Parliament not infrequently endorsed more-or-less wandering railways gave the Highland a supporting argument. Their lines north and west of Inverness were "optimum" *because* they were indirect – laid out to touch the places where scanty traffic might be concentrated and economic development gradually stimulated. Cut-offs, even an ambitious "direct" line from Central Scotland to Inverness, might be justified one distant day. To offer these prematurely would be irresponsible and must reduce both victim and attacker to beggary.

The Highland system certainly qualified as "optimum" in the sense just described. Indeed, the term was applicable, in some degree, to their Perth–Inverness main line, which drew additional traffic from the Moray frontier where Highland and Great North of Scotland collided. The company's internal revenues, though boosted by the needs of sporting estates, were barely adequate during much of the year. Solvency required that through traffic on the Perth route be maximised – passengers, mail, general goods, fish and livestock. But

Sheltered Oban bay (from which the town took its name) was early a target for railway promoters. Completion of the cross-country line from Callander in 1880, after many difficulties, accelerated Oban's development as a tourist centre and a principal port, year-round, for the Hebrides This photograph shows the station as later enlarged.   (A B MacLeod)

detouring by Forres meant a Glasgow–Inverness journey of over 200 miles, and a shorter through line in rival hands might spell disaster – as much from inevitable rate-reductions in the face of competition as from business lost. Installed as chairman of the united Highland Railway, Alexander Matheson had been blunt:

> [Our] lines already made [are] far from safe so long as another
> Company [can] push into the north from the south.[9]

Although there was no immediate westerly danger, Mitchell's warning came to be heeded – Lochaber was the Highland's unguarded flank. By way of insurance in this quarter, the Inverness & Aberdeen Junction Company had contemplated taking over the Caledonian Canal.[10] That proposal went no further; but it would become the Highland's standard formula that neither a railway down the Great Glen nor a branch from Strathspey into Lochaber was urgently wanted. For connection with its system, the canal steamers, together with the Fort William–Kingussie mail coach, were provision enough. Critics, more numerous with the years, would come to see in this not prudential policy but blameworthy indifference. The Highland, acknowledging the obligations of monopoly, ought to encourage new lines within the territory which they claimed for themselves, and neglect of Fort William and Lochaber would be cited as a particular shortcoming. All admitted that much had been achieved – but had the Highland Company's own endeavours reached their limit? On that score, even admirers grew doubtful, while detractors urged the spur of competition.

* * *

Meanwhile, the dogged efforts to retrieve a through line to Oban had eventually succeeded, in the shape of the Callander & Oban Railway, authorised in 1865. A cross-country extension of the little Dunblane, Doune & Callander (1858) and a client of the Scottish Central, this promised a very roundabout, but arguably "optimum" Glasgow–Oban route. Genuinely a landowners' promotion, on the model of the Highland's own constituents, albeit with "outside" support, the Callander & Oban became almost at once a Caledonian dependant, thanks to the great amalgamations. In consequence, the newly formed Highland Company no doubt breathed more easily – the Caledonian could be trusted, for the foreseeable future, to discourage any dangerous westerly designs on Inverness. Highland fears would have been all the greater had the Oban party won the support of the Edinburgh & Glasgow Company and the patronage of their North British successor for a shorter route from Clydeside, by Loch Lomond or by Strathblane and Aberfoyle. In that event the Oban line would have provided a "direct" Glasgow–Crianlarich stem, pointing in the direction of Glen Coe and the Great Glen – surely a standing temptation for the North British, irresolute though they might be.

Construction of the Callander & Oban was go-stop-go, pausing first at Glenoglehead (at that time called "Killin", though the village was several miles distant). An abandonment act was obtained in 1870, on the basis that the line would halt at Tyndrum which was reached in 1873. Initially ambivalent about the obligations which they had inherited, the Caledonian eventually resolved that, with fresh powers from Parliament, their protégé should be completed to the west coast as first

Looking west from Callander & Oban Tyndrum, the "end of the line" between 1873 and 1877. The promoters of the Glasgow & North Western Railway looked to exploit the redundant yard (right) for exchange traffic. When building onwards to Dalmally and Oban resumed, the station had been resited (left). Construction westward to Loch Awe was relatively easy (cf. the challenge of Glen Ogle to the east) but beyond lay the Pass of Brander and the final up-and-over by Glen Cruiten.   (LGRP)

intended. From 1880, finished at last, the Callander & Oban would compete in some measure with the Dingwall & Skye, besides capturing Lochaber's principal mails, hitherto routed via Perth. Though the Kingussie coach continued to operate, Fort William's passenger and parcel traffic also tended to the new railhead, using David MacBrayne's mail steamers. But Caledonian – Highland relations were not seriously strained, and neither company wanted to disturb their broadly amicable partnership at Perth. The Caledonian were in no haste to take up the coastal branch into Lochaber, from Connel Ferry by Appin and Ballachulish, pledged by the Callander & Oban promoters in their early over-confidence, some twenty years before. (MacLean of Ardgour had commissioned a forlorn preliminary survey.[11]) Nor was it at all likely that the Caledonian would entertain a more ambitious Oban–Fort William–Inverness line through the Great Glen.

Until the definitive legislation of 1896, "light railway" would remain an imprecise term, and narrow gauge had been rejected for the Dingwall & Skye; but those who argued that light or narrow-gauge railways were best suited to the western Highlands had found a new voice while the fate of the Callander & Oban hung in the balance. Among the several engineers who flourished pet schemes, Sean McBean urged the dispassionate assessment of a westerly light line from Glasgow via Fort William to Inverness – as a secondary route which need not damage the Highland Company. He also envisaged, but obscurely, a branch from Invergarry by Glen Shiel to Kyle of Lochalsh, and his subsequent proposals included a

Glasgow–Inveraray–Oban–Fort William line. MacBean, who genuinely sought debate, approached the Caledonian, the Highland and the North British, though perhaps with small expectation of success. All three proved dismissive.[12] William Moore, who thought in the most basic terms, did not aim at Inverness; his narrow-gauge "West Highland & Glen Coe Tramway", reaching to Fort William, would have terminated at Banavie on the Caledonian Canal.[13] There were also those who assumed that the standard gauge Callander & Oban would halt permanently at Tyndrum. They saw opportunity in narrow gauge feeder lines, and one such was the proposed "Fort William, Ballachulish & Tyndrum Railway", which progressed to a preliminary notice in 1873, only to fade away when westward construction of the Callander & Oban resumed.[14]

Shaping every calculation at the beginning of the 1870s had been the possibility that the Caledonian and the North British would amalgamate, crowning all the mergers of the 1860s.[15] Though might-have-beens are always suspect, there can be little doubt that subsequent railway development across much of Scotland would have been fundamentally reordered and senseless competition much reduced, had the two come together. When the moment passed, their old enmities became even more the central fact of Scottish railway politics on into the 1890s – and the Caledonian decision to commit wholeheartedly to the Callander & Oban was certainly influenced by the prospect of North British intervention. In the expectation that construction would end at Tyndrum, speculative interest in a complementary Glasgow–Oban line via Loch Lomond had inevitably revived.[16] The North British might well have hesitated to commit unreservedly to such a scheme, but would they look benevolently on an independent promotion and perhaps offer a guarantee or working agreement?

* * *

Speculative activity, once stimulated, did not die down. Almost as soon as the Callander & Oban was completed, attention turned to improvement of the new route in the shape of a Glasgow–Crianlarich cut-off. Caledonian and North British alike had advantages to gain, preserves to safeguard, and were bound to be drawn in sooner or later. In adopting such a line, the Caledonian would strengthen their grip on the Callander & Oban, at the same time invading North British territory north-of-Clyde; by "going to Crianlarich" the North British could protect their near monopoly of Dunbartonshire and Loch Lomond and, for good measure, claim a share of Oban traffic. Conflict loomed in 1882 when the Strathendrick & Aberfoyle Company, their line newly opened, made it known that a "Crianlarich extension" was in prospect. Though the North British had agreed to work the Strathendrick & Aberfoyle (nominally independent until 1891) their connivance is not proven. The scanty evidence suggests that other parties, by manipulating the little company's directors, counted on pushing the North British into action.[17]

The Highland directors had taken no alarm to see the Caledonian finally established at Oban (above), and a North British bid to share in Oban traffic, if that went no further, need not have troubled them. But the argument of public interest, besides justifying a Crianlarich cut-off, lent itself to an attack on their own less than direct main line; and a vastly greater promotion was soon to overtake the tentative Aberfoyle–Crianlarich link. Preceded by only a few weeks of rumour, the Glasgow & North Western Railway Bill, lodged for the parliamentary session 1882-3, would combine an Oban cut-off with a 160-mile westerly line to Inverness. This highly ambitious and unashamedly "outside" scheme meant deadly danger for the Highland Company and presented both Caledonian and North British with difficult choices.

Laid out by engineer Thomas Walrond-Smith and sponsored by the firm of Wilkinson & Jarvis, the Glasgow & North Western ran by Loch Lomond's eastern shore, Crianlarich (where it intersected the Callander & Oban), Blackmount, Glen Coe, Fort William and the Great Glen (see panel on next page). John Wilkinson and James Jarvis were themselves contractor-engineers; financier Edwin Gerard and Robert Read, sometime secretary of the Somerset & Dorset Joint Railway, were the other named promoters. Their bill sought a startling £2 million in capital powers.[18] Walrond-Smith's best-known achievement is the eastern part of what became the Midland & Great

Stromeferry, well inside Loch Carron, was from 1870 the Dingwall & Skye Company's less than satisfactory terminus for train-steamer interchange. With Oban as a competitor for Hebridean traffic, Strome would never develop into a railway village such as Kyle of Lochalsh (from 1897) or West Highland Mallaig (from 1901) were later to become.

(George Washington Wilson/University of Aberdeen)

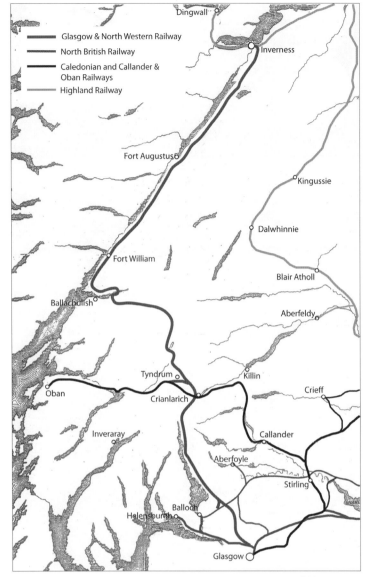

Glasgow & North Western Railway as proposed in 1882.

GLASGOW & NORTH WESTERN RAILWAY, 1882-3

The line as presented to Parliament began at Maryhill – a spur connected with the North British Company's Milngavie branch – and struck for Loch Lomond through the Kilpatrick Hills, intersecting the Forth & Clyde Junction Railway at Drymen, with junctions in all four directions. First keeping to the lochside by Balmaha, it rose steadily from Inversnaid and thus obtained a gradient of 1 in 70 through Glen Falloch. At Crianlarich, it spanned the Callander & Oban Railway then ran parallel through Strathfillan, on a somewhat lower alignment than the West Highland Railway as subsequently built. A junction spur across the valley led to Callander & Oban Tyndrum. On either side of the intermediate summit between Strathfillan and Glen Orchy (County March), the gradient remained 1 in 70, necessitating a short tunnel. From Bridge of Orchy the line rounded Loch Tulla to Inveroran then climbed to its ultimate summit on the edge of Blackmount. Skirting the western margin of Rannoch Moor, it swung behind Kingshouse and descended Glen Coe to Loch Leven, which it crossed at the Dog Narrows, not Ballachulish Ferry. The ruling gradient over Blackmount (Inveroran to Loch Leven) was 1 in 50. Powers were sought to serve Ballachulish village and slate quarries by a "steam ferry" from Callart on the opposite shore.

Now running by the sea coast, the line touched North Ballachulish, Onich and Corran Ferry, then followed Loch Linnhe to Fort William. A more-or-less level course was taken all along the south-eastern side of the Great Glen, by the River Lochy, Loch Lochy, Loch Oich and Loch Ness; and here, as on Lochlomondside, no gradient exceeded 1 in 180. Entry to Inverness was by Culduthel and Millburn (cf. Millburn Junction and flyover, for the Aviemore cut-off as subsequently built). The promoters sought running powers into the Highland Company's station, which they promised to enlarge.

Lesser bridges apart, Walrond-Smith planned eleven viaducts, the longest (some 200 yards) at the Dog Narrows. With few exceptions, curves would have been at least 20 chains radius. Seventy tunnels were required in all, but their aggregate length was less than one mile. One viaduct dramatically fronted the Glas waterfall (Glen Falloch); another straddled the confluence of the Rivers Lochy and Spean at Mucomir (Gairlochy). Below Glen Coe's Aonach Eagach ridge the plans showed the line terraced on the mountainside, with elaborate protection works (avalanche shelters and very brief tunnels). There was terracing also on Lochness-side, between Fort Augustus and Foyers.

Based on the evidence of Thomas Walrond Smith, engineer, evidence, Glasgow & North Western Railway Bill, Commons, 8-10 May 1883, NRS/BR/PYB (S)/1/325.

Northern Joint Railway; and why this syndicate turned its attention from East Anglia to Scotland remains a question with no satisfactory answer, save that other opportunities across mainland Britain were dwindling. Arguably, the speculative flurry first generated by the uncertain fortunes of the Callander & Oban had suggested a venture on a much larger scale. The North British were the promoters' main hope and before long would declare themselves an interested party. It does not follow, however, that the Glasgow & North Western was North British-inspired, and it seems that the aggrieved Highland directors judged accurately:

> *This line came on the public by surprise. It was never asked for, and is promoted not by the Proprietors and others in the district, but by speculators in London for purposes of their own.[19]*

The promoters aimed to set Caledonian against North British, and Caledonian and North British against the Highland Company. They suggested, not implausibly, that their scheme could be fulfilled in stages – first between Glasgow and Balmaha on Loch Lomond, where outer-suburban and summer-season traffic would develop rapidly; then from Inverness down the Great Glen, bringing rail connection to Lochaber. The middle portion, completing the

On the West Highland line, a south-bound timber train descends from County March summit (in the middle distance). By tunnelling, the Glasgow & North Western Railway would have obtained a less testing passage from Strathfillan into Glen Orchy.   (Tom Noble)

new through route and benefitting Oban, would come last, by which time the Highland, recognising that an all-round increase in railway business must result, would be reconciled to competition.[20] Put more cynically, the syndicate counted on at least part of their scheme being taken up. Both Caledonian and North British were sure to estimate the "residential" traffic which might be won north of Glasgow; and one of the two might adopt the proposed line as far as Crianlarich or Tyndrum – perhaps as far as Fort William, if only to forestall the other. As for the Highland, by adopting the final sixty miles through the Great Glen, they could keep Inverness in their own hands, and Fort William might become another Perth, where through traffic was exchanged.

Powers were offered to every established company with any conceivable interest in the new line (including the Great North of Scotland). In the Glasgow & North Western Bill as finally presented, this was narrowed down to a working and maintenance agreement with the North British, which at once roused the Highland's suspicions. Andrew Dougall, their veteran secretary-manager, pressed John Walker, the North British general manager, to promise that "friendly relations" would continue:

[Considering] the large traffic we send over your Line annually, [my] Directors hope your Company will insist on the Promoters deleting this provision…[21]

The North British gave no pledge, and in Walker's reply old resentments burst out:

[If] the Highland Railway had been as open to us as to the Caledonian and the traffic of both treated impartially…we should not have countenanced any Line competing with yours and…I cannot understand why a…fairly prosperous company…should, for the sake of £5,000 a year,* sacrifice its independence.

The North British, he reiterated, had not encouraged the Glasgow & North Western scheme. However, negotiations were now in progress:

You cannot expect us to reject an independent route to Inverness when it is presented to us."[22]

In Walker's negotiations with the Glasgow & North Western promoters, Samuel Mason, his predecessor as North British general manager, was in some way an intermediary. The course of events suggests that Walker and his chairman, Sir James Falshaw, swithered between affecting support, as a lever to secure better terms at Perth, and backing the project unreservedly. The Bill reached the House of Commons Committee without an agreement, because the North British insisted on entry to their Glasgow Queen Street Station via Balloch and Dumbarton or via Milngavie.[23] Presumably the intention was to reduce the Glasgow & North Western to a biddable client, in case the Caledonian took a hand. (Relatively modest new construction together with running powers would have sufficed to connect the Caledonian system with the promoters' chosen line by Strathendrick.) A further twist arose when the board of the City of Glasgow Union Railway (eventually to be partitioned between the Glasgow & South Western Company and the North British) offered access to Glasgow St Enoch, ostensibly of their own volition.[24]

One may read into the parliamentary record a North British game of subterfuge and double-dealing which somehow misfired. And there was an English dimension. The Midland Company's relations with the Glasgow & South Western had long been intimate (the two twice came close to amalgamation), while the North British had a foot in two Anglo-Scottish camps – both East Coast and Midland. There are hints that the Midland Company, perhaps with North British encouragement, weighed the advantages of a second route – Glasgow & South Western with Glasgow & North Western – for its traffic from Carlisle into the North of Scotland. The East Coast allies, for their part, feared North British treachery, while the Caledonian feared North British aggrandisement. It is to be remembered, nevertheless, that the North British and all their English partners, Midland, Great Northern and North Eastern, were heavily committed to the Forth Bridge, on which construction had just begun, and thus to the future development of the Perth route north from Edinburgh – which must have coloured the attitude of all concerned to the prospect of a competing westerly line.

The Highland Company stood implacably opposed; and loyalty (or self-interest?) impelled the Caledonian to make common cause. Save in Lochaber, landed opposition was almost unanimous. (A few proprietors in the Glasgow hinterland

---

*   This figure represented the Stanley Junction–Perth tolls which the Caledonian remitted (above).

Dropping northwards from County March, the West Highland line describes a dramatic horse-shoe curve round Auch Glen. By contrast, the Glasgow & North Western Railway would have descended towards Bridge of Orchy on much the same alignment as the modern A82, from which this photograph was taken.

(Keith Fenwick)

welcomed the possibility of "residential" feuing). John Fowler, the Highland's eminent consulting engineer, dismissed the Glasgow & North Western, with some exaggeration, as a "glorified tramway", but there was also dispassionate criticism of Walrond-Smith's layout, and his examination in Parliament revealed that the surveys had been in part perfunctory.[25] A host of repetitive witnesses enthusiastically paraded their own hopes for the new line, but they were ill-prepared to counter the down-to-earth arguments of the Highland and Caledonian. Facing defeat, the promoters changed tack. Having already promised the early addition of a branch to the west coast, they now pledged to recast their scheme as a Loch Lomond (Ardlui)–Crianlarich–Fort William–Arisaig line, primarily for the relief of crofters and fishermen. ("Arisaig" in this context meant the whole district north from Ardnamurchan to Morar; Walrond-Smith contemplated a railway harbour on Loch-nan-Uamh.) The syndicate's speculative hopes persisted. Their line, if so modified, would have fed the Callander & Oban, inviting Caledonian support; and attempts to fill the Glasgow–Ardlui gap were sure to follow, embroiling Caledonian and North British. But the promoters' retreat meant that Highland Company were no longer under frontal attack, and an Arisaig railhead, rivalling Stromeferry, was soon out of the reckoning. The House of Commons Committee, rejecting the Glasgow & North Western, ruled that the altered scheme required a fresh bill in another parliamentary session.[26]

* * *

The Glasgow & North Western scheme might have fared better had it been delayed by just one year. In 1883 distress and unrest in the western Highlands and Islands impelled the then Liberal Government to appoint an investigating commission, headed by Lord Napier. Extensive evidence was gathered, amid wide publicity, and the ensuing Napier Report of 1884, though concentrating on land reform, did not ignore transport and communications. Without dwelling on details,

the Commissioners implied that the Highland Company, and the Caledonian too, had not done their whole duty. In effect, the Report recommended a return to the policy of earlier decades, which had underwritten the Parliamentary Roads and the Crinan and Caledonian Canals. (Both these waterways, still subsidised, were in the care of the Caledonian Canal Commission.) Government subsidy, deployed selectively, would achieve a more coherent rail and steamer network. Specifically, they suggested that, if private enterprise could bring a railway to Lochaber, state aid might be forthcoming for its extension to a third harbour on the west coast, supplementing Oban and Stromeferry.[27] Railway development as the answer to socio-economic problems in both Ireland and Scotland would remain a lively political topic for more than twenty years. However, Walrond-Smith and Wilkinson did not try again. The latter found his next opportunities in Sweden. In 1887-8, with the campaign for the West Highland Railway just begun (below), he would offer the Glasgow & North Western plans to the activists of Fort William – it seems without result.[28]

In the aftermath of the 1882-3 contest, the Highland directors' first instinct was to occupy the Great Glen. But an Inverness–Fort William "block" line promised poor returns at best and might defeat its own purpose by encouraging fresh attempts to reach Fort William from the Central Belt, whereupon the dangers of a competing through railway to Inverness must arise again. They chose instead to improve their Perth–Inverness route, and in 1884 the Aviemore cut-off was authorised, a heavily-engineered line over Slochd Mhuic which shortened the journey by twenty-five miles. (When the necessary powers had been acquired, the Highland board felt sufficiently insured against renewed westerly attack and would made no haste to complete their expensive cut-off.) In addition, double-tracking from Blair Atholl to Dalwhinnie, over Druimuachdar summit, promised more efficient operation. The Far North companies (above) were formally absorbed by the Highland in 1884, which implied a renewed commitment to the remoter communities

The Glasgow & North Western Railway, completing its descent through Glen Coe, was laid out to turn up Loch Leven, doubling back on the northern shore after crossing at the Dog Narrows, seen here in the centre of the photograph. To surmount Glen Coe directly, from sea level at Ballachulish, would have been an even greater engineering challenge.

(A Johnstone)

which the Highland served. (Canvassing for support in Ross-shire, Sutherland and Caithness, the Glasgow & North Western promoters had argued that a competing line to Inverness would ensure a better, cheaper service for all the districts north and west, while the repeated claims of the Great North of Scotland for access to Inverness had been couched in similar terms.) As for the Highland's Dingwall & Skye route to the Hebrides, improved buoying and lighting in Loch Carron meant that the Portree and Stornoway steamers from Stromeferry would operate more reliably.[29]

That the Highland Company must look to their all-round defences was at once confirmed by an *easterly* assault, in the shape of a Ballater–Tomintoul–Nethy Bridge line. It is unnecessary to describe the proposed Strathspey, Strathdon & Deeside Railway (1883-4) in detail or to assess the all too likely difficulties of construction and operation. More to the point, its supporters thought in terms of an extension to Inverness, by Carrbridge and Slochd Mhuic, which would have furnished a second through route from Aberdeen. This threatened to duplicate (and might even have pre-empted) the Highland's Aviemore cut-off. The unsuccessful Morayshire & Perthshire Direct Junction Railway twenty years previously had left a legacy of unconvincing projects to connect both Strathisla with Deeside and Donside with Strathspey. Now the latest promoters, like the Glasgow & North Western syndicate, were in earnest – though no doubt they too would have compromised to serve their speculative ends; and the Great North of Scotland Company, while ambivalent about the full-blown Deeside to Inverness scheme, pondered how to turn the situation to advantage (cf. how the North British had wavered over the Glasgow & North Western). Could the Highland be pressured into joint ownership of the Aviemore cut-off (with a connection at Carrbridge from the Great North's Strathspey line)? Would they concede running powers from Elgin to Inverness if the Great North desisted?[30]

Parliament, having dismissed the Glasgow & North Western, also rejected the Strathspey, Strathdon & Deeside. Both were latter-day, so-called contractors' lines. The classic (largely English) examples of earlier date had added appreciably to the basic railway network already laid down before the 1860s; and by the late 19th century the Scottish Highlands had come to offer preconditions favourable to such schemes, i.e. inter-company conflict, either active or readily rekindled, together with poorly served and otherwise dissatisfied districts, eager for their own line or perhaps a competing one. That the case for assisted transport development was gaining ground may well have influenced the men who framed these two audacious projects. Nevertheless, the Glasgow & North Western promoters had not sought (and did not want?) the subsidy tentatively recommended, after the event, by the Napier Commission. Their parliamentary counsel, questioning the efficacy of government intervention, made a robust (and calculated?) defence of traditional capitalism, without apology for the scheme's speculative origins:

It will prove of more advantage to... a suffering population... than any amount of emigration or eleemosynary relief could bestow, even [when] provided by [the state].

Not every contractors' line had been above board, he admitted, and unwary investors had sometimes paid the price, but the community at large invariably gained when private enterprise, with all its risks, was left untrammelled:

There are... lines which have been sheer swindles but... when made have been an unmixed benefit...[31]

* * *

Though nothing on a like scale followed the parliamentary battles of 1882-3 and 1883-4, the climate of manoeuvre and suspicion intensified, and the North British Company, who

Unlike the modern A82, the military road and its public successor followed the south-eastern side of Loch Ness, as seen here looking north from Fort Augustus; the Glasgow & North Western Railway would have done likewise, with much rock-face terracing. (A Johnstone)

had been caught unprepared by the Glasgow & North Western promotion, showed a new determination to shape events. Completion of the Tay Bridge (the *second* Tay Bridge, after the notorious disaster of 1879) and the Forth Bridge was by now assured, boosting North British confidence. John Thomas, in his well-known general histories, has argued that they aimed at "the conquest of the West" and a decisive trial of strength with the Caledonian.[32] Though Thomas oversimplifies the complex railway politics of the day and overstates the North British conversion to a pro-active strategy, a bolder blend of defensive and expansionist calculation was certainly manifest. In 1886-7 the landed promoters of the Clyde, Ardrishaig & Crinan Railway* obtained a North British guarantee and working agreement.[33] The proposed Glen Falloch Railway (1887-8) presaged a Helensburgh–Crianlarich cut-off in North British hands – which the Caledonian were able to frustrate.[34] And in 1889 the North British backed the West Highland Railway, from Clydeside to Fort William – offering a guarantee, a working agreement and a contribution to capital. A 30-mile extension, not for the moment covered by the North British guarantee, was included in the West Highland Bill of 1888-9, taking the proposed line to Roshven (Loch Ailort) on the Arisaig seaboard.[35]

West Highland success, against strong Caledonian and Highland opposition, had several ingredients: a disciplined case was prepared; the burgh of Fort William and the key proprietors along the route spoke as one; and the North British were engaged beforehand. In the House of Lords the Bill prevailed but with the Roshven extension struck out, so that the promoters faced the second House with concealed misgivings. Nevertheless, the Commons Committee pronounced that a railway terminating temporarily at Fort William was justifiable,

both on its merits and as a "large step" towards the western sea. August 1889 saw the West Highland Company established, and construction would begin that October. The line as authorised ran from Helensburgh (strictly, Craigendoran) via the Gare Loch, Loch Long and upper Loch Lomond to Crianlarich, then onwards by Bridge of Orchy, over Rannoch Moor and down Glen Spean. There was provision for a connecting spur to the Callander & Oban Railway at Crianlarich. Caledonian and Highland were handicapped by the perception that they had too long ignored Fort William and Lochaber. And both companies miscalculated in expecting that the West Highland scheme would fail comprehensively on the vexed question of government aid for its Roshven arm, which after all turned out to be expendable – though at some risk to the whole project, after the promoters had paraded their intention to provide a new railhead for the west-coast fishery. That the North British commitment stopped at Fort William largely explains the Lords' decision to disallow the Roshven line, and advance to the Atlantic seaboard was postponed, pending a government declaration of policy on state subsidy.[36]

This time, the Highland directors could not readily plead mortal injury. Their core territory was for the moment safe; with Roshven gone, their traffic by Stromeferry faced no immediate challenge. Judging the battle lost, they chose negotiation before the Commons Committee met, leaving the Caledonian to fight on alone in defence of the Callander & Oban. Heeding North British advice, the West Highland promoters dropped their proposed connection from Spean Bridge to Loch Lochy on the Caledonian Canal, which the Highland were sure to see as a preliminary probe towards Inverness. A Fort William–Banavie link was substituted, to be covered by the North British guarantee. Together with a deviation in the Spean Valley and another approaching Fort William, the little branch would be approved by the supplementary West Highland Act of 1890. A

* From Hunters Quay, with ferry connection from North British Craigendoran and a second ferry on Loch Fyne.

treaty neutralising the Great Glen was drafted in July 1889, on which basis the Highland ceased their opposition:

1.   *The Highland Company to withdraw.*
2.   *The North British Company and the promoters of the Bill undertake not to promote, directly or indirectly, nor to support the promotion by any other company or persons, nor to contribute to nor work, any railway north or east of Banavie for ten years after the opening of the West Highland Railway to Fort William.*
3.   *The Highland Company and the North British Company to revise the existing agreement between them, and to renew it on revised terms so that it shall expire at the end of ten years from 1 March 1890, provided that such revised terms be not more onerous to the Highland Company than the terms of the existing agreement.*
4.   *£500 to be paid by the North British Company to the Highland Company towards the Highland's costs of opposing the present Bill.*
5.   *Formal agreement to be prepared by the parties' legal representatives.*

Signed, Donald Cameron of Lochiel, for promoters; John Walker, for North British Company; Andrew Dougall, for Highland Company, 3 July 1889.

Addendum
6.   *The restriction in article 2 shall not apply to any railway between the West Highland line at or near Inverlair (Glen Spean) and the Highland Railway at any point between Kingussie and Dalwhinnie.*[37]

The North British, it seems, did not press for large concessions at Perth under article 3 – and throughout all the strife to follow Highland and North British would remain partners in through traffic there. Though soon known as the Ten Years Truce, the Great Glen Agreement implied a term of some fifteen years – i.e. counting ten from the completion of the West Highland (article 2); and the signatories can have had little confidence that their bargain would endure for that length of time – which may well explain the Addendum. If government or public opinion were eventually to denounce the pact, a link line by Loch Laggan into Strathspey might sufficiently meet complaints; it would give new cross-country connections, while Inverness would remain the Highland Company's citadel and the Great Glen a no-man's-land. But against an independent promotion, designed to undermine the 1889 Agreement, there could be no perfect insurance.

References

J. McGregor, *The West Highland Railway: Plans, Politics and People*, Birlinn (John Donald), 2005, cited as PPP.

1.   For example:- NRS/BR/PYB(S)/1/325, Lord Abinger, evidence, Glasgow & North Western Railway Bill, Commons, 3 May 1883.
2.   NRS/BR/PROS(S)/1/1/15, memorandum revival of Inverness–Perth railway scheme, 1852-3.
3.   Joseph Mitchell's *Reminiscences* (ed. I. Robertson), David & Charles, 1971, vol. 2, pp. 210-1.
4.   Lochiel Papers, Lochaber Archive, CL/A/3/2/73/5, Bruce to Donald Cameron of Lochiel, 23 October 1863.
5.   CL/A/3/2/73/5, Matheson to Lochiel, 4 October 1863. P. Fletcher, *Directors, Dilemmas and Debt*, GNSRA and HRS, 2010, chapter
6.   CL/A/3/2/73/5, D. MacLaren to Lochiel, 7 November 1863.
7.   H. Parris, *Government and the Railways in Nineteenth-century Britain*, RKP and University of Toronto Press, 1965, chapters 1-3.
8.   Fletcher, op.cit.
9.   *Herepath's Railway Journal*, 4 November 1865.
10.   NRS/BR/IAJ/1/1, Inverness & Aberdeen Junction Railway minutes. 17, 22 and 29 February 1860.
11.   A related map is preserved in Fort William's West Highland Museum.
12.   *Railway News*, 7 November 1874 and 19 June 1875. NRS/BR/NBR/1/24, North British Railway minutes, 14 June 1878. See also Fletcher, op. cit., Chapter 15.
13.   Ian Thornber collection.
14.   NRS/RHP 46426/3, Fort William, Ballachulish & Tyndrum Railway. *Edinburgh Gazette*, 21 November 1873.
15.   D. Ross, *The North British Railway*, Stenlake, 2014, pp.90-1.
16.   NRS/BR/PYB(S)/1/394, Charles Forman, evidence, Callander & Oban Railway Bill, Commons, 2 April 1897 (alluding to earlier schemes in which engineers Formans & McCall had been involved).
17.   PPP, p.26. NRS/BR/NBR/1/30, North British Railway minutes, 19 January 1883, noting letter from Keyden, Strang & Girvan.
18.   NRS/BR/PYB(S)/1/325, Glasgow & North Western Railway Bill, clause 13.
19.   Author's collection, Highland Railway, memoranda on Glasgow & North Western Railway.
20.   NRS/BR/PYB(S)/1/325, Glasgow & North Western Railway Bill, Commons, evidence and speeches by counsel, May 1883.
21.   NRS/BR/NBR/8/1764/Box 6, general manager's files relating to West Highland Railway, Dougal to Walker, 3 January 1883.
22.   NRS/BR/NBR/8/1764/Box 6, general manager's files relating to West Highland Railway, Walker to Dougall, 5 January 1883.
23.   NRS/BR/PYB(S)/1/325, statement by counsel for promoters, Glasgow & North Western Railway Bill, Commons, 24 May 1883.
24.   ibid.
25.   NRS/BR/PYB(S)/1/325, Thomas Walrond-Smith, evidence, Glasgow & North Western Railway Bill, Commons, 8-10 May 1883.
26.   NRS/BR/PYB (S)/1/325, proposal by counsel and chairman's response, Glasgow & North Western Railway Bill, Commons, 1 June 1883.
27.   Napier Report, Parliamentary Papers c.3980.
28.   MacKenzie Papers, West Highland Museum, Wilkinson & Jarvis to Donald Boyd, 31 December 1887. D. Watts, Thomas Walrond-Smith, civil engineer, 1843-1919, *Joint Line*, M&GNS Magazine, Summer 2021.
29.   NRS/BR/HR/1/4, Highland Railway minutes, 3 July, 7 August, 4 September, 2 October and 4 December 1883. NRS/BR/PYB(S)/1/326, Highland Railway (New Lines) Bill, 1884.
30.   NRS/BR/PYB(S)1/62, Strathspey, Strathdon & Deeside Junction Railway Bill, 1884. NRS/BR/PYB(S)/1/328, Great North of Scotland Railway (New Lines) Bill, 1884 (cf. NRS/BR/PYB(S)/1/326). NRS/BR/RHP 25442, Great North of Scotland Railway, Nethy Bridge-Inverness extension, 1884.
31.   NRS/BR/PYB(S)/1/325, introductory speech, counsel for promoters, Glasgow & North Western Railway Bill, 30 April 1883.
32.   J. Thomas, *The North British Railway*, David & Charles, 1975, vol. 2, chapter 6.
33.   NRS/BR/MPS(S)/5/1, map of Clyde, Ardrishaig & Crinan Railway. NRS/BR/NBR/1/34, North British Railway minutes, 13 January and 9 June 1887.
34.   PPP, p.36 and p.61.
35.   PPP, chapter 3.
36.   ibid.
37.   NRS/BR/NBR1/36, North British Railway minutes, 11 July 1889, and NRS/BR/HR/1/6, Highland Railway minutes, 7 August 1889.

Fort Augustus, in 1931, with the Abbey towers in the middle distance. Passengers at the prow of *Gondolier*, the MacBrayne Company's summer-season steamer on the Caledonian Canal, wait to descend the locks onward to Loch Ness (a tedious business which took an hour at least). The railway swing bridge lies open, out of use.   (John Roake collection)

Of necessity, the MacBrayne Company's vessels carried passengers, mails and general goods, including private cars and small commercial vehicles. All were craned on and off – a year-round performance at the three western Highlands railheads (Oban, Mallaig and Kyle of Lochalsh) until the 1970s, when the era of roll-on/roll-off ferries began. Heavier cargoes were shipped direct from the Clyde. This 1950 photograph at Kyle of Lochalsh barely hints at future containerisation.

(Cyril Herbert, courtesy Science Museum Group)

Rannoch station, West Highland Railway, c.1895, looking north to the highest section of the new railway across Rannoch Moor. The West Highland invader re-ignited Great Glen conflict.

(Glenfinnan Station Museum Trust)

CHAPTER TWO

THE WEST HIGHLAND COMPANY IN BEING, NEXT MOVES 1889-94

Among the promoter-directors of the West Highland Company were two seasoned campaigners, Donald Cameron of Lochiel and the third Lord Abinger, who owned the Inverness-shire estate of Inverlochy. They had actively encouraged every previous railway project aimed at Lochaber, or capable of extension in that direction. By their joint efforts, every large proprietor along the West Highland route had been persuaded to declare in favour or, at worst, stand neutral. Lochiel had been Conservative MP for Inverness-shire from 1868 until 1885 and he had served on the Napier Commission. Abinger's personal involvement in railway matters dated back to the Mont Cenis Pass project of the 1860s. He used his City contacts to obtain a preliminary assessment of the proposed Craigendoran–

Fort William–Roshven line by the prestigious contracting firm of Lucas & Aird, and he would become the West Highland's first chairman. Banker-solicitor Nigel MacKenzie was factor for half-a-dozen estates in the western Highlands, Lochiel's included. As provost of Fort William, he helped broker the understanding whereby town and "country" (i.e. the Lochaber landlords and their sporting tenants) joined forces behind the West Highland scheme. In association with MacRae, Flett & Rennie (Edinburgh), the principal agents, he then precognosed parliamentary witnesses and shaped the promoters' case, becoming afterwards the company's agent in Lochaber. In 1883 Abinger had testified exuberantly for the Glasgow & North Western promoters, applauding their decision to revive the Glasgow–Inverness line "which ought to have been originally constructed". With the Napier hearings in progress, detaining the Commissioners in Scotland, MacKenzie had given equally positive evidence at Westminster on Lochiel's behalf.[1]

The West Highland Railway was the principal achievement of Charles Forman, from 1874 a partner

Donald Cameron of Lochiel, 24th chief of Clan Cameron (d.1905), who saw diplomatic service and became a Conservative MP. He was a member of the Napier Commission (1883-4) and subsequently a promoter-director of the West Highland Railway (1888-1905). His statue stands in The Parade, Fort William.   (Graham Maxtone)

alongside his father, James Forman, in the engineering firm of Formans & McCall. The elder Forman, a prominent critic of the cross-country Callander & Oban, had always advocated a shorter route; the younger man's earliest surveys included a "direct" Glasgow–Oban line via Loch Lomond, calculated to complement (or supersede?) the Caledonian's struggling client. It is likely that he also helped lay out the narrow-gauge "Fort William, Ballachulish & Tyndrum Railway", another Formans & McCall initiative of the mid-1870s (see Chapter 1). Speculative promotions were to Charles Forman's taste, and the Strathendrick & Aberfoyle Company's mooted cut-off to Crianlarich, which he engineered in his own right, was almost certainly in that category. Engaged by the landowners of South Argyll, with the North British Company somewhere in the background, he undertook the Clyde, Ardrishaig & Crinan Railway, which won Parliament's approval – though it was never to be begun. (Denied additional North British support, the company was wound up in 1892.) Forman's West Highland surveys, first by Glen Coe but subsequently by Rannoch, grew out of an earlier commission to investigate a modest line from Helensburgh to Garelochhead and Arrochar for the Colquhouns of Luss. His ability was already recognised, so too his ready eye for opportunities to set company against company; and he was unlikely to rest content with the West Highland as authorised, or long respect the Great Glen Agreement. For their part, contractors Lucas & Aird were not without a speculative bent. They had enthusiastically endorsed Forman's plans and their tender to build the Craigendoran–Fort William line was accepted.[2]

* * *

There follows an overview of the four years from October 1889, with the West Highland under construction. The other

Lochaber landowners on the West Highland board were soon replaced by North British nominees. Abinger, though he remained a director until his death in 1892, made way for the Marquess of Tweeddale, who thereafter chaired both companies, while North British secretary George Wieland, a figure of importance later in the Great Glen story, added West Highland business to his duties.[3] In 1891, following John Walker's sudden death, John Conacher became the North British general manager. Conacher's instincts were more cautious, and that same year saw the so-called Peace Agreement (properly, New Lines Agreement), whereby Caledonian and North British sought a tolerable coexistence – after both of them had been seriously chastened by their barren contest, through two parliamentary sessions, to possess the Glasgow & South Western Railway. No previous treaty between them, defining "exclusive" and "shared" districts, had lasted long. Although time would show that the latest version (twice renewed before 1914) was more robust, it meant détente, scarcely peace.[4]

Like the Ten Years Truce in the Great Glen concluded with the Highland Company two years earlier, the 1891 Peace Agreement implied a North British reassessment of the proactive strategy which Walker had pursued and perhaps second thoughts about their West Highland commitment. But to dispassionate observers Fort William seemed no sort of resting place. Whatever the North British Company's first intentions, whatever their later thinking, only by extending the new railway – to Inverness, if not to the west coast – could revenue be enhanced. As construction costs mounted, Conacher and Lord Tweeddale increasingly doubted that the West Highland would ever pay. Averse to further adventures, they did not share Lochiel's conviction that revival of the Roshven line would bring financial salvation. Nevertheless, extension westward to a new fishery harbour would enlarge the West Highland's traffic, reducing the burden on North British shareholders and justifying a further (strictly finite) outlay, if government assistance in some form were first assured.[5]

The weight of opinion now favoured Mallaig bay, at the mouth of Loch Nevis and 40 miles from

Charles Forman, engineer (d.1901)
(Author's collection)

Banavie, as the West Highland's ultimate terminus.[6] However, a rival scheme was already well-advanced. In origin a landowners' project and comparable with the Clyde, Ardrishaig & Crinan, the Garve & Ullapool Railway (branching from the Dingwall & Skye) had won Parliament's approval in 1890. The Highland Company were supportive in so far as they needed a counter to any new West Highland promotion; but their aid was limited to the advice and assistance of company engineer Murdoch Paterson.[7] Anxious that the Garve & Ullapool might become the unchallenged candidate for state aid, John Baird of Knoydart joined with other landlords in western Inverness-shire and Skye to sponsor the Loch Eil & Mallaig Railway, for which engineer Alexander Simpson made a fresh survey, following Forman's earlier layout as far as Kinlochailort. (The firm of Simpson & Wilson had close ties with the wider Baird family, industrialists in the Central Belt.) Their project was soon restyled the West Highland Mallaig Extension, whereupon Lochiel assumed the lead, on behalf of the West Highland Company. From the North British, however, Baird could obtain only the bald terms of a 50% working agreement.[8]

In short, the Highland Company and the North British both temporised. Meanwhile, Lochiel's prediction that subsidy was sure to come had been borne out. The Conservative Government of 1886-92 were brought to concede that the western Highlands merited equal treatment with Ireland, where their policy of "killing Home Rule with kindness" included state support for transport improvements. Both the Lothian Commission (1889-90) and the ensuing Treasury Committee (1890-1) declared for two new lines, one south and one north of the Highland Company's Dingwall & Skye route to Stromeferry. It was assumed that the North British would commit to the Mallaig Extension as the only serious "south of Strome" contender; but for Conacher and Tweeddale it remained essential that a sure and sufficient Treasury contribution be in place first. The Government's preference "north of Strome" was a Lochinver line, from Garve via Ullapool or cross-country from Culrain on the Highland's Far North route. Achnasheen–Aultbea and Invershin–Loch Laxford had also been assessed. In response, the

John Conacher, general manager of the North British Railway from 1891 to 1899.
(*The Bailie*, 4th November 1891)

Highland directors offered to take up any one of these "Lothian lines", provided that the Mallaig railway received no assistance, a stipulation which the Treasury rejected.[9]

In 1889 the Great North of Scotland Company had attempted a devious bid for access to Inverness by sponsoring a Black Isle branch and a complementary Ardersier–Fortrose ferry. Sensing another opportunity, they declared themselves willing to work the Garve & Ullapool (and presumably its extension to Lochinver), given the necessary running powers over the Highland system west from Elgin.[10] The Caledonian stood ready to argue that, by virtue of the well-established steamer services out of Oban, the Inverness-shire coast north from Ardnamurchan ought to remain a district shared with the North British under the Peace Agreement.[11] But the Government wanted no such complications and negotiations moved towards compromise, whereby all the "north of Strome" schemes were eventually put out of the reckoning. To offset a Treasury Guarantee for the West Highland Mallaig Extension, the Highland Company would obtain a parliamentary grant whereby the Dingwall & Skye could advance some ten expensive miles to Kyle of Lochalsh, the terminus first projected.[12] Though inevitably caught up in the politics of subsidy for these competing schemes, John Conacher and Andrew Dougall, the Highland's secretary-manager, kept the Great Glen treaty in sight. They desired to preserve it – and the first challenge would come in the autumn of 1893, when completion of the West Highland to Fort William was still several months away.

* * *

The Great Glen had been "shut up". On the more populous north-western side of Loch Ness, disappointed when in 1882 the Glasgow & North Western promoters chose the south-eastern side, hopes for a local line had persisted. However, expectations of a West Highland advance towards Inverness proved strongest in Fort Augustus and Glen Garry. David MacBrayne's Caledonian Canal steamers were slow, and every railhead was more-or-less remote. To travel via Inverness and Forres meant a circuitous journey; connection with Kingussie (by Spean Bridge and the Fort William–Kingussie coach) could not be counted on; and Oban was best reached by a second vessel, from Corpach or Fort William. The more generous steamer timetable of the summer months catered for tourists and did not meet local needs. Traders and shopkeepers, who could not fulfil orders expeditiously, were forced to hold large stocks; to deal in game or other perishables had proved impossible. There were other complaints. It constituted "almost a denial of justice" (so Lord Abinger had put it, on his tenants' behalf, when testifying in support of the Glasgow & North Western Railway) that attending the county rating appeal court, like other pressing business in Inverness, might require two days' absence – which few could afford. Distiller Donald P MacDonald, who was Fort William's principal employer, claimed that during the winter months the only regular sailing from Banavie, where the canal vessels turned, was of little practical use.[13]

Inverness solicitor Charles Innes, partner in the firm of Innes & MacKay, had repeatedly attacked the Highland

Company's standard argument that the Glen's northern half was adequately served by MacBrayne's boats. He stood with prominent local figures such as Leo Linse, Lord Abbot of the Benedictine monastery at Fort Augustus, who complained that to answer urgent letters often meant "staying up all night". The Loch Ness mail steamer, scheduled to arrive in the late afternoon, suffered long delays whenever the intermediate piers "had a heavy cargo"; and it left again for Inverness very early the next day. Connecting with the Oban steamers at Fort William, the Invergarry mail cart had a likewise inconvenient timetable.[14] Of similar stamp to fellow-lawyer MacKenzie, Innes was a man of many parts. Though radical in opinion and something of a crofters' champion, his politics were Unionist (see page 37). He represented both the dowager Lady Seafield (Glen Urquhart) and the British Aluminium Company, whose pioneering smelter at Foyers would begin production in 1896. He had been ready (like Nigel MacKenzie) to work with the Glasgow & North Western promoters; and he had been employed on occasion by the Great North of Scotland in their repeated sallies towards Inverness. Moreover, Innes had acted for Baird of Knoydart during the first stages of the Loch Eil & Mallaig scheme, when Baird's aim was to bring the Scottish Office, the Treasury and the North British to a common purpose.[15]

A concerted Great Glen campaign defeated all Innes's ingenuity. Any railway which served Invermoriston and Glen Urquhart could not touch the aluminium plant on the opposite shore of Loch Ness. Among Great Glen proprietors, Grant of Glenmoriston and Lady Seafield acknowledged the local demand for rail connection, but their sympathies lay with the Highland Company, while Lord Lovat, Fraser-Tytler of Aldourie and Baillie of Dochfour were Highland directors and had acquiesced in the Ten Years Truce. Though Lovat could not ignore the discontents of Fort Augustus, he saw a sufficient answer in the new railhead at Spean Bridge which the West Highland would provide. The Glengarry (Ellice) Trustees and widowed Mrs Ellice (see panel below) were much of Lovat's mind. In 1882-3 she had been ready to oppose the Glasgow & North Western Bill. Suspecting the long-term intentions of the North British, she also resisted the West Highland scheme until the promoters' Spean Bridge–Loch Lochy branch had been dropped.[16] At the Lochaber end of the Glen, Abinger and Lochiel, whose properties marched on the River Lochy, were West Highland directors and constrained, like their Highland

THE ELLICES OF INVERGARRY

Edward Ellice (d.1863) acquired Glenquoich in 1840 and Glengarry in 1860. His son, also Edward Ellice (d.1880), Liberal MP for St Andrews, may have introduced engineer Thomas Bouch to the Lochaber landowners interested in the proposed Fort William Railway (1862-3). The younger Ellice's second wife Eliza Hogart (d.1910) is the "Mrs Ellice" of this text. With the Glengarry estate in trust, he was succeeded by his cousin, Captain Edward Ellice (1858-1934), a promoter-director of the Invergarry & Fort Augustus Railway. From 1903 to 1906 Captain Ellice too was Liberal MP for St Andrews.

Glenquoich Lodge, over many years Lord Burton's base in the Scottish Highlands. In the mid-20th century, the building and its immediate policies succumbed to the Garry-and-Quoich hydro-electric scheme.

(D Whyte post card)

counterparts, by the 1889 Agreement. Continuation of the West Highland to Mallaig, with Treasury aid in place, was Lochiel's priority – he was anxious that the North British should once again be fully committed, with no other distractions.[17]

The Truce did not bind Lord Burton, who leased the Ellices' Glenquoich together with a portion of Lochiel's Glenkingie. In 1883, then Sir Michael Bass MP, he had joined in formally introducing the Glasgow & North Western Bill, besides offering his supporting testimony.[18] In 1888-9, however, Burton had appeared ambivalent about the West Highland scheme (though he gave evidence in its favour in the House of Commons, after the Bill had passed the Lords). He declined to join the West Highland board. As a Midland Railway director, he may have judged this inappropriate, but subsequent events suggest that he resented the interval of years which the Great Glen pact prescribed.[19] His own tedious and expensive journeys between Burton-on-Trent and Glenquoich via Perth took at least 28 hours; and in his opinion West Highland Spean Bridge, though an improvement of sorts, would have little advantage for the districts west of Invergarry. Closely associated with Burton was George Malcolm, who factored the Glengarry and Glenquoich estates and took sole charge of the latter out-of-season. As secretary of the Highland Property Association, he was a figure of importance in his own right. For a decade at least, Malcolm had urged an acceleration of the morning mail train north from Perth and the earlier departure of the connecting Loch Ness boat. The Great Glen, he complained, was "caught between the cupidity of the Highland Railway and the niggardliness of the Post Office". Admitting the relative poverty of many landowners in the western Highlands, he held that wealthy shooting tenants like Burton were better able to encourage and support new lines.[20]

Malcolm had been complicit in the Glasgow & North Western scheme, undeterred by its questionable credentials. Though not privy to the promoters' calculations, he assumed (correctly) that they aimed to engage one or more of the "great companies". Having advised Walrond-Smith on the best layout along Loch Oich, he obtained early sight of the engineer's finished plans.[21] But Mrs Ellice, "quite horrified" at the prospect of a railway opposite her windows, had threatened "unflinching opposition" unless the line was thoroughly disguised. Malcolm found himself in disgrace with the Ellice family when, encouraged by Bass (Burton), he too consented to support the Glasgow & North Western Bill in Parliament.

In the end, he did not testify.[22] A major player in the West Highland promotion during 1887-9, Malcolm had cajoled both Burton and Mrs Ellice to support it. His own part therein was controversial, and he had earned the angry reproaches of the Caledonian Company for concealing the early involvement of the North British.[23] Malcolm bowed to the 1889 Great Glen treaty but made no secret of his conviction that, before long, a railway must supersede the Caledonian Canal. Like all the other activists, he pictured a transformed Lochaber and a flourishing, rail-served Fort William (see panel below).

Prospectively the only centre of any size on the Glasgow & North Western route, Fort William had glimpsed a great future. On the benefits of a West Highland bid for Inverness, however, opinion was divided. All remembered how Oban of the 1880s had thrived as a rail-and-steamer interchange, drawing away Lochaber business. Although the town was now to have its own railway, that tale might be repeated. If the West Highland became primarily a Glasgow–Inverness line, striking from Glen Spean into the Great Glen, Fort William would be bypassed and could expect only a lesser role in management and operation. Both Oban and Inverness were sure to benefit, should a through line between the two eventually materialise,

---

GEORGE MALCOLM, INVERGARRY, TO DONALD BOYD, MERCHANT, FORT WILLIAM, FEBRUARY 1888

I [am sending] the first volume, 1804 to 1811, of the Reports of the [Caledonian Canal] Commissioners [which] contains the original instructions given to Telford the Engineer…It would seem that [he intended] the formation of a Harbour and Docks at Fort William [which] I [now] hope may be…carried out. No doubt when the Railway is arrived (sic)…it will soon be pushed forward to Inverness and to the west coast, in development of the fishings, which sooner or later Government will have to assist…to the extent of forming or largely contributing to…suitable harbours and breakwaters…

Source: Lochaber Archive, Glenquoich letter books, CL/A/12/1/8, 10 February 1888

but would an intermediate town fare so well? A Spean–Laggan link into Strathspey, recalling the abortive scheme of 1862-3 (see Chapter 1), might better complement the Mallaig Extension and secure Fort William's long-term growth, by opening up cross-country routes to Perth and Aberdeen.[24]

* * *

That Burton and Malcolm were ready to destroy the Ten Years Truce is not certain; but Charles Forman needed no encouragement. During 1893 he would undertake several surveys along the Great Glen with a view to an independent promotion extending the West Highland line. In late October a "meeting of gentleman interested in the proposal" took place at the chambers of solicitors Anderson & Shaw, Inverness, when Forman assured them that detailed plans and other necessary preparations could be completed in time to submit a bill that November. However, the parliamentary timetable was tight, and subscriptions were yet to be gathered. It might be better in the first instance to pursue a more modest "half-way" scheme, connecting the new railway with Fort Augustus and Loch Ness. Behind much protestation of honest purpose ("satisfying local needs") was a clear intention to undermine the 1889 treaty, thus embroiling the Highland Company and the North British, and then to sell to one or the other. For that the "half-way" option would suffice. Moreover, it would postpone a potentially divisive question – whether to aim for Inverness via Invermoriston and Glenurquhart or via Foyers (above).[25]

And there was a wider context. To North British dismay, the incoming Liberal Government (1892-5) had proved hostile in principle to a Treasury Guarantee for the West Highland Mallaig Extension, as pledged by the Conservatives just before their general election defeat. Though the permanent civil servants considered this offer binding (which the Liberal ministers eventually accepted), there was no speedy decision. A late bill had taken the scheme forward in parliamentary session 1892-3, only for it to be frustrated by the procedural tactics of the Caledonian and Highland, who were certain to renew their opposition in the next parliamentary round (1893-4), and there was as yet no indication that the Chancellor of the Exchequer, Sir William Harcourt, would relent.[26] Construction of the Mallaig line could not begin for many months; and Forman may well have judged the moment right to test the mutual forbearance of the principal subscribers to the treaty of 1889. Could the North British be tempted to adopt his Inverness (or Fort Augustus) project? He had prepared Spean–to–Spey plans too, and so possessed a second string.[27] On the assurance that his Great Glen project would be set aside, the Highland and North British might be levered into endorsing a Loch Laggan

David MacBrayne (d.1907), who took over the Hutcheson steamer company in 1878. "MacBraynes", diversifying into road transport, would remain a family firm until 1928, when the London, Midland & Scottish Railway (LMS) assumed part ownership. (Author's collection)

line – which the Highland regarded as much the lesser evil.

Though openly at odds over the Mallaig Extension, behind the scenes Conacher and Dougall intended, if they could, to maintain the Great Glen Agreement. Dougall was persuaded that his company should not oppose a West Highland branch into Strathspey, allowable under the terms of 1889 – so much can be inferred from his interview with Lochiel on 21st October 1893, touching on new railways "towards Inverness and Kingussie". This Dougall recounted to the Highland board four days later, and meanwhile there had been a further survey along Loch Laggan, on the West Highland Company's instructions. Whether North British engineering staff were involved does not appear. These developments overlapped Forman's negotiations with the prospective private backers of a Great Glen promotion; and mid-November saw reports appear that, for the moment, a Spean Bridge–Inverness (or Spean Bridge–Fort Augustus) scheme would not be pursued.[28]

Without full North British support, no West Highland promotion could proceed, and Conacher was poised to retreat from the prospective Loch Laggan line as soon as he judged it safe to do so. On 16th November he wrote urgently, and confidentially, to secretary Wieland:

Mr Dougall has just been here, and...according to his information...the Promoters of the Fort William & Inverness Line (sic) have [been] advised to defer their scheme... If we can be assured of this, [nothing] further should be done in the Kingussie scheme...

Conacher was too late to prevent publication (18th November) of the preliminary notice for a "West Highland Inverlair & Kingussie Extension". (For "Inverlair" read "Tulloch" – see below.) Against misunderstanding or suspicion of treachery, he wrote personally to assure Dougall that no bill would follow. Having informed the Highland directors, Dougall returned his thanks, though with a barbed postscript:

I am glad that the projected Inverlair & Kingussie Line is to be withdrawn. I hope before long you will be able to make a similar announcement in regard to the Mallaig [railway].[29]

Was Forman out-manoeuvred? Coincidentally or not, his relations with Conacher thereafter deteriorated markedly. Both Formans & McCall and Lucas & Aird were hard pressed when the North British insisted that the West Highland must be ready before the summer season of 1894 ran out. With traffic begun, arguments over the work unfinished would persist into 1896. Adding to bad feeling was another Forman project – a funicular connection from Whistlefield to Portincaple (Loch Long), at the southern end of the new railway, which the North British would not entertain. The scheme found support, to Conacher's

Looking north east in 1914 towards Loch Laggan from the down platform at Tulloch (briefly "Inverlair") in upper Glen Spean. This is the direction in which the West Highland Company's Inverlair & Kingussie Extension would have run. From Tulloch, Glasgow-bound trains turn east then south, to climb by Loch Treig into Rannoch Moor.
(J B Sherlock)

embarrassment, among the influential "residenters" (largely Glasgow businessmen) of Carrick Castle and Lochgoilhead.[30] When in July 1894 Parliament finally approved the Mallaig Extension, engineering responsibility would remain with Alexander Simpson, who had conducted the Loch Eil & Mallaig survey (above). Forman had looked to be involved; but, belatedly reimbursed for his Fort William – Roshven plans, he withdrew in Simpson's favour.[31]

At the West Highland's official opening on 11th August 1894, Lord Tweeddale emphasised how North British shareholders had done their duty. They could expect no early reward for sustaining the West Highland Company, and any input to the Mallaig Extension meant an additional sacrifice. The future welfare of a large region was at stake and the Liberal Government should play their part by accelerating the vital Treasury Guarantee, which at last they had promised to honour. He claimed Lochaber for the North British, who were alive to local needs – in the medium term, additional to the Mallaig line, other projects would be considered. Tweeddale implied, however, that the Great Glen Agreement would remain in force – because both the Highland Company and the North British had their hands full. The Highland, he suggested, ought to reconsider one or more of the "Lothian lines" which fell indisputably within their territory. Meanwhile the North British would make sure, with subsidy in place, that the West Highland was completed as quickly as possible to the Atlantic coast. Closing the gap between Fort William and Inverness was for the longer term when other obligations had been fulfilled.[32]

Despite these emollient words, Tweeddale and Conacher knew that the previous year's muted crisis in the Great Glen had been imperfectly resolved. Lochiel thought it likely that, by way of insurance, the North British would be obliged to revive the fleeting West Highland Kingussie Extension. The proprietors affected must be kept amenable and, to this end, in an otherwise petty quarrel, he was ready to appease The Mackintosh, who had demanded that Inverlair station in Glen Spean be renamed Tulloch – as it was from 1895.[33] And Forman, who had by no

means given up, could well find other opportunities – he might entangle Caledonian and North British, their Peace Agreement notwithstanding, besides North British and Highland. Five years earlier the Caledonian Company, glossing over their own dilatory record, had warned that approval of the West Highland route would prevent their ever again sponsoring the "more useful" Callander & Oban coastal branch from Connel Ferry to Ballachulish and Fort William, which, they protested, had always been their intention.[34] But these were tactics, with the West Highland Bill still in the balance. Now the West Highland was accomplished fact and politics had moved on. The 40 miles between Oban and Fort William had become, like the Great Glen, a no-man's-land – though not formally so defined – and what might the Caledonian do next?

* * *

In 1893 the Highland directors had not been called upon to tolerate a Spean-to-Spey link in West Highland (i.e. North British) hands; and it is questionable whether in the end they would have assented. Remembering how in 1888-9 they had underestimated the danger which the West Highland promotion posed, they were resolved not to repeat their mistake. Had Dougall been too trustful in his dealings with Conacher? Had the deceitful North British, ostensibly eager to preserve the Great Glen Truce from "outside" assault, colluded with Forman after all? Were they readying their next move and would this follow the opening of the West Highland? (It was another goad that further resistance to the Mallaig Extension Bill had proved useless.) Apprehensive and resentful, the Highland board had come to contemplate pre-emptive occupation of the Great Glen, and rumours of a fresh survey to Inverness, to be carried out by Forman under North British instruction, may have been the final provocation. Less than a month after the West Highland's opening-day celebrations, they resolved to lodge the necessary bill, instructing company engineer Murdoch Paterson to prepare parliamentary plans.[35]

The Callander & Oban, too, were ready to set the pace.

Caledonian overlordship was lightly exercised (by contrast, the West Highland was regarded dismissively, from the first, as "the North British by another name") and secretary-manager John Anderson, whose long career bears comparison with Dougall's, enjoyed a large freedom of action. In 1888-9 he had resisted the West Highland promotion vigorously, but he intended to make what he could of transfer traffic and thought it pointless to bicker over the Crianlarich spur (which would lie unused into 1897). Anderson judged that an Oban–Lochaber connection, like exchange at Crianlarich, would be modestly worthwhile and, on balance, more advantageous to the Caledonian than to the North British. At his prompting, the Callander & Oban directors set aside £1,500 for an up-to-date survey between Connel Ferry and Fort William, continuing (if money permitted) to Fort Augustus or even to Inverness, and this decision coincided – by accident or otherwise – with the Highland's abrogation of the Great Glen Agreement in the autumn of 1894.[36]

Though the Mallaig line had won its act, the vital Treasury Guarantee faced an uneasy parliamentary passage, and it may be that Anderson had hit on a more subtle policy than outright opposition. Events had overtaken both the Ten Years Truce and the Peace Agreement, as contractor John Aird reminded Conacher. The North British, who might have anticipated Forman's intrigues of 1893, should have kept the initiative by terminating the 1889 treaty and backing a West Highland bid for Inverness.[37] Instead, they had been forced onto the defensive. Given powers to reach Fort William, the Callander & Oban or their Caledonian patron, and the Highland too, might plausibly claim some share in the West Highland Extension as effectively a "government line", funded by taxpayers who deserved value for money – it would carry the maximum traffic if connected with Inverness and Oban.

The proposed line from Connel Ferry into Lochaber was itself a candidate for subsidy. Lord Tweeddale, in his speech at Fort William that August, had urged the opponents of the Mallaig project to desist, devoting their energies instead to other desirable schemes on which the Government might look with favour; and Anderson could claim to have heeded the advice of the North British-cum-West Highland chairman, an irony that did not escape notice. State funding in any shape for a Great Glen line was quite out of the question – on that the Highland Company had no illusions – while a railway through Benderloch, Appin and Ballachulish, on Anderson's own figures, would find adequate local business. However, a strong case for aid lay in the cost of bridging Loch Etive, Loch Creran and Loch Leven. If dual-purpose structures were adopted, carrying a roadway, central government or local authority assistance for the Callander & Oban could surely be justified? Sir John Wolfe-Barry (of Tower Bridge fame), who had served on the Lothian Commission, was enlisted to design these sea-loch viaducts, while the general plans for what emerged as a Connel Ferry to Banavie branch were entrusted to Charles Forman. Press coverage proved broadly sympathetic. Although the Highland Company, by common consent, had done most for the North of Scotland, the Caledonian, in sustaining the Callander & Oban, had opened up the western Highlands, where the North British were latecomers. In consequence of the Lothian Commission findings, both the Highland and North British looked to receive specific help, for extension of the Dingwall & Skye and the West Highland respectively. The Caledonian would benefit only indirectly from the additional traffic at Oban generated by the enhanced steamer timetable which the Commission had recommended, and assistance for a needful line along the Linnhe coast would square the account.[38]

Earlier (c.1890) Anderson had encouraged a superficial survey for an unlikely 60-mile line from Connel Ferry to Ardnamurchan (Kentra), which would have required a fourth sea-loch viaduct at Corran Ferry.[39] The circumstances are shadowy, but he may have seen Kentra as another potential railway harbour "south of Strome" for the attention of the Lothian Commission. That in 1894 he really looked beyond Fort

Sporting estates and their upkeep generated rail traffic both in and out of season, but the conversion of previously "cleared" land from sheep farming to shooting and fishing remained controversial. The *Illustrated London News* of Saturday 30th September 1905 shows King Edward VII on a deer drive. The King was accompanied by Henderson, Lord Burton's retired head stalker. The scene of the drive was the district round the head of Glen Quoich, traditionally a deer sanctuary for MacDonell (MacDonald) of Glen Garry.

Looking across Corran Ferry into Ardgour at the Loch Linnhe Narrows, c.1960. The bus waiting on the slipway carries the distinctive MacBrayne livery. John Anderson of the Callander & Oban Company scouted a 60-mile line from Connel Ferry to Ardnamurchan (Kentra), requiring four expensive sea-loch viaducts, one of them at this spot. On the never-to-be-built West Highland Ballachulish Extension, Corran would have become a railhead for the Ardgour hinterland.
(John Sinclair collection)

William, save to wrong-foot the North British, seems improbable. Nevertheless, newspapers and even sober professional journals saw an impending drama. Let the suddenly-announced projects, Highland and Callander & Oban, be combined and a through Oban–Fort William–Inverness railway would result – quite excluding the West Highland Company. To the more excitable commentators it seemed poetic justice that the North British invader, newly established in Lochaber, now in turn faced invasion. The Caledonian Company, who had neither encouraged (so they said) nor forbidden Anderson's initiative, could afford to wait-and-see, relishing North British discomfiture – and the Callander & Oban contemplated working their new line themselves, which made Caledonian detachment more believable.[40] It was remarked that the public stood to gain a secondary route from the Central Belt to Inverness, via Crianlarich, Connel Ferry, Ballachulish and the Great Glen – which must temper the Highland Company's outdated monopoly but would not threaten them with ruin. At all events, if the Highland retreated from their hasty Great Glen scheme, a Callander & Oban presence at Fort William would help ensure that the way to Inverness was not again closed off for years ahead.

Under pressure both in and out of Parliament, the Liberal Government had conceded in principle that "we must carry out the undertaking...given by our predecessors". Finalising the Treasury Guarantee for the Mallaig line, they now said, was only a matter of time and procedure. But these were the assurances of a weak and divided administration, who might seize on any complication as an excuse for procrastination.[41] There can be little doubt that Anderson and Dougall were playing politics, the former with the Caledonian's blessing. Though the Great Glen was Dougall's prime concern, together they saw a fresh opportunity to frustrate or at least delay the West Highland Extension. Forman would lay out his Callander & Oban line to terminate at Banavie, and a bid for running powers or joint ownership onwards to Mallaig was clearly implied. Indeed, the Callander & Oban Bill would specify powers to this effect, though probably without genuine intent. The Highland's Great Glen plans, prepared by Paterson, included a Banavie spur – with similar, if unstated, implications.

For Tweeddale and Conacher, ultimately answerable to the edgy North British board, it was all-important that the West Highland Company should retain absolute control of the Mallaig line, so as to secure the whole balance of its revenues after the conditions of subsidy had been met. But, confident in the knowledge that the Treasury would not entertain any joint arrangement, they could brave this latest threat. What to do in the Great Glen was a different matter. The wording of the 1889 Agreement (see Chapter 1) on the face of things left the Highland Company at liberty to resile, leaving the North British and West Highland tied. Only a strained reading could sustain the argument that the Highland had admitted the West Highland's right to full possession in return for a 10-year breathing space. James Watson, the North British company solicitor, thought the matter "very difficult":

> I do not see how the West Highland...can get out of it and there is nothing express (sic)... which could prevent the Highland... going on with a line. [It] must be the West Highland ...case that there is implied in the Agreement [how] a line to Inverness was in the scope of their intention, a view acquiesced in by Mr Dougall on behalf of the Highland Company [but] postponed as a concession...

The Highland would maintain, he warned Conacher, that they had entered into the treaty on the understanding that they were free to bring forward their own Great Glen promotion whenever they chose.[42]

These conflicting positions were widely reported, attracting much editorial comment. On 14th September *The Scotsman* carried the North British version, while a Highland rejoinder appeared in the next day's *Aberdeen Free Press*. It was noted, too, how the Caledonian Company had so far stood aloof (*Glasgow Herald*, 14th September). The authoritative *Railway Times* (15th September) declared that the action of the "conservative" Highland Company was out-of-character and ill-advised; their enthusiasm for "this wonderful Fort William Extension" did not convince; "dread of southern competition" was the only explanation, and they would discover that they were no longer their own masters, if obliged to come to terms with the Callander & Oban. On 22nd September the *Oban Times* took up the same theme – whatever the Highland's reasons, their "autocratic monopoly" would not easily be restored, and a Callander & Oban–Highland agreement for a through line to Inverness was the likely outcome. Anderson's bold step, the editorial continued, had been welcomed in every district between Connel Ferry and Fort William. This was contradicted by other reports, which discovered a strong local feeling in favour of a West Highland branch south to Ballachulish and into Appin, because in the past the Callander & Oban (more accurately, the Caledonian) had blown hot and cold.

References

J. McGregor, *The West Highland Railway: Plans, Politics and People*, Birlinn (John Donald), 2005, cited as PPP.

NRS/BR/LNE/8/764 – because the Treasury's Mallaig Guarantee ran till 1931, the North British general manager's files relating to the West Highland Extension were reclassified "LNE" from 1923.

Notes 16 and 19-23 – the Cameron of Lochiel Papers (Lochaber Archive) include the Glenquoich estate Letter Books, which contain much of George Malcolm's correspondence.

1. PPP, chapters 2 and 3. NRS/BR/PYB(S)/1/325, Lord Abinger, evidence, and Nigel MacKenzie, evidence, Glasgow & North Western Railway Bill, Commons, 3 and 7 May 1883.
2. PPP, chapter 3.
3. PPP, pp.67-8. NRS/BR/WEH/1/1, West Highland Railway minutes, 5 March 1890.
4. PPP, pp.11-4 and 97. NRS/BR/SPC/9/1, Conacher Papers, Marquess of Tweeddale to John Conacher, 15 August 1891. NRS/BR/NBR/3/15, New Lines Agreement, 1891, cf. *Glasgow Herald*, 23 October 1891, reporting Caledonian Railway-North British Railway negotiations.
5. PPP, chapter 4.
6. For example:- NRS/BR/LNE/8/764/Box 1, general manager's files relating to West Highland (Mallaig Extension) Railway, Alexander MacDonald, to George Wieland, secretary, North British Railway, 4 May 1891 – with copy of MacDonald's evidence to the Lothian Commissioners, 22 May 1890.
7. PPP, chapter 4. NRS/BR/HR/1/6, Highland Railway minutes, 26 April 1889.
8. NRS/BR/LNE/8/764/Box 1, Wieland to John Baird, 9 and 13 November 1891.
9. PPP, Chapter 4. NRS/BR/LNE/8/1764/Box 6, general manager's files relating to Mallaig Extension, Andrew Dougall, to G.J. Goschen MP, 1 June 1892 – copied to Lord Lothian, Secretary of State for Scotland. Ibid, H. Babbington-Smith (H.M.Treasury) to Dougall, 2 June 1892.
10. Jack Kernahan, *The Black Isle Railway*, The Highland Railway Society, 2013. PPP, chapters 4 and 5.
11. PPP, p.120.
12. Ibid., chapter 4.
13. NRS/BR/PYB(S)/1/325, Donald P. MacDonald, evidence, and Lord Abinger, evidence, Glasgow & North Western Railway Bill, Commons, 1 and 3 May 1883.
14. MacKenzie Papers, West Highland Museum, Rev. Leo Linse, Fort Augustus, Proof for West Highland Railway Bill, 1888-9.
15. NRS/BR/PYB(S)/1/386, Invergarry & Fort Augustus Railway Bill, evidence, various witnesses, May 1896. Andrew Perchard, *Aluminiumville*, Crucible, 2012, pp. 26 and 137. Lochiel Papers, Lochaber Archive, CL/A/3/2/31, items relating to proposed Glasgow & North Western Railway. Kernahan, op.cit., chapter 2. NRS/BR/LNE/8/764/Box 1, W.C. Dunbar to Innes & MacKay, 16 April 1892.
16. CL/A/12/1/8, George Malcolm to Lord Abinger, 5 November 1888, cf. Malcolm to Lord Burton, 15 November 1887.
17. PPP, p.146.
18. NRS/BR/PYB(S)/1/325, Glasgow & North Western Railway Bill, Commons, 25 April 1883. Ibid., Sir Michael Bass (subsequently Lord Burton), evidence, 2 May 1883.
19. CL/A/12/1/8, Malcolm to Burton, 15 November 1887; to Lord Abinger, 5 November 1888. NRS/BR/PYB (S)/342, Burton, evidence, West Highland Railway Bill, Commons, 4 July 1889.
20. CL/A/12/1/5 Malcolm memorandum, (?) May, 1881. NRS/BR/PYB(S)/1/342, Malcolm, evidence, West Highland Railway Bill, Lords, 27 March 1889.
21. CL/A/12/1/5, Malcolm to Bass, 9 August 1882. NRS/BR/PYB (S)/1/325, Thomas Walrond-Smith, evidence, Glasgow & North Western Railway Bill, Commons, 8 May 1883.
22. CL/A/12/1/5, Malcolm to Bass, 6 October 1882, 3 February 1883 and 3 April 1883.
23. PPP, Chapter 3. CL/A/12/1/8, Malcolm to Burton, 15 November 1887; to Donald Boyd, 10 February 1888; to Abinger, 5 November 1888 and 26 April 1889; to Lochiel, 26 January 1889. NRS/BR/PYB(S)/1/342, Malcolm's cross-examination, West Highland Railway Bill, Lords, 27 March 1889, and Commons, 4 July 1889.
24. PPP, p.153. *Oban Times*, 22 September 1894.
25. *Inverness Courier*, 27 October 1893.
26. PPP, pp.102-3.
27. *Inverness Courier*, 24 and 27 October 1893.
28. *Inverness Courier*, 24 October 1893. NRS/BR/HR/1/7, Highland Railway minutes, 25 October 1893.
29. *Inverness Courier*, 14 November 1893. NRS/BR/LNE/8/764/Box 1, Conacher to Wieland, 16 November 1893. Ibid., Wieland to Conacher and Conacher to Wieland, telegrams, 18 November 1893; Conacher to Andrew Dougall, 27 November 1893; and Dougall to Conacher, 28 November 1893. NRS/BR/HR/1/7, Highland Railway Minutes, 6 December 1893.
30. PPP, p.143.
31. NRS/BR/LNE/8/764/Box 1, Simpson & Wilson to Conacher, 3 March 1893; and Tweeddale to Conacher, 6 March 1893.
32. *Glasgow Herald*, 9 August 1894, reporting that a bill to authorise a Treasury Guarantee for the Mallaig Extension would be introduced. *The Scotsman,* 13 August 1894, reporting in full Tweeddale's speech at Fort William.
33. NRS/BR/WEH/4/4, Tulloch station dispute.
34. NRS/BR/PYB(S)1/342, Joseph Bolton evidence, West Highland Railway Bill, Lords, 3 April 1889; James Thompson evidence, West Highland Railway Bill, Commons, 5 July 1889.
35. NRS/BR/NBR/8/1764/Box 6, general manager's files relating to the West Highland Railway, William Arnott to Conacher, 29 August 1894. NRS/BR/HR/1/8, Highland Railway minutes, 5 September 1894. *The Scotsman,* 6 September 1894. NRS/BR/PYB(S)/1/378, Highland Railway, Spean Bridge & Fort William Extension, 1894-5 (with press cuttings etc.)
36. NRS/BR/COB/1/5, Callander & Oban Railway minutes, 5 and 26 September 1894 1894.NRS/BR/PYB(S)/1/378, Callander & Oban Railway, Ballachulish, Fort William & Banavie Extension, 1894-5 (with press-cuttings etc.).
37. 37. NRS/BR/NBR/8/1764/Box 6, John Aird to Conacher, 14 September 1894.
38. NRS/PC91, press cuttings relating to the West Highland Railway, 13 September, 3 October and 28 November 1894. *Oban Times*, 22 September 1894. *Railway Times*, 20 October 1894. *Financial Times,* 30 October 1894. *Dundee Advertiser*, 5 December 1894. *Glasgow Herald*, 7 December 1894.
39. Scottish Railway Preservation Society Collection.
40. *Glasgow Herald*, 14 September 1894. Railway News, 15 September 1894. NRS/BR/COB/1/5, Callander & Oban Railway minutes, 9 November 1894. NBR/8/1764/Box 4, Thompson to Conacher, 28 November 1894 and Conacher to Thompson 30 November 1894.
41. NRS/BR/LNE/8/764/Box 1, Durnford & Co. to Conacher, 20 July 1894. NRS/BR/NBR/8/1764/Box 3, Lochiel to Conacher, 23 July 1894.
42. NRS/BR/NBR/8/1764/Box 6, Watson to Conacher 7 September 1894.

Banavie basin on the Caledonian Canal (see p.36) was sited above the seven locks of "Neptune's Staircase", which is seen here in 1973 with the railway swing bridge on the Mallaig line prominent at centre right. Passenger vessels did not make the tedious passage but turned in Banavie basin, beyond the top lock (see pp. 36 and 53). Interchange with the Oban steamers at Corpach was traditionally by "horse omnibus". From 1895 the West Highland Banavie branch permitted passengers to transfer instead via Fort William.   (Keith Fenwick)

Lines and proposed lines at Fort William – the implausible tangle of 1894-5, with the West Highland Mallaig Extension newly approved, the Banavie branch unfinished and both Callander & Oban and Highland schemes in prospect. They are superimposed on the 1947 Ordnance Survey map, which also shows the West Highland proper, opened in August 1894.

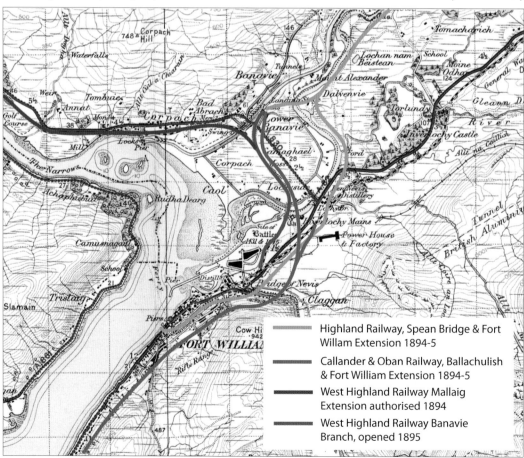

Highland Railway, Spean Bridge & Fort Willam Extension 1894-5

Callander & Oban Railway, Ballachulish & Fort William Extension 1894-5

West Highland Railway Mallaig Extension authorised 1894

West Highland Railway Banavie Branch, opened 1895

CHAPTER THREE

PATCHED-UP QUARRELS, 1894-95

The Highland Company claimed that the 1889 Agreement had left them free to occupy the Great Glen, should self-defence so require. In taking countermeasures the North British would face the accusation that they and not the Highland had broken the treaty. Nevertheless, North British solicitor James Watson favoured a swift and firm response:

The West Highland Company should promote a line to Inverness following exactly the same route as the proposed new Highland line, at all events where it passes through the property of any landowner...likely to give trouble in a West Highland scheme...[1]

If rival projects coincided, the proprietor must resist them both or admit bias – Watson's tactics were obvious. But a parliamentary contest would be chancy, and the best *strategy* was another matter. The North British had pledged to make good the loss of Roshven, provided that the Liberal Government gave assistance, and the Lothian Commission, in identifying the Mallaig Extension as a desirable project, had reinforced their claim to the districts west of Fort William. By contrast, their pretensions in the Great Glen had been consigned to the vague future. Lord Tweeddale confided to general manager John Conacher that he foresaw a protracted conflict. The North British chairman, who sat on the Highland board (by virtue of the two companies' common interests at Perth), found the other directors in belligerent mood. Once competing bills were lodged, he feared that there would be no early negotiations. If the threat of a rival promotion was not enough to make the Highland Company retreat, would North British shareholders see out a parliamentary battle which might end in new obligations?[2]

Victory for the West Highland, but with no immediate imperative to build a Great Glen line, was Tweeddale's ideal outcome. Tantamount to restoration of the 1889 truce on North British terms, this would exclude the Highland from Lochaber for as long as the West Highland Company's powers endured, and the North British would be able to argue, at least for the time being, that Parliament had acquiesced in the postponement of all Great Glen schemes. Cameron of Lochiel, on the other hand, thought the situation very hazardous. He wanted the earliest possible compromise. The critics of the Mallaig Extension had not been silenced and for the West Highland Company to pretend that another costly promotion was affordable would reinvigorate their opposition. (Was subsidy for the Mallaig line necessary after all? Should the Treasury's contribution be reduced?) The Highland must be persuaded not to "risk the issue in Parliament".[3]

John Walker (for the North British Company) and the Cameron chief (representing the West Highland promoters) had signed the Great Glen Agreement in 1889. With Walker dead, it would be Lochiel's responsibility to sustain the dubious position that the Highland had already surrendered the Great Glen in principle and must give way to the West Highland. Could he refute, under cross-examination in Committee, the inevitable argument that North British and West Highland were still tied by the treaty? Could he face down the charge that "as a Director I have repudiated what I undertook as a Promoter"? Moreover, Lochiel dreaded an embarrassing victory and could not see "how we are to raise the capital for [a railway] to Inverness". If empowered to build a Great Glen line, the West Highland Company must turn to their North British parent, whose further benevolence would be severely tested. He deprecated all complexity until the Mallaig Extension was safe. Tweeddale responded (with more confidence than he truly felt) that, when the time came, the North British would rewrite their guarantee to include an approved West Highland extension to Inverness. In placatory tone, Conacher explained that no irrevocable decision had been taken. However, the Highland Company must be kept under pressure by making ready a competing scheme.[4]

For Tweeddale and Conacher, and for Lochiel too, it was the worst of all possibilities that Callander & Oban and Highland might join forces at Fort William, in joint possession of an Oban–Inverness line. There was no ensnaring treaty to prevent the immediate promotion of a West Highland "blocking" branch to Ballachulish, whereby John Anderson and the Callander & Oban board might be brought to terms. But no lasting settlement would result without the acquiescence of the Caledonian Company – who for the moment affected detachment, while the Callander & Oban ostensibly looked to work the new line themselves and had appointed their own agent in Fort William.[5] Not without apprehension, the North British directors chose patience. The Caledonian must show their hand before long. Meanwhile, in a curious about-turn, Charles Forman's Great Glen plans of 1893, unwanted by the Highland, had been purchased by the North British, and thus he added a new West Highland brief to his Callander & Oban appointment.[6] No doubt this reinforced the Highland's earlier suspicions, which had brought them to denounce the Ten Years Truce; but it does not follow that the North British had all along intrigued with the opportunistic engineer.

Callander & Oban and Highland together might have argued (see Chapter 2) that their respective schemes added up to a useful, though roundabout, supplementary route to the North; and parliamentary recognition of their joint interest in the Great Glen would have disposed of the West Highland Company's claim to sole possession. (A secondary route via Aberdeen, of course already existed, its value limited by the intermittent hostilities of the Highland and the Great North of Scotland.) Forman, whose long-term programme certainly included a through Oban–Fort William–Inverness line, may have hoped that Callander & Oban and West Highland would become allies. But that twist of events is hard to imagine – the Caledonian, who would dictate Callander & Oban policy in the end, were unlikely to leave the Highland in the lurch for the sake of a fractious Great Glen partnership with the North British. Might the Caledonian have been ready to redefine their long association with the Highland Company so that Fort William, with the Callander & Oban established there, became a lesser point of exchange, supplementary to Perth? Arguably, such an outcome would have given the Highland security for the long term, ensuring the "least worst" division of their closely guarded traffic. It is probable that any Caledonian calculations went no further, but probable too that the Highland were unconvinced. The West Highland were already ensconced in Lochaber and Parliament might well prescribe equal treatment. A Great Glen accord, Callander & Oban and Highland, with the West Highland as a third party, would not bar the North British decisively from Inverness.

Certain Highland directors were rumoured to have encouraged a complementary Callander & Oban promotion, perhaps as an answer of sorts to the inevitable charge that their own bill was a blatant "blocking" measure.[7] However, there is little or no evidence that John Anderson and Andrew Dougall had colluded in detail. The Highland secretary-manager was wary of any entanglement, and a prolonged Great Glen contest would invite intervention by the Great North of Scotland Company, who might turn the situation to advantage. Dougall preferred a forthright strategy, asserting the superiority of the Perth–Inverness main line and his company's right to defend it against all-comers. On paper, West Highland-cum-Great Glen constituted the shorter through route and would do so still, by a narrower margin, when the Highland's Aviemore cut-off was

completed; but journey times were another matter, and Dougall intended to expose all the limitations of the West Highland's exacting 90 miles between Craigendoran and Glen Spean. In search of ammunition, he requested that the Board of Trade provide copies of all their reports on the condition of the newly opened railway, only to have his "most unusual application" indignantly refused, as undermining the Board's impartiality.[8]

After the initial flurry of suspicions, accusations and counter-accusations, would all three bills proceed? Nervous investors shied away from Highland and North British stock and the Caledonian too were affected. At the North British statutory half-yearly meeting in late September, Tweeddale had fallen back on the convenient fiction of West Highland independence and made no firm commitment to a Great Glen promotion. Aeneas Mackintosh of Raigmore, chairman of the Highland Company, addressed his shareholders early in October, and he also gave little away, beyond "hopeful reference" to a Fort William line. He dwelt instead on the satisfactory earnings of the Strathpeffer branch and the progress of the Aviemore cut-off. After years of deliberately slow advance, work on the latter would be pressed on, in response to the new uncertainties which completion of the West Highland had created, and the powers first obtained in 1884 must be renewed one last time.[9]

* * *

Meanwhile debate continued in the correspondence columns of the press, ranging over the original West Highland project and the findings of the Lothian Commission besides the battles immediately in prospect – and with not a few editorials too (see panel below). Poetic justice was a recurring theme. The North British Company, by ill-advisedly backing the West Highland, had invited the retaliation which they now faced, but the Mallaig Extension, in the opinion of most commentators, ought to be built, because the hoped-for economic and social benefits of the new routes could not be fully realised without it. Yet this must entail further injury, in some degree, for both the Caledonian (Callander & Oban) and the Highland (Dingwall & Skye), compounding their

---

Railway Times, editorial, 15th December 1894

[The West Highland Company and the North British are justified in trying to reach Mallaig] but the case for [their] extension to Inverness stands on a wholly different footing...Of its own motion the North British has gone out into the wilderness and... cannot justly complain if it fails to find there the means of sustenance. In truth it may be shrewdly doubted whether Inverness and the Highlands require a second railway or could adequately support it.

Railway Times, letter, 29th December 1894 from P. Campbell-Ross

Would you deprive the people living north of the Grampians of the advantages which competition for their traffic would give them, and...on the strength of information given by those whose interest it is to maintain [an] injurious monopoly? [The Kyle of Lochalsh extension] adds mileage to the Highland system; but it will have no other advantage. It was a blunder to attempt it merely with the view of putting the extension of the West Highland to Mallaig out of court; for [the latter] is to be proceeded with...

Railway Times editorial, 29th December 1894

If [competition] is brought about by building railways in excess of local requirements, then it will inevitably be found in the long run, that a temporary advantage has been purchased at the price of a permanent disability...The ultimate cost of such mistakes must be shared between the capitalist and the community. For the fierce competition engendered by reckless construction must in the end give place to an agreement to maintain rates, and the trader and the travelling public must alike be taxed in the endeavour to earn some interest on misspent money...One fairly prosperous railway is likely to afford better facilities than would be given by two companies engaged in a perpetual struggle with bankruptcy.

righteous resentment. Though Mallaig traffic would improve the West Highland's balance sheet, the North British could not expect to recoup sufficiently until they reached Inverness, in stark competition with the Highland Company. In that event, although the Perth–Inverness line might retain its primacy, the Highland must suffer lasting harm, and the Caledonian's share of through traffic must diminish. The Post Office, for example, would come under pressure to modify the existing mail contracts in favour of the shorter route. At the extreme, the Highland might be driven to amalgamation. Would union with the Great North of Scotland offer a way out? Or would Caledonian and North British fight over the spoils?[10]

The Highland found fiercely partisan apologists, who extolled the company's reliable dividends and defended a "justified monopoly". North British domination of Fife, argued some, had been much more objectionable. (Kirkcaldy's Liberal MP, though not unfriendly to the West Highland, doggedly opposed state assistance for the Mallaig Extension, as an undeserved reward for their paymaster.) And what had Caledonian and North British to show for decades of tit-for-tat competition? Small-investor earnings would be depressed if West Highland and North British capital were unproductively enlarged to finance railways so obviously ahead of their time. The entire North owed the Highland Company a debt of gratitude, and if management had become hidebound (as many admitted) then completion of the Aviemore cut-off would bring reinvigoration. Let those who thought otherwise ponder the consequences of a forced amalgamation – company offices and railway-related activities, especially locomotive building, would almost certainly depart Inverness, to the town's great loss. All this brought the rejoinder that the Highland's solid reputation had been achieved at the expense of traders and travelling public. Spending on facilities and rolling stock was undeniably overdue and the company's antiquated passenger vehicles drew unflattering comparison with the West Highland's new compartment-cum-saloon bogie coaches. Threats alone produced action. Half-hearted improvement, plus a few new branches like the Black Isle line (1894), had been prompted by the Great North's intermittent probing. The Glasgow & North Western challenge a dozen years before had brought a temporary vigour. The Highland Company, wrote one critic, "never move except under the lash".[11]

In the to-and-fro of debate, the disappointed interests "north of Strome" made themselves heard, though no one "Lothian line" emerged as the preferred candidate for reassessment. P. Campbell-Ross, an embittered supporter of the Garve & Ullapool Railway Company (wound up in 1893), condemned the Highland's panicky behaviour (see panel on page 28). When the Treasury proved amenable, Dougall and his directors had settled much too hastily for extension of the Dingwall & Skye route; and they had gone on to precipitate a needless confrontation with the North British. A Great Glen contest would divert resources from more useful schemes and extinguish the last hopes of the Garve & Ullapool syndicate (cf. Lochiel's fears for the West Highland Mallaig Extension, as not yet fully secure).[12] That first the Aviemore project and next the Lothian Report had too much preoccupied the Highland board was another complaint – the directors had "neglected" the weary route to Wick and Thurso

and now their attention would be fixed on further defensive measures. If the North British prevailed, could they be persuaded to take a hand beyond Inverness, as the Great North had tried but so far failed to do? Might they find the resources to eliminate the long detours by Lairg and Forsinard?[13]

The Highland Company, said critics, deserved small sympathy. The board had been notoriously make-do-and-mend, while investment in buildings and equipment became ever more urgent. Partial funding for the Kyle of Lochalsh scheme was a mere "sop" wheedled from the previous Government, after it had been made clear that the Mallaig line would receive assistance, and the Dingwall & Skye, when extended to Kyle, would serve the rail-less districts to the north-west no better than before. The Highland ought to have embraced purposefully at least one "north of Strome" scheme. Instead the directors had fudged the matter, opting insincerely for Lochinver only to ensure that the Treasury did not close with the Great North's offer to work the Garve & Ullapool. Moreover, the Highland ought long since to have pushed the Aviemore cut-off more energetically, instead of deploring its necessity. The Kyle line, despite the assurance of a parliamentary grant, required a sizeable input. If this already meant financial over-stretch, by what logic could an unrewarding 60-mile "block" scheme in the Great Glen be justified? ("Let them show that they can creditably manage what they already have in charge.")[14]

For many it remained axiomatic that the well-being of the Highland Railway and the well-being of Inverness and the North were one and the same. But others strongly differed, asserting that the company's landowner-directors inevitably put their own interests first. The Garve & Ullapool party claimed that the Highland's short-lived endorsement of a Culrain–Lochinver line, disingenuous in any case, revealed the influence of the Duke of Sutherland, who, they alleged, had tried to manipulate the aged Liberal premier, William Gladstone, in the matter of subsidy.[15] If the overall transport needs of the region had outstripped the resources which the Highland Company could command, then their independence could not long continue, and a costly victory in the Great Glen would be meaningless. When Parliament approved the West Highland Mallaig Extension (the "first successful assault on the Highland's monopoly"), the board had convinced themselves, on slender evidence, that a North British attack on Inverness was bound to follow, and their decision that the Aviemore cut-off should be quickly finished was likewise an error, bringing conflict with contractors and subcontractors and injury to the local businesses who supplied them. Litigation had ensued, which could only mean more delay. In sum, the Highland's blinkered and defensive instincts reflected the mentality of the landed proprietors too long in control, whose own status and income were no longer assured. More modern management was urgently needed.[16]

* * *

In mid-November 1894 preliminary notices announced the Callander & Oban Ballachulish, Fort William & Banavie Extension; the Highland Spean Bridge & Fort William Extension; and the West Highland Inverness Extension. All three Bills were duly lodged, and the Great North of Scotland

Company weighed in too: their Bill, by no means the first of its kind, sought running powers to Inverness and Muirton basin (on the Caledonian Canal) – this time on the basis that connection with either Great Glen scheme must be in the public interest.[17]

Callander & Oban:- Commencing with a triangular junction at Connel Ferry, Forman and Wolfe-Barry laid out a line to Ballachulish Ferry almost identical with the Ballachulish branch as later built. Crossing Loch Leven, it continued through Onich to Corran Ferry and along Loch Linnhe. Approaching Fort William, where the West Highland had occupied the seafront, it rose to a hillside station behind the town and dropped again to Nevis Bridge. It then paralleled the West Highland Banavie branch (on which traffic would not begin until June 1895). For goods sidings and a locomotive depot at Fort William, accessed by a spur from Nevis Bridge, the Callander & Oban proposed to acquire the then Victoria Park (today the site of the town's swimming pool). Another spur joined the West Highland in the direction of Spean Bridge. A light line to East Laroch (for Ballachulish village and quarries) diverged at Ballachulish Ferry.[18]

Highland:- From a junction on the Aviemore cut-off, just outside Inverness, Murdoch Paterson's Great Glen line swung south, then spanned the canalised River Ness at Bona Ferry. To Fort Augustus, it took the north-western side of Loch Ness, continuing by the south-eastern shores of Loch Oich and Loch Lochy. At Gairlochy it divided. For through running in the Glasgow direction, one arm followed the River Spean, crossed at Highbridge, to reach the West Highland at Spean Bridge; the other followed the River Lochy (as the Glasgow & North Western Railway would have done), and paralleled the West Highland from Lochy Bridge into Fort William, with a spur for access to the pierhead station. There was a connection, across the Lochy, to the Caledonian Canal at Banavie. In addition, the Highland sought their own Fort William terminus on Loch Linnhe, together with a new pier, to be reached by a three-quarter mile tunnel.[19]

West Highland:- Forman's line, based on his plans of 1893, penetrated the Great Glen from Roy Bridge; it climbed the shoulder separating Glen Spean from Glen Gloy, then descended to Loch Lochy. For some 40 miles thereafter, to the neighbourhood of Lochend and Dochgarroch, it was almost identical with Paterson's layout – because the latter matched Forman's earlier surveys. Entry to Inverness was by Tomnahurich, where the line bridged the Caledonian Canal, and the West Highland station would have fronted the River Ness. For through running from Fort William, a two-mile connection across the Spean (Achindaul–Stronaba) was included – with Forman's Highbridge viaduct sited a little downstream from Paterson's.[20]

That Fort William would come to possess three stations was scarcely to be believed. To simplify the tangle just described, the West Highland's Banavie branch might have passed into joint ownership, while Callander & Oban and Highland might have shared either the former's hillside alignment or the latter's improbable tunnel, with common facilities at Victoria Park.

Bills of 1894-5

Callander & Oban Railway, Ballachulish, Fort William & Banavie Extension

No.1 Connel Ferry–Ballachulish Ferry, 25 miles (Facing junction from Callander direction.)

No.2 Connel Ferry, western spur, 250 yards (For through running between Oban and Fort William.)

No.3 Continuation of No.1 to Ballachulish (East Laroch), 2½ miles (To be built light, under Act of 1868.)

No.4 Continuation of No.1 to Fort William (Nevis Bridge), 13½ miles

No.5 Fort William (Nevis Bridge)–Fort William (Victoria Park), ½ mile

Nos.6 & 7 Fort William (Nevis Bridge)–Banavie (pier on Caledonian Canal), 2 miles

No.8 Connection to West Highland Railway east of Banavie Junction, ¼ mile ("Banavie Junction" to 1901, subsequently "Mallaig Junction", today "Fort William".)

No.9 Banavie, spur from No.7 to West Highland Railway, Banavie Branch (No measurements: needed only if the Callander & Oban came to share the West Highland Mallaig Extension.)

Highland Railway, Spean Bridge & Fort William Extension

No.1 Inverness (junction with Aviemore cut-off)–Spean Bridge (junction with West Highland Railway), 55 miles

No.2 Gairlochy (Mucomir farm)–Fort William (Victoria Park), 8 miles

No.3 Continuation of No.2 to Fort William station and pier (Loch Linnhe), ¾ mile (tunnel)

No.4 Connection from No.2 to West Highland Railway west of Banavie Junction, 250 yards

No.5 Connection from No.2, west of Torcastle to Banavie (Caledonian Canal), 2 miles.

West Highland Railway, Inverness Extension

No.1 Glen Spean (junction west of Roy Bridge)–Fort Augustus (pier on Loch Ness), 24 miles

No.2 Fort Augustus–Inverness (Caledonian Canal, Tomnahurich drawbridge), 29 miles

No.3 Continuation of No.2 to station (River Ness), 1 mile

No.4 Inverness (Tomnahurich) to Muirton (Caledonian Canal), 1 mile

No.5 Inverness, spur (eastern) from No.4 to Highland Railway, 450 yards

No.6 Inverness, spur (western) from No.4 to Highland Railway, 500 yards

No.7 Inverness, spur from No.3 to No.4, 700 yards

No.8 Achindaul (on West Highland proper) to No. 1 near Stronaba (junction west of Invergloy), 2 miles (For through running between Fort William and Inverness.)

NRS/BR/PYB(S)/1/378, Callander & Oban, Highland and West Highland Bills of 1894-5.

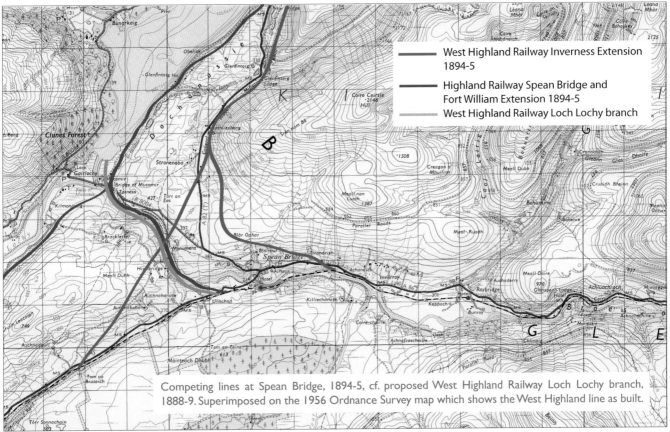

Competing lines at Spean Bridge, 1894-5, cf. proposed West Highland Railway Loch Lochy branch, 1888-9. Superimposed on the 1956 Ordnance Survey map which shows the West Highland line as built.

Legend:
— West Highland Railway Inverness Extension 1894-5
— Highland Railway Spean Bridge and Fort William Extension 1894-5
⋯ West Highland Railway Loch Lochy branch

Nonetheless these were by any test extravagant projects, which could not but recall the Railway Mania half-a-century earlier. The *Dundee Advertiser*, in jocular mood, captured the "bubble" quality of the three promotions:

> *Very soon a Lochaber man will be able to boast that all railways lead to Fort William...Why the metropolis of 'Long John' will become another Perth or Carlisle and Cockney tourists in great numbers will sample the local manufacture* at the station as they wait for trains.*[21]

At Inverness, Forman's provision far exceeded the requirements of station-to-station transfer: there were junctions with the Highland in both directions, making a triangle between the River Ness and the Caledonian Canal, and the West Highland was to have independent access to Muirton basin. This surely implied that the North British looked to filch a large proportion of the Highland's established traffic. It all suggested, too, regular exchange with the Great North of Scotland, if that company's latest Elgin–Inverness bid succeeded.

At Banavie, by contrast, the North British found themselves under attack. The Callander & Oban Bill specified future running powers westward to Mallaig (which the Caledonian Company might exercise) and also the option of applying to Parliament for "a joint and equal interest" in the West Highland Extension when the promised Treasury Guarantee was enacted. Though the Highland Company's Bill contained no corresponding clauses, their proposed link to the canal at Banavie basin presaged a similar claim. But the combined assault was essentially a sham. With no expectation that the

Treasury would endorse their intervention and no real wish to share in the Mallaig scheme, the Callander & Oban Company and the Highland sought only to discomfit the North British – and the disarray of the Liberal Government had tempted them to do so.

Over the Mallaig line the North British faced frustration and delay, not defeat. (Parliament would authorise the Treasury Guarantee in 1896 and building would commence the following year.) In the short run their West Highland woes soon multiplied. All along the route, sidings, station buildings and railwaymen's houses were variously unfinished, while some of the completed work was revealed as over-hurried – the consequence of North British insistence that traffic begin, come what may, in 1894. (Only the Board of Trade's indulgence had made opening possible). That October, most of what remained to be done was given over to the company engineer, whose remedial efforts were protracted. With January of 1895 came arctic weather over much of Scotland. Before winter receded, the West Highland would be thrice blocked by snowfall more formidable than anything experienced during the four-and-a-half years of construction.[22]

* * *

By withdrawing from the 1889 Agreement, the Highland Company had invited a Great Glen struggle and it was the local belief that the North British meant business. Charles Innes and George Malcolm, two men of influence (see Chapter 2), were quickly in touch with Tweeddale and Conacher. Whatever their involvement in Forman's earlier Great Glen ventures, they were poised to campaign for his latest line as soon as it emerged in West Highland colours. At public

---

* "Long John" whisky was the "manufacture" in question. Distiller Donald P. MacDonald, son of the eponymous Long John, had been a West Highland promoter.

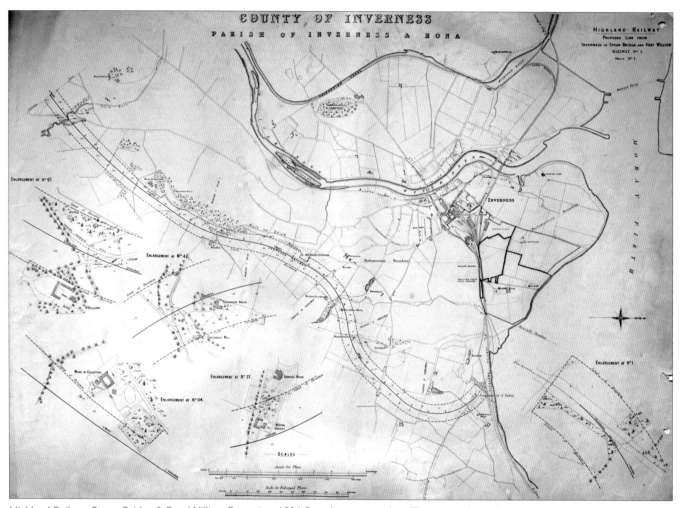

Highland Railway, Spean Bridge & Fort William Extension, 1894-5, parliamentary plans. The upper sheet shows the proposed line at Inverness, where it swung away from the Aviemore cut-off; the lower sheet shows the proposed tunnel, terminus and company pier at Fort William. The West Highland station appears in the centre.   (Highland Railway Society collection)

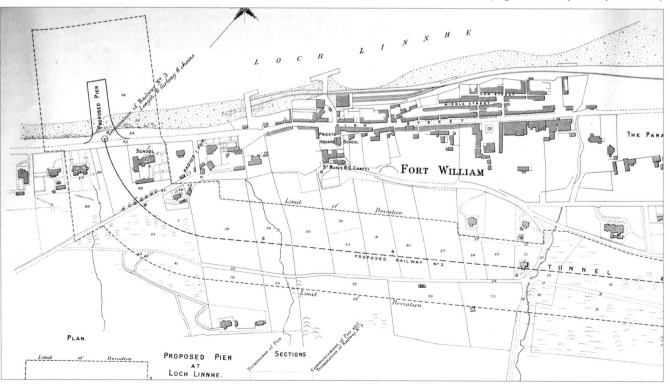

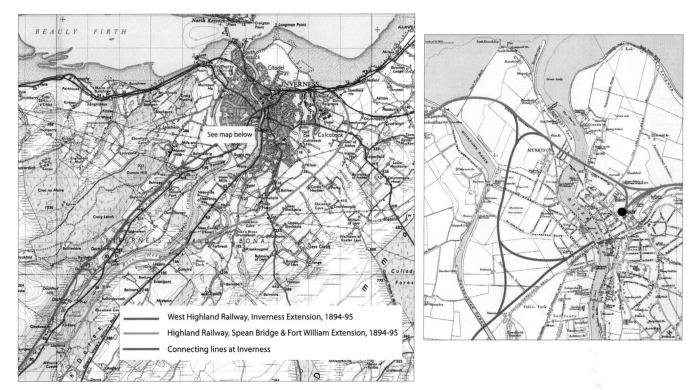

Competing lines at Inverness, 1894-5. Spanning the Caledonian Canal at Tomnahurich, the proposed West Highland line terminated at a new station on the River Ness. It connected with the Highland Railway west of the Ness viaduct. By contrast, the Highland's proposed line to Spean Bridge and Fort William rounded the then eastern edge of the town before crossing the canalised river at the foot of Loch Ness (Bona Ferry/Lochend). Thence to Invergloy, the two lines largely coincided.

(1958 Ordnance Survey map on left, town map on right from Ward Lock's Shilling Guide, 1922)

meetings all along the valley, Innes assured his audiences that the North British were fully engaged and would achieve what the Glasgow & North Western promoters had so rightly attempted in 1882-3 – a through railway to Inverness. The Highland Company ought to give way. They intended, he was convinced, to reserve such powers as Parliament might award them and would not build their line unless compelled to do so.[23] Malcolm spread the same message, with every encouragement from Lord Burton. Appointed an additional agent for the West Highland Company, Innes made ready to cooperate with Nigel MacKenzie of Fort William in precognosing parliamentary witnesses. All the activists, and Charles Forman too, seem to have ignored the early signs that the Highland and the North British were both inclined to think again.[24] In the first weeks of 1895 the Great Glen "bubble" would deflate rapidly, while the Caledonian and North British would begin, with much recrimination, to seek a frontier between Oban and Fort William by which Callander & Oban and West Highland might abide.

The parliamentary process had been initiated but could be halted, and solicitor Watson advised that the North British board should delay no longer in confronting their Caledonian counterparts, in whose power it lay both to deter the Highland directors and to make sure that the Callander & Oban Bill went no further.[25] On 22nd November Conacher wrote formally to James Thompson, the Caledonian general manager:

[Do] your Company admit that the proposed lines are new lines...in the district of the North British Company within the meaning of the [1891] Agreement...and [are] your Company prepared...to discourage and oppose the two applications..?[26]

Though asserting the North British "right" to the Great Glen and the Caledonian's duty to uphold it, Conacher was primarily concerned to halt Anderson's scheme. He reminded Thompson how the Caledonian, in resisting the West Highland Mallaig Extension, had invoked the Peace Agreement to argue that their intimate involvement with the Callander & Oban conferred a clear interest and locus standi. To shrug off responsibility now, said Conacher, was a contradiction: they must take action before their client's forthcoming Wharncliffe meeting (i.e. formal shareholders meeting) endorsed the Ballachulish, Fort William & Banavie Bill:

Control of the Callander & Oban Company's application to Parliament is in your hands, and I trust your Company will arrange for the withdrawal of the Bill without the necessity of [new] proceedings.[27]

The Caledonian's answer hung fire, but on 2nd January 1895 a telegram from Thompson promised a decision the following week. (He made no comment on the Highland Company's Bill.) The next day, judging that the Caledonian would continue to stall, Conacher put in preparation a North British application to Lord Watson,* arbiter under the Peace Agreement.[28]

Tweeddale chose a direct approach to the Highland chairman, ahead of the board meeting fixed for 5th December. He denied that the North British had been the aggressor:

*I regret that I cannot be with you on Wednesday** [because] I would far rather speak than write about your decision to go to Fort William. [It] was not until the...announcement*

---
* Not to be confused with the North British solicitor.

** Attending as North British representative on the Highland board (above).

of the intention of the Highland Company...appeared in the papers and had been confirmed by Mr Dougall that the West Highland even considered [promoting] a Bill next session. If [you] persist...money, time and perhaps temper will be expended quite needlessly. Is it not possible to avoid or at least postpone the fight?[29]

The Great North of Scotland, added Tweeddale, were "on the warpath" and would seize their opportunity, to the Highland's undoing. In reply, Mackintosh of Raigmore welcomed the possibility of "a friendly arrangement". Tweeddale's letter had been read and held over, pending a better-attended board in the New Year. Forman's machinations during 1893-4, he implied, had forced the Highland's hand:

My belief was and is that [a Great Glen] scheme was to have been brought forward by an independent Company and that any delay would have put us at a disadvantage.[30]

To Tweeddale's displeasure, first the *Glasgow Herald* and then other newspapers learned of his "private and confidential" overture – which would be rejected, according to some reports, as incompatible with the "understanding" said to subsist between the Highland and the Callander & Oban.[31] On 20th December Mackintosh, reiterating his wish for a "friendly solution", wrote once more:

We have no arrangements with the Callander & Oban and Caledonian Companies on the subject of the Fort William Line.[32]

Here the facts are uncertain. The "understanding", if it existed, involved only a few members of the Highland board. The Marquess of Breadalbane, with Caledonian, Callander & Oban and Highland directorships, may have been the key figure. Both Anderson and Dougall had recognised the need to agree a shared layout at Fort William; but that was a matter of practicalities and does not prove prior plotting.[33]

In mid-January 1895 came Lord Watson's ruling: the Caledonian could claim no interest north of Ballachulish Ferry.[34] This eased the challenge to the West Highland's hold on Lochaber; and the Caledonian confirmed that they would veto the Callander & Oban Bill. The arbiter's decision also gave additional reassurance that the Mallaig Extension would remain entirely a West Highland project. However, John Anderson proposed a compromise, halting the Callander & Oban scheme at Loch Leven, which Thompson at once conveyed to Conacher:

[They] will drop Railways 4 to 9 inclusive...and restrict their Bill to Railways 1 to 3 constituting the Line from Connel Ferry to Ballachulish [village] ; and they will give [an] undertaking that...the Bill will be amended in Committee [to this effect].[35]

The Caledonian, he warned, were not unwilling to court another battle. They saw the districts of Benderloch, Appin and Kentallen as exclusively theirs and were ready to seek a further decision from Lord Watson unless the North British so conceded. Meanwhile the Callander & Oban Wharncliffe meeting had been postponed.

Conacher had been prepared for this gambit, as his telegram to Tweeddale (who had gone to London) shows:

Caledonian have offered to drop [their] line north of Ballachulish...Opportunity of imposing the [terms] I mentioned...Our making the line Fort William to Ballachulish [becomes possible].[36]

On 25th January, with his chairman's approval, he wrote again to Thompson. The North British, though unwilling to forgo absolutely a territorial interest south of Loch Leven, might tolerate a Callander & Oban branch to Ballachulish Ferry. Caledonian and Callander & Oban must abstain for ten years from any new promotion aimed at Fort William, giving no support of any kind to any independent project; for the same period, North British and West Highland must be free to promote a Fort William–Ballachulish branch; and any connecting line from Ballachulish slate quarries to Ballachulish Ferry must be jointly owned. With the debatable Great Glen Agreement in mind, Conacher wanted to bind the Caledonian tightly.[37]

In response, Thompson sought immediate discussions whereby a Connel Ferry–Ballachulish bill agreeable to the North British might proceed that session. ("A committee of my Directors would...be ready to meet a Committee of your Directors in Edinburgh".) But it was now Conacher's turn to stall and the Caledonian reluctantly gave in.[38] On 8th February the Callander & Oban Bill was abandoned. By way of insurance, Conacher had engaged William Black, a supreme court solicitor and Callander & Oban shareholder, to attend the adjourned Wharncliffe meeting and demand a general vote if the board attempted to persevere.[39] These tetchy exchanges nevertheless pointed to a Loch Leven frontier – which Caledonian and North British were indeed to achieve in 1896.

Lochiel had believed all along that the Callander & Oban and Highland schemes were interdependent. He was sure that the Highland Company would retreat, if unable "to get any forwarder (sic)" towards Oban:

This places us in a much stronger position...I apprehend that [they] will be only too glad to back out...We must not allow them to [represent this] as a "concession" [but] press for the status quo ante...

The North British should avoid any commitment, in or out of Parliament, to early construction of the West Highland Inverness Extension:

I entirely concur in the steps which have been taken [so far] as no one feels more strongly the importance of being heard [at Westminster]; but getting terms...is one thing, making the railway ourselves is a very different thing.[40]

In his lengthy memorandum to Conacher, Lochiel argued that a Great Glen line guaranteed at 3½% could not pay. The North British had settled on this figure for the entire Craigendoran – Mallaig route, reduced from the 4% originally applied to the West Highland proper, when they finally committed to the West Highland Extension. Despite constant complaint, Inverness and the North would retain "a partiality" for the Highland Company; and when the Aviemore cut-off came into use the West Highland-cum-Great Glen route would have "no decided advantage". There need be no fears if the Highland Bill succeeded – limited to an Inverness–Spean Bridge scheme. Without a connection south to Oban, the Highland's case for independent access to Fort William would be weak. Without their Gairlochy–Fort William line and Banavie spur, they could not readily share in the Mallaig Extension. Their Great Glen "branch" (sic), once built, might become an underused "block" line; but they must run some trains, feeding local and tourist traffic to the West Highland at no cost to the

North British. If, withdrawing their Bill, they refused entirely to bargain, it would demonstrate that "blocking" had always been their purpose, which must strengthen the West Highland's hand in any future bid for Inverness. Lochiel proposed quitting the field, on three strict conditions – the Highland to complete their line within five years; a sole connection with the West Highland, at Spean Bridge; and provision for arbitration to ensure a minimum number of connecting trains.[41]

On 13th February 1895 "representatives of the Highland, West Highland and North British Companies", meeting in Edinburgh, contrived a face-saving formula: the time was inopportune for large capital commitments and therefore both the Highland Bill and the West Highland Bill would be withdrawn.[42] Having nothing to lose, the Great North of Scotland continued their Bill, but without serious expectation of success. (Their closer involvement in the Great Glen battles of 1895-6 and 1896-7 is treated in later chapters.) On 14th February both Highland board and North British board approved the draft of a restored Great Glen Agreement, modified to deter any disruptive "half-way" promotion such as Forman had contemplated in 1893. The new form of words may have owed something to Lochiel's memorandum. However, nothing had come of his suggestion that the Highland be allowed, on tight terms, to occupy the ground.

The tortured text ran thus:

The Highland Railway Company, the West Highland Railway Company and the North British Railway Company agree not to introduce into Parliament, nor to support, assist or countenance, directly or indirectly, in Parliament, any Bill for powers to construct any Railway between Fort William, Banavie and Spean Bridge, or the neighbourhood of these places, on the one hand and Inverness or any point on or near the proposed Railway Routes between Inverness and Fort William, Banavie and Spean Bridge, or the neighbourhood thereof, on the other hand without giving the other two Companies notice of their intention.

It was signed by George MacPherson-Grant for the Highland Railway, Tweeddale for the North British and Lochiel for the West Highland.[43] (MacPherson-Grant would succeed to the chairmanship of the Highland Company in 1896.)

The *Railway News* that same week carried a magisterial summing-up of the Great Glen anti-climax and its context. The tottering Liberal Government must fall soon, making the outcome of any prolonged parliamentary battle in the current session doubly hazardous. The Callander & Oban and Highland had not consolidated their never more than tentative alliance against the West Highland. To isolate and defeat the latest Great North attack, the Highland needed peace with the North British. Although the Aviemore line, in sight of completion at last, promised the Highland greater security, they were necessarily apprehensive of the new burden which duplicate provision by the Forres route must entail. And the North British had their own reasons to go warily. January's snows had emphasised the West Highland's operating and maintenance costs; years must pass before the projected earnings of the Mallaig Extension could bring relief; and Inverness had proved an at once elusive and ensnaring target.[44]

References

J. McGregor, *The West Highland Railway: Plans, Politics and People*, Birlinn (John Donald), 2005, cited as PPP.

1. NRS/BR/NBR/8/1764/Box 6, general manager's files relating to West Highland Railway, James Watson to John Conacher, 7 September 1894.
2. NRS/BR/NBR/8/1764/Box 6, Marquess of Tweeddale to Conacher, 17 September 1894.
3. NRS/BR/NBR/8/1764/Box 6, Cameron of Lochiel to Tweeddale, 14 September 1894.
4. NRS/BR/NBR/8/1764/Box 6, Tweeddale to Conacher, 17 September 1894. Conacher to Lochiel, 19 September 1894.
5. NRS/BR/COB/1/5, Callander & Oban Railway minutes, 23 October and 9 November 1894.
6. NBR/BR/NBR/8/1764/loose, general manager's files relating to West Highland Railway, George Wieland to Conacher, telegram, 19 September 1894,
7. NRS/BR/PYB(S)/1/378, press cuttings relating to Great Glen railway schemes, September and October 1894.
8. The National Archives (Kew), MT6/1414, Andrew Dougall to Railway Department, Board of Trade, 5 October 1894, and resulting Board of Trade memorandum.
9. *The Scotsman*, 28 September and 25 October 1894.
10. NRS/BR/PYB (S)/1/378, press cuttings relating to Great Glen railway schemes, September and October 1894.
11. PPP, p.144.
12. *The Scotsman*, letters from "Fact", 10 September 1894, and "Pro Bono Publico", 24 September 1894.
13. *The Scotsman*, letter from "Civis", 13 October 1894.
14. *The Scotsman*, letter from "Observer", 7 September, 1894.
15. *The Scotsman*, letter from "Fact", 20 September 1894.
16. *The Scotsman*, letters from "Fact", 10 September 1894, "Invernessian", 15 September 1894, "Progress", 24 September 1894, "Civis", 13 October 1894, and P. Campbell-Ross, 5 December 1894.
17. NRS/BR/PYB(S)/1/143. Great North of Scotland Railway Bill, 1894-5
18. NRS/BR/PYB(S)/1/378, Callander & Oban Railway, Ballachulish, Fort William & Banavie Extension Bill, 1894-5.
19. Ibid., Highland Railway, Spean Bridge & Fort William Extension Bill, 1894-5.
20. Ibid., West Highland Railway, Inverness Extension Bill. 1894-5.
21. *Dundee Advertiser*, 5 December 1894.
22. NRS/BR/NBR/8/1764/Box 2, general manager's files relating to West Highland Railway, Conacher to Charles Forman, 16 and 19 October 1894, and Forman to Conacher, 16 and 20 October 1894. NRS/BR/NBR/8/1764/Box 4, general manager's files relating to West Highland Railway, William Arnott, Fort William district superintendent, to Conacher, telegrams, 7, 8 and 14 January 1894, and reports, 11 January and 11 February, 1894.
23. *Northern Chronicle*, 14 November 1894. *Inverness Courier*, letter from "Expert", 16 November 1894.
24. *The Scotsman*, 6 December 1894. *Glasgow Herald*, 7 December 1894.
25. NRS/BR/NBR/8/1764/Box 4, general manager's files relating to West Highland Railway, Watson to Conacher, 21 November 1894. NRS/BR/1/40, North British Railway minutes, 22 November 1894.
26. NRS/BR/NBR/8/1764/Box 4, Conacher to James Thompson, 22 November 1894.
27. NRS/BR/NBR/8/1764/Box 4, Conacher to Thompson, 21 December 1894.
28. NRS/BR/NBR/8/1764/Box 4, Conacher to Thompson and Thompson to Conacher, letters and telegrams, 31 December 1894 and 2 January 1895.
29. NRS/BR/NBR/8/1764/Box 6, general manager's files relating to West Highland Railway, Tweeddale to Mackintosh of Raigmore,

chairman, 3 December 1894.

30. NRS/BR/NBR/8/1764/Box 6, Mackintosh to Tweeddale, 6 December 1894.

31. NRS/BR/NBR/8/1764/Box 6, Tweeddale to Mackintosh, 19 December 1894. *Glasgow Herald,* 7 December 1894. *Railway Times*, 15 December 1894. *Central News*, 19 December 1894.

32. NRS/BR/NBR/1764/Box 6, Mackintosh to Tweeddale, 20 December 1894.

33. NRS/BR/COB/1/5, Callander & Oban Railway minutes, 17 and 23 October 1894.

34. NRS/BR/NBR/8/1764/ Box 4, general manager's files relating to West Highland Railway, submission to Lord Watson by North British Railway under New Lines Agreement (1891), 3 January 1895, and Watson to Conacher, 14 January 1895.

35. NRS/BR/NBR/8/1764/ Box 4, Thompson to Conacher, 22 January 1895. NRS/BR/COB/1/5, Callander & Oban Railway minutes, 22 January 1895.

36. NBR/BR.NBR/8/1764/Box 4, Conacher to Tweeddale (telegram), 23 January 1895.

37. NRS/BR/NBR/8/1764/ Box 4, Conacher to Thompson, 25 January 1895.

38. NRS/BR/NBR/8/1764/ Box 4, Conacher to Thompson and Thompson to Conacher, letters and telegrams, 28 January - 5 February 1895.

39. NRS/BR/COB/1/5, Callander & Oban Railway minutes, 8 February 1895. *Glasgow Herald*, 9 February 1895. NRS/BR/NBR/8/1764/ Box 4, William Black, supreme court solicitor, to Conacher, 6 February 1895, and John Anderson, secretary-manager, Callander & Oban Railway, to Black, (?) February 1895.

40. NRS/BR/NBR/8/1764/Box 6, general manager's files relating to West Highland Railway, Lochiel to Conacher, 29 January 1895.

41. Ibid.

42. NRS/BR/HR/1/8, Highland Railway minutes, 14 February 1895. NRS/BR/NBR/1/40, North British Railway minutes, 14 February 1895. NRS/BR/NBR/8/1764/Box 6, joint press statement, Highland Railway, North British Railway and West Highland Railway, 13 February 1895. PPP, p.147.

43. NRS/BR/NBR/1764/8/Box 6, memorandum of Edinburgh meeting, 13 February 1895, subsequently endorsed by all three companies.

44. *Railway News*, 16 February 1895.

Banavie Pier station – "Banavie" until 1901 – terminus of the terminus of the 1½ mile West Highland branch. The footpath to the Caledonian Canal basin is clearly visible (see also p.53). The ample goods yard was in some degree "political"; with the proposed Roshven extension lost in Parliament, here was a railhead for all the districts west to Arisaig, pending the promotion and completion of the state-aided Mallaig Extension, which was to have its own Banavie station. (LGRP)

CHAPTER FOUR

A BUSY YEAR IN PARLIAMENT, 1895-96

Parliamentary session 1895-6 saw no fewer than five measures integral to this study. The Light Railways Act reached the statute book, as did the Treasury's long-delayed Guarantee for the West Highland Mallaig Extension. Both the Callander & Oban Ballachulish branch and the West Highland Ballachulish Extension (sic) were authorised – the latter a branch in conception but literally an end-on extension southwards of the West Highland's foreshore layout at Fort William. And the Invergarry & Fort Augustus Railway won approval, as an independent Great Glen promotion.[1]

* * *

From the mid-1880s Ireland's future had dominated the British political scene; but the divide for and against Irish Home Rule roughly corresponded to the divide between those wedded to free trade and private enterprise and those ready to experiment with etatist policies. Both in Ireland and in the Scottish Highlands, landowners tentatively embraced state-sponsored transport improvements to stimulate economic growth, reduce poverty and contain unrest. They hoped thereby to avoid or at least postpone fundamental land reform. Meanwhile the advocates of protection for agriculture and fishing had chimed in – given reliable transport, Scotland's west-coast crofter-fishermen might be professionalised, *"committing entirely to the sea"*. The Hebridean fishery, dominated by east coast boats, could expand in its own right if additional railheads were established, helping to feed the cities and reducing Britain's dependence on imported foodstuffs. Though reform of land tenure was central to the Scottish crofters' agitation, campaigners also called for investment in general "improvement", including better communications. They demanded equal treatment with Ireland, where relatively lavish expenditure was assigned to "killing Home Rule with kindness".

By enfranchising the crofter, the third edition of 19th century parliamentary reform (1884-5) had ensured election victories for Crofter-Liberal candidates in a swathe of Highland constituencies, including Inverness-shire – a transformation foreseen by Cameron of Lochiel, who had held the seat for the Conservative Party since the 1860s. Convinced that only by identifying with "improvement" could the landed class retain their position, he had joined the Napier Commission and re-engaged with railway politics. Landlords and Crofter-Liberals made distrustful partners. The former encouraged emigration and increasingly drew their income from sporting leases; the latter sought to reverse depopulation and expand crofting tenancies. With no particular animus for the Highland Company, the new MPs were, like many other Liberals,

suspicious of the railway industry's power and wealth. If the Highland and North British had resources enough to do battle in the Great Glen, why call on the public purse and not their own reserves to sustain respectively a Lochinver line, reputedly the Highland's first-choice "Lothian" option, and the West Highland Mallaig Extension? The Caledonian, too, could well afford to underwrite a Callander & Oban branch into Lochaber. When landowners in the western Highlands and Islands spoke of sacrifices in sustaining the local economy or railway managers complained of scanty returns, the Crofter-Liberals were apt to see a sinister alliance of vested interests, set on evading real change.

During 1886-92 the anti-Home Rule Liberal Unionists, alienated when Gladstone declared for Irish devolution, had given conditional support to Lord Salisbury's Conservative Government. Joseph Chamberlain, the Liberal Unionist leader in the House of Commons, favoured an interventionist programme for the Highlands and Islands, imitating the placatory measures applied in Ireland. He had endorsed both the West Highland Railway (its Roshven extension included) in 1889 and the Garve & Ullapool Railway a year later; and he welcomed the findings of the Lothian Commission.[2] But from 1892 it rested with a minority Liberal Government, sustained in the House of Commons by the Irish Nationalists, to develop the Commission's recommendations and implement the Mallaig Extension Guarantee provisionally offered by the Conservatives before their election defeat. Gladstone's priority was a second attempt to carry Irish Home Rule. Failure finally ended his long career, leaving Lord Rosebery's ensuing administration disheartened and divided. On transport subsidy the Crofter-Liberals had no one view; but Dr Donald MacGregor, who now represented Inverness-shire*, pressed for a Treasury statement on the Government's position.[3] Though MacGregor earned the thanks of the West Highland directors, Lochiel's distaste for all land-reform "radicals" was no secret.

The abortive Home Rule campaign had put out of reach any rebuilding of the old Liberal Party. In the general election of 1895 Conservatives and disaffected Liberals came together under an ambiguous but effective "Unionist" banner, which implied preservation of the United Kingdom and domestic socio-economic reforms to complement imperial policy. The victorious Unionist Government, essentially a Salisbury–Chamberlain coalition, were to enjoy a wider freedom of action than any of their recent predecessors, but they did not aspire to a thorough re-examination of the railway companies'

---

* Charles Fraser-MacKintosh, Inverness-shire's MP from 1886, had been a prominent Crofter-Liberal but he lost in 1892, having turned Liberal-Unionist.

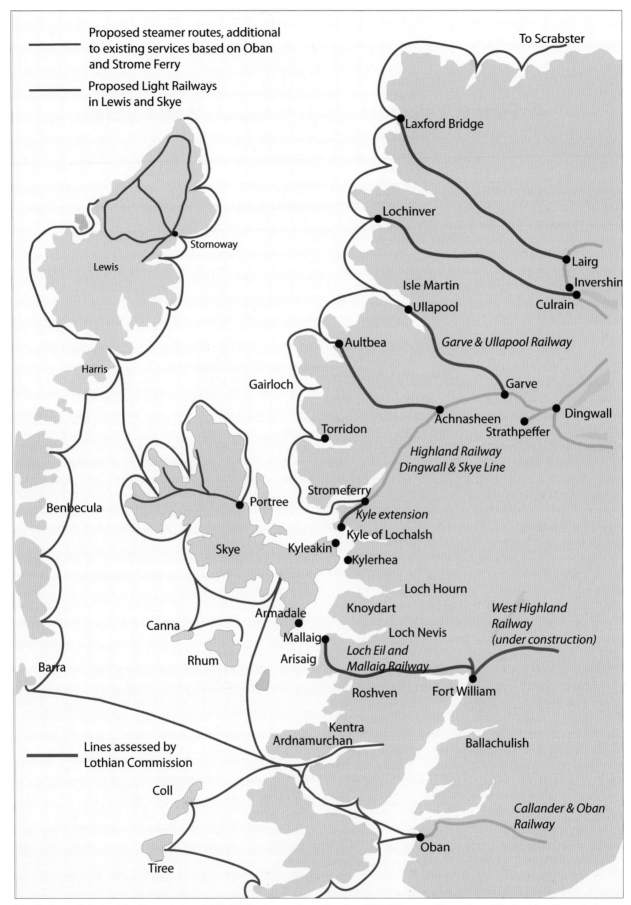

Proposed steamer routes, additional to existing services based on Oban and Strome Ferry

Proposed Light Railways in Lewis and Skye

Lines assessed by Lothian Commission

To Scrabster

Laxford Bridge

Lochinver

Lairg

Invershin

Culrain

Isle Martin

Ullapool

Garve & Ullapool Railway

Aultbea

Gairloch

Garve

Dingwall

Achnasheen

Strathpeffer

Torridon

*Highland Railway
Dingwall & Skye Line*

Lewis

Stornoway

Harris

Stromeferry

Kyle extension

Kyle of Lochalsh

Benbecula

Portree

Skye

Kyleakin

Kylerhea

Loch Hourn

Knoydart

*West Highland
Railway
(under construction)*

Loch Nevis

Canna

Armadale

Mallaig

*Loch Eil and
Mallaig Railway*

Arisaig

Rhum

Roshven

Fort William

Barra

Kentra

Ardnamurchan

Ballachulish

Coll

*Callander & Oban
Railway*

Oban

Tiree

The findings of the Lothian Commission (1889-90), further evaluated by the 1890-1 Treasury Committee. The Lothian Commissioners included Sir John Wolfe-Barry and Sir James King, deputy-chairman of the Caledonian Railway.

relationship with the state. There would be no serious rationalisation of competing rail routes, no guidance as to filling the remaining gaps in the network such as the Great Glen presented, save that the Light Railways Act of 1896 would simplify the promotion of lesser lines designed for a limited traffic. This well-intentioned measure replaced imprecise and outdated legislation of thirty years standing – but it also signalled that the new administration, though pledged to enact the Mallaig Guarantee, would make no like commitment to other new railways. (A rare exception was the Wick & Lybster Light Railway, which would obtain a Mallaig-style Treasury Guarantee in 1903.) Responsibility for assisting light projects in Scotland fell to the recently reformed county authorities, in conjunction with the Board of Trade. Central Government retreated from the time-consuming and controversial decisions thrust upon them in 1890-1 by the Lothian Commissioners and the Treasury Committee.

The departing Liberals had resigned ahead of their general election defeat. In this situation, unfamiliar today, it was within the rules of Parliament to continue Sir William Harcourt's Mallaig Guarantee Bill as an "uncontentious measure". But a group of intractable Liberal members, principled or partisan, vowed to maintain their opposition, while several embittered Irish Nationalist MPs refused all cooperation. In Inverness-shire disgruntled Liberals alleged that Lochiel had exerted undue influence in favour of the successful Unionist, James Baillie of Dochfour, who was already the sitting MP, having won the by-election occasioned by MacGregor's quitting Parliament. A Great Glen proprietor at the north end of the valley and the son-in-law of Lord Burton, Baillie was also a Highland Railway director, but he pledged to support the Mallaig Guarantee. With a consensual bill out of reach, the Unionists had no choice but to begin again in the following session. Sir Michael Hicks-Beach, their Chancellor of the Exchequer, refused to modify the Conservatives' formula of 1892 whereby the Treasury kept first call on the earnings of the West Highland Mallaig Extension – which diluted the real cost of subsidy. The North British directors hesitated – they had hoped to ring-fence a proportion of their working costs – but settled for minor concessions. Last-ditch opponents of the Guarantee spun out the parliamentary process by submitting that the scheme be fundamentally reassessed under the impending Light Railways Act. They pressed, too, for a Treasury representative on the West Highland Board, a condition unacceptable to the North British. By way of compromise there was provision for annual inspection of the Mallaig line by the Board of Trade while the Guarantee remained in being.[4]

* * *

In May 1895 bad-tempered negotiations between Caledonian and North British were resumed – only to be interrupted by the general election, which preoccupied the MP-directors on both sides.[5] Nevertheless, both a Connel Ferry–Ballachulish Ferry line (Callander & Oban) and a Fort William–North Ballachulish line (West Highland) were proposed for parliamentary session 1895-6, complementary after a fashion although each company would enter formal objections to the other's bill. Both schemes derived from Charles Forman's survey of 1894 (see Chapters 2 and 3), and his latest plans for the West Highland Company included a "low level swing bridge" across Loch Leven, carrying the public road and a tramway. The latter, continuing to Ballachulish quarries and shared with the Callander & Oban, might convey both slate and Glen Coe excursionists. It was the North British hope that the proposed frontier at Ballachulish Ferry could be pushed south to Kentallen, with the tramway extended to that point – a plausible idea in that Kentallen offered interchange with David MacBrayne's steamers and the traffic of a granite quarry, which both Callander & Oban and West Highland might exploit. But this the Caledonian rejected, indicating their wish for a shared "high level viaduct", clear of shipping, at the Ballachulish Narrows, against future reconsideration of a through railway.[6] Though Parliament passed both lines (see panel below), the connecting swing bridge was rejected, so too the West Highland tramway and the Callander & Oban's preferred alternative – a "light" extension from Ballachulish Ferry to the slate workings. In session 1896-7 the Callander & Oban would obtain revised powers continuing their branch, as a conventional railway, to

---

BALLACHULISH BILLS, 1895-6

West Highland Railway Ballachulish Extension
No.1 Fort William, pierhead–North Ballachulish, near Loch Leven Temperance Hotel, 12 miles
No.2 Bridge (for public road), Loch Leven narrows, Ballachulish Ferry, ¼ mile*
Nos.3 & 4 Tramways (1'11" gauge), North Ballachulish–Ballachulish quarries, 3¼ miles*
No.5 Tramway (1'11" gauge) Ballachulish Ferry–Kentallen, 2½ miles.*
NRS/BR/PYB (S)/1/385

Callander & Oban Railway, Ballachulish Branch
No.1 Connel Ferry Junction–Ballachulish Ferry, near Ballachulish Hotel, 25¾ miles
No.2 Connel Ferry western spur ¼ mile **
No.3 Continuation of No.1 to Ballachulish quarries and East Laroch pier – to be built light, in consultation with Board of Trade, 2¼ miles.*
NRS/BR/PYB (S)/1/380

*Disallowed. The extension of C&OR No.1 to Ballachulish village was authorised in 1897.

** Remained unbuilt.

Approximate route of the West Highland Ballachulish Extension, approved in 1896. through Nether Lochaber, superimposed on 1956 Ordnance Survey map.

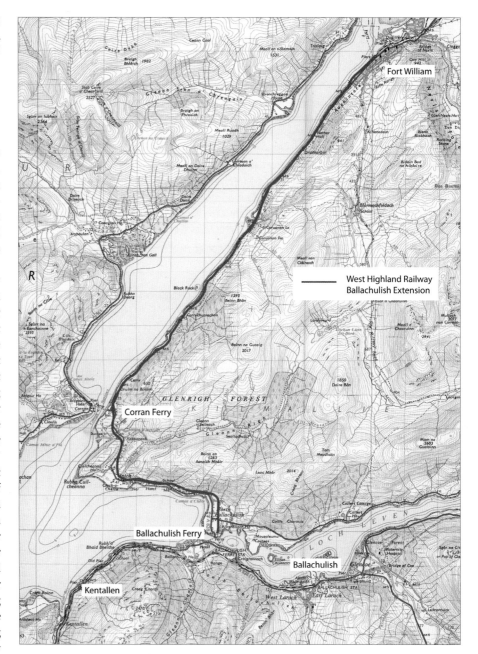

Ballachulish village, with connection to the quarries.[7] Construction promised to be relatively easy, save for the Loch Etive and Loch Creran bridges; the 27-mile line would open throughout in 1903. By contrast the West Highland Ballachulish Extension (so-called) was never to be built.

Anxious for a strong hand to play and fearful of procedural quirks which might give the Callander & Oban a clear field, the North British insisted that the West Highland Ballachulish Bill be prepared at their dictation and without delay – exposing the pretence of West Highland independence and angering Cameron of Lochiel, the proprietor principally affected. There was little consultation, and his tenants in Nether Lochaber, like the "villa residents" along Loch Linnhe south from Fort William, faced severance or loss of amenity.[8] In Parliament the North British would down-play all suggestion that they must eventually cater for through traffic, and general manager John Conacher pictured a purely local service, usefully tapping the Ardgour hinterland at Corran Ferry and feeding the West Highland – for which purpose the locomotives and rolling stock lying over at Fort William between Glasgow turns could sustain a sufficient timetable.[9] And the North British would soon judge (perhaps they had always so calculated?) that West Highland powers-in-hand were safeguard enough against any renewed Callander & Oban thrust beyond Loch Leven. Better a 12-mile buffer zone as far as Fort William, with the West Highland's right-to-build as insurance, than a bridgeable gap measured in yards at Ballachulish Ferry.

Kentra Bay (Ardnamurchan), 30 miles from Corran, had been scouted by John Anderson of the Callander & Oban as a railway harbour with advantages over both Roshven and Mallaig (see Chapter 2); but from 1896 this little-known scheme disappears from the record.[10] Anderson's motives, beyond a resolve not to surrender his company's interest in the districts of Morvern, Moidart and Arisaig, are uncertain. Whether the Caledonian Company in all circumstances would rest content at Ballachulish was a different matter. And what of Forman? He was confident that events would serve his purpose. Sooner or later public opinion must insist that the West Highland either build their

North Ballachulish line or yield to a fresh Callander & Oban bid for Fort William. Or renewed strife between Highland and North British might revive the shadowy Highland–Callander & Oban understanding of 1894-5 – and Forman had the means of shaping that scenario by attacking the restored Great Glen Agreement.

* * *

The Invergarry & Fort Augustus Railway was presented as a bona fide landowners' scheme. Neither the Highland nor the North British, the promoters asserted, could be injured by a venture designed first and foremost to serve a dozen estates on or within reach of their proposed line. The proprietors together with their sporting lessees possessed the means to help themselves; they could call on other public-spirited investors; and they were not disposed to wait. Moreover, they would provide an additional steamer on Loch Ness, complementing their railway. Communities all along the Great Glen must

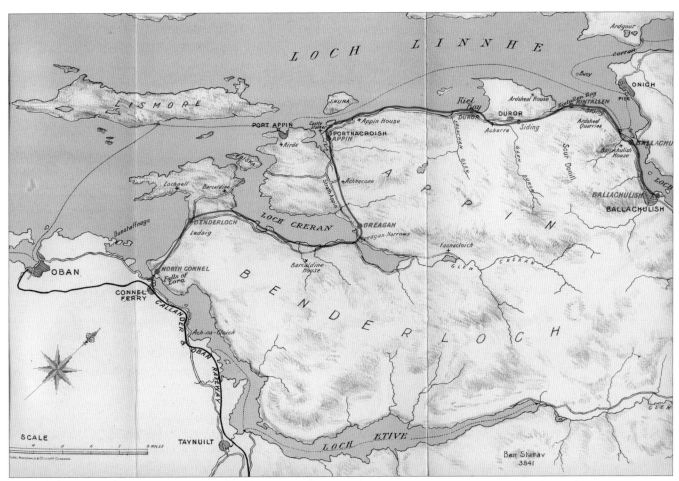

The Callander & Oban Company's Ballachulish branch, approved in 1896, as completed in 1903. Its extension beyond Ballachulish Ferry was authorised in 1897. (Highland Railway Society collection)

benefit, by obtaining in one direction interchange with the West Highland and in the other better access to Inverness. By easing local transport needs, the project would afford a breathing space in which to find the best long-term answer. Afterwards the Invergarry & Fort Augustus could become part of a new route to the North, no matter in whose hands. The Highland and North British had given vague assurances that a through rail link would be built eventually, but their arrogant attempts to proscribe any independent endeavour lacked legal force. Why not take them at their word and help them towards a speedier resolution?[11]

As a "half-way" scheme, the Invergarry & Fort Augustus recalled Charles Forman's tactics of 1893. He now re-surveyed a line 24 miles in length, feeding the West Highland at Spean Bridge. To Mucomir his revised layout followed the River Spean, which it spanned at Highbridge, on the alignment adopted by Murdoch Paterson for the Highland Company's Great Glen scheme of 1894-5. It climbed behind Glenfintaig, descending again by Invergloy and along Loch Lochy, where the Glasgow & North Western Railway (and Paterson's line too) would have kept more closely to the water's edge. At Fort Augustus it bridged both the Caledonian Canal and the River Oich, ending at a new pier on Loch Ness. The concluding mile, though disproportionally expensive, pointed onwards to Inverness by the Great Glen's north-western side, the alignment which most activists had come to favour. This fitted

the promoters' argument that their project must assist, and could not hinder, the completion one day of a through westerly rail route. Forman discarded the more direct entry to the Glen from Roy Bridge (direct, that is, for traffic to and from the South) which he had chosen for his West Highland Inverness Extension; but a cut-off to Invergloy could be reinstated in due course. A junction spur in the direction of Fort William might be contrived also, but for the time being local trains between Fort William and Fort Augustus would reverse, with little inconvenience, at Spean Bridge, where exchange of passengers and light goods was expected to outweigh through workings.[12]

The very mixed reactions of the proprietors in question made "landowners' line" a doubtful description. The fourth Lord Abinger (who had succeeded in 1892) lent his name as a promoter. He regarded a station at Mucomir (Gairlochy) as generally useful to the area and welcomed the prospect of a junction at Spean Bridge, where he owned the Abinger Arms Hotel; however he spent little time in Lochaber and would take little active part.[13] Captain Walker of Tirindrish, who had resisted the West Highland Inverness Extension, required an undertaking that neither his land nor General Wade's dilapidated 18th century arches (the original High Bridge) on the River Spean would be harmed.[14] The Glenfintaig (Belford) Trustees, who managed Fort William's Belford Hospital, abstained from opposition – on the promise of accommodation works, facilities at Mucomir, and a minor deviation to protect

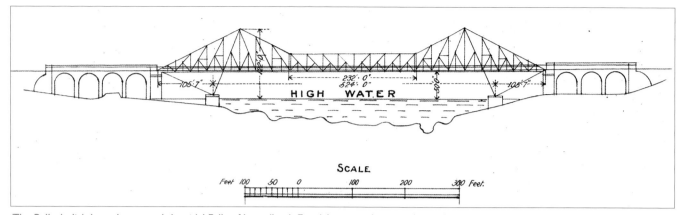

HIGH WATER

SCALE

Feet 100   50   0   100   200   300 Feet.

The Ballachulish branch spanned the tidal Falls of Lora (Loch Etive) by a cantilever viaduct, which subsequently became dual-purpose, carrying the public road. No subsidy for this provision was forthcoming and the tolls charged drew hostile comment. The road today remains single carriageway.   (Highland Railway Society collection)

their arable land – but they gave no positive support.[15] On the former Letterfinlay estate (now partitioned), three owners stood neutral. Two others voiced support – Lachlan MacKintosh, merchant and former provost of Kingussie, and Lewis Miller of Crieff, a sometime timber contractor. They both made troublesome demands; and Miller's bargain for the eventual clearance of mature woodland at Corriegour would trouble the London & North Eastern Railway (ultimate successor to the Invergarry & Fort Augustus Company) a quarter of a century later.[16]

A showing of active support by the Glengarry Trustees (see Chapter 2) was essential. Captain Edward Ellice proved a reluctant recruit. He declined to become a promoter until the family solicitors had drafted an agreement limiting his financial obligations and bestowing special rights at the future Invergarry station. Forman thought the latter requirement unreasonable but urged acquiescence in the short run – delay would have doomed the whole scheme.[17] Mrs Ellice feared the loss of the old military road along Loch Oich, which provided a secluded drive for her summer guests. She obtained a promise that all the railway embankments visible from Invergarry House would be grassed or screened.[18] Lord Lovat refused even token support. Conceding the long-standing defects of local transport, he remained of opinion that West Highland Spean Bridge made an adequate remedy. His personal objections to the new line, which threatened the amenity of Inchnacardoch Lodge as it approached Loch Ness, were resolved with no great difficulty, whereupon he withdrew his hostile petition; but he offered no positive encouragement.[19]

With a lease for many years, Lord Burton could be counted a resident promoter. He occupied the Ellices' Glenquoich – the lodge lay 14 miles beyond Invergarry village – every sporting season. Angelo of Culachy (Glen Tarff), once satisfied as to

James Scarlett, 4th Lord Abinger, (d.1903), promoter-director of the Invergarry & Fort Augustus Railway.

Forman's layout approaching Fort Augustus, declared himself in favour. Birkbeck of Loch Hourn, which opened on the sea west from Glen Quoich, offered his testimony. The landlords of Glen Moriston and Glen Urquhart, whose several properties were more-or-less distant from a Fort Augustus railhead, displayed little interest or reiterated their Highland Railway loyalties; their shooting tenants were unenthused. On the Glengarry estate, Lord Portman rented Aberchalder Lodge while the Duke of Portland leased the Oich and Garry fishing rights; though in principle favourable to a railway, they made no commitment. The promoters saw Baillie of Dochfour, now intimately linked with Burton but constrained by his Highland directorship (above), as a tacit sympathiser. They hinted that Lochiel, a West Highland director, was similarly constrained and could not admit that the Invergarry & Fort Augustus was a sound and above-board venture.[20] But this scarcely lent the project a convincing landed tone and did not offset Lovat's displeasure. Burton's conspicuous part exposed how tepid by contrast were the Ellice Trustees, with factor George Malcolm caught – not for the first time – between his two employers.

The Highland Company and the North British quickly ascertained what would become the basis of their concerted opposition – that the scheme hung on the capital to be provided by three "outside" businessmen–promoters.[21] Such a description fitted both John Nielson, identified as "Glasgow ironmaster", and Sir Donald Matheson, whose interests included the Turkey Red dye-works in the Vale of Leven. However, John Cunninghame of Craigends (Renfrewshire) could not be categorised so readily. Though prominent in the Ayrshire iron industry, he came from an old landed family and owned another property at Foyers. Matheson was already a director of the Lanarkshire & Dumbartonshire Railway, Cunninghame a director of the Lanarkshire & Ayrshire. They could not be dismissed as naïve investors entrapped by Forman. Both these companies were satellite to the Caledonian Railway; both companies were engineered by Formans & McCall and opened in stages – the Lanarkshire & Ayrshire between 1888 and 1904, the Lanarkshire & Dumbartonshire between 1894 and 1896. Cunninghame had sold part of his Foyers estate on Loch Ness to the British Aluminium Company, whose engineer-managing director, Emmanuel Ristori, became another Invergarry & Fort Augustus promoter. Lord Burton, though wealthier than any of the three "outsiders" and fated to become the mainstay of the Invergarry & Fort Augustus Company, made a smaller initial contribution.

* * *

Malcolm would testify before the House of Lords Committee how, when the West Highland Inverness Extension Bill was withdrawn, he "cast about…to find some other means".

Lord Burton (d. 1909), formerly Sir Michael Bass, as depicted in *Vanity Fair*.

Introduced to Glasgow solicitors G. Strang-Watkins and David Reid of Keyden, Strang & Girvan, he had "invited them to… see some of the people in the district", including Lord Burton and a reluctant Mrs Ellice. The Invergarry & Fort Augustus promotion had grown from there – it was, he emphasised, a truly independent enterprise, not a smokescreen for Highland, North British or Caledonian.[22] Forman, it seems certain, had been Malcolm's unidentified intermediary. Keyden, Strang & Girvan (formerly James Keyden & Co.) were old allies of Formans & McCall and they had become agents for the two Caledonian client-companies just described. In October 1895, before Burton came south for the winter, a further meeting had taken place at Glenquoich when it was decided in principle to lodge a bill, with Strang-Watkins as principal agent. And Charles Innes, who had campaigned so strenuously for the West Highland Inverness Extension, had been eager to assist.[23]

Perhaps the promoters' first intention was to test and once more bring down the Great Glen Agreement, without proceeding to Parliament. In cajoling the Ellice Trustees and other landowners, Strang-Watkins and Reid had affected to believe that the scheme could pass unopposed, as a bona fide local promotion, self-evidently desirable. Highland, North British and West Highland might all be refused a locus, which would isolate other objectors and ensure a favourable hearing.[24] But the renewed Highland–North British treaty stood, and the Invergarry & Fort Augustus Bill was finalised, with its protagonists schooled to argue that they faced mistaken resistance and would rescue the Highland and North British from interminable deadlock. When a parliamentary case came to be made, coordination was no simple task. Away from Glenquoich, Lord Burton divided his time between London and Rangemore Hall, near Burton on Trent. Lord Abinger lived

mainly in Surrey and Edward Ellice in Sussex, while the three "outside" capitalists, though Glasgow-based, were frequent travellers. In the Great Glen, Innes and Malcolm began negotiations to purchase land, fix accommodation works and settle compensation – which necessitated a correspondence triangulating Glasgow, Invergarry and Inverness. A general meeting in London, attended by Forman and Malcolm, was organised (with some difficulty) for mid-January 1896. Agreement with the Invergarry Trustees had not yet been finalised and Ellice took no part. Ristori left early. That evening Cunninghame and Neilson held a dinner party at the Conservative Club, St James's, for which Burton was requested to "remain in town", in order that (as Strang-Watkins put it) "*the promoters may know a little more of each other*". Matheson presided, as chairman-designate of the prospective Invergarry & Fort Augustus Company.[25]

Should they cast a wider net – perhaps by urging The Mackintosh and the other landowners affected by the Aviemore cut-off that the Highland Company would respond more briskly to their grievances if a competing Great Glen route became a serious possibility? But this implied early designs on Inverness, which the promoters were at pains to deny. Instead, Strang-Watkins pondered an approach to Sir John Stirling-Maxwell, the new owner of Corrour on the West Highland line – might he become an Invergarry & Fort Augustus subscriber? It constituted a Great Glen interest that Stirling-Maxwell had been co-opted to the Glenfintaig and Glengarry Trusts; moreover, Malcolm had been appointed factor for Corrour estate, additional to Glengarry and Glenquoich, and could use his influence.[26] Forman proposed that powers be sought to acquire the Caledonian Canal, strengthening the promise of better integrated transport along the Great Glen. If, as Reid suggested, a hint was dropped to the Canal Commissioners, nothing resulted.[27] However, the idea lingered. Perhaps Forman hoped that the Invergarry & Fort Augustus would inherit the government subsidy which sustained the waterway?

Public meetings in the Great Glen were nearly an afterthought, and by February 1896 these had become urgent. Cunninghame, with local knowledge and some local standing, was the preferred spokesman for the promoters; but he was engaged elsewhere. Matheson and Neilson, relying on Malcolm's latest notes, set out to "see the locality"; and on 11th March they accompanied Forman and Reid to Spean Bridge (fortified by a substantial luncheon hamper for the 4-hour West Highland journey). The whole party continued the next day to Fort Augustus. At both venues, Forman and Innes were the main speakers.[28] Arrangements at Spean Bridge were last-minute. William MacLennan, Lord Abinger's factor,

Downstream from Roy Bridge, the West Highland line crossed to the left bank of the River Spean; diverging at Spean Bridge, the Invergarry & Fort Augustus Railway crossed back again, by a substantial viaduct just upstream from General Wade's 18th century High Bridge.

(Courtesy Science Museum Group)

had hastily arranged for the distribution of handbills, after a misjudged, almost farcical, attempt by Strang-Watkins to engage Nigel MacKenzie of Fort William, the West Highland Company's Lochaber agent. (Strang-Watkins had encountered his fellow-solicitor only as secretary of the Glenfintaig Trust; Innes and Malcolm, who knew better, had not been consulted in time).[29] MacKenzie, already busily assembling ammunition for the North British, seized the opportunity to organise a rival meeting (unashamedly bogus) and afterwards planted press reports that local opinion at the southern end of the Great Glen was hostile to the Invergarry & Fort Augustus. Though Strang-Watkins and Reid were outraged and invoked the Procurator-Fiscal at Fort William, MacKenzie escaped retribution.[30]

Innes and Malcolm had secured a sufficient pool of prospective witnesses with local credentials – clergymen, innkeepers, hoteliers, general merchants and tenant farmers, together with a few professional men. William MacLennan (above) and Thomas Wilkinson, who leased the Abinger Arms, were primed to prepare supporting data. ("Insert full notes…of the traffic of the district in cattle, sheep, wool, manure, feeding stuff etc…within your personal knowledge.")[31] No equivalent input could be expected from Lord Lovat's factor. At Fort Augustus, Abbot Linse and the Reverend John McKay, minister of the local Free Church, formed an incongruous but effective campaigning partnership. Strang-Watkins was alarmed to learn that Lord Burton was "going abroad for his health" and might not give evidence in person, but the Ellice family had been won over after a fashion and Malcolm could speak with authority

for all Glen Garry and the districts westward.[32] The Reverend Donald Cameron, Church of Scotland minister at Blarour (Spean Bridge), provided estimates of livestock numbers across his Kilmonivaig parish, which embraced Glen Spean, Glen Roy and the Great Glen south of Aberchalder, and these were double-checked by his namesake, the auctioneer-owner of Fort William mart. (See also page 103) But Cameron "wavered" and looked hopefully to the North British – what if, after all, the Invergarry & Fort Augustus Railway was fated to remain for ever a minor branch? He considered the West Highland Inverlair & Kingussie Extension, so very briefly in prospect two years earlier, a much superior scheme, as making certain a through (though indirect) rail link between Fort William and Inverness and opening up other possibilities eastward from Strathspey:

> If no such extension…is in contemplation, I would not be opposed to the present Bill, as…better than nothing. But it is not to be compared…with the proposed [line] from Tulloch (Inverlair).[33]

Fort William to Inverness via Kingussie and the Aviemore cut-off was about 85 miles, against 65 miles by the Great Glen.

Opinion across Lochaber tended to the same reservations. Parliament, it seemed, was about to clear the way at last for construction of the West Highland Mallaig Extension; approval for a rail link to Oban was also in prospect, albeit a link interrupted for the time being at Loch Leven; and a line into Strathspey was much to be hoped for, permitting development in due course of several cross-country routes besides giving an adequate connection with the North. Altogether this must ensure Fort William's further expansion as a railway hub. A Fort Augustus line promised less. Its absorption into a West Highland-cum-Great Glen route to Inverness might remain indefinitely at the mercy of railway politics; and, if that day came, Glasgow–Inverness traffic would diverge at Roy Bridge or Spean Bridge, to the obvious disadvantage of the town. For good measure, Fort William was unconvinced that an Oban–Inverness railway via the Great Glen would be altogether advantageous; Oban and Inverness, at either end of the through route, stood to benefit more.

*   *   *

George Malcolm's search for "other means" (above), which he did not explain in full, had brought him in September 1895 to an interview with William Moffatt, secretary-manager of the Great North of Scotland Railway. Would the Aberdeen company condemn the Highland–North British Agreement and countenance, even sponsor, a fresh Great Glen promotion, complementing the Great North's next bid for access to Inverness? Forman attended, and probably arranged the meeting. At this stage, all three plotters may have calculated that the re-established Highland–North British pact would succumb to the first pressure. A month later (7th October) Moffatt saw Forman again, accompanied this time by David Reid, who posed a different question. With the Invergarry

& Fort Augustus scheme now in its early stages, would the Great North acknowledge an interest and contribute to the preliminary expenses? More exchanges followed, conducted through Keyden, Strang & Girvan, until in mid-November the Great North board decided that to engage with a Great Glen project stopping short of Inverness was imprudent. They resolved, however, to keep "the whole situation" in view and await the outcome of the Invergarry & Fort Augustus Bill.[34]

For Malcolm the Great Glen took priority, but Forman had his own agenda and was not wedded solely to a remodelled "half-way" project. After his schemes of 1893 had been frustrated, he maintained contact with Moffatt, as his best hope for their revival. It is not impossible, had the fleeting West Highland Inverlair & Kingussie Extension Bill gone forward in parliamentary session 1893-4, that the Great North would have petitioned to claim a say; and in December 1894, when rival Highland and West Highland schemes for the Great Glen seemed in serious preparation, the landowners of Badenoch had pressed the Aberdeen company not to forget "the proposed Inverlair–Newtonmore railway" (sic).[35] Moffatt, it appears, gave serious consideration to a Fort William connection, whether via the Great Glen or via Strathspey; and no doubt he had noted the Caledonian Company's mischievous suggestion that the Mallaig line, as a subsidised "government road", ought to be shared by all-comers. In August 1895 he made an unannounced visit to Lochaber, accompanied by several of his directors – i.e.

The Invergarry & Fort Augustus viaduct on the River Oich, seen from the Caledonian Canal towpath. Fated never to carry a through railway to Inverness, this stylish structure saw less than five years of regular use. The Reverend John McKay's Free Church stands on the hillside.

(Highland Railway Society collection)

A.1342.   CASTLE URQUHART, LOCH NESS.

Both long and deep, Loch Ness is also for the most part fully a mile wide. This view of *Gondolier* provides a scale. The paddle steamer is north-bound past Castle Urquhart and about to call at Temple Pier.

(J B White, Dundee, postcard)

before his meeting with Forman and Malcolm. Moffatt's party explored the route of the West Highland Extension as far as Glenfinnan. In October, a group of Great North officers made a similar expedition, returning to Aberdeen by Tulloch and Kingussie – and some bruit of what all this portended may have reached the Reverend Cameron (above). The neighbouring Church of Scotland minister at Corpach (Kilmallie parish) was certainly alert to rumour.[36] From November, with no assurance of any Great North commitment, the Invergarry & Fort Augustus promoters moved towards the position which they were to adopt when their Bill came to Committee the following year – if the Highland Company proved tolerant and the North British offered practical cooperation, they would need no other engagements. But it is entirely likely that Forman, never averse to a second string, continued to urge on Moffatt the attractions of a route from Moray via Strathspey into Lochaber, whence onward connection to Mallaig (and Oban too?) could be counted on before too many years elapsed.

The renaissance and expansionist ambitions of the Great North of Scotland Company under Moffatt's management are not the subject of this study. It should be remembered too that a proportion of Inverness traffic always passed by Aberdeen – which the Great North would not willingly put at risk. If Moffatt genuinely wanted access to Fort William, it was the more straightforward option that he pledge co-operation with any Great Glen scheme which Parliament might approve. A link with the West Highland via Craigellachie, Boat of Garten, Kingussie and Loch Laggan could not be established without

controversial running powers over the Highland main line along upper Strathspey. On the other hand, applying for these rights would have put the Highland Company on the defensive; and the Great North's offer to work the Garve & Ullapool Railway, given the necessary running powers through Inverness to Garve, had been a comparable gambit – not to mention their earlier threat to duplicate or contest the Aviemore cut-off over Slochd (see Chapter 1). Might the Highland have traded better facilities west of Elgin against withdrawal of the application? Might they have surrendered in Strathspey, the better to defend Inverness? And the argument that cross-country rail links with Lochaber could be better developed via Laggan than via Inverness was equally available to Moffatt.

The North British were willing in principle that the West Highland should eventually join hands with the Great North, and John Conacher was unalarmed. On 18th September 1895 he made a brief examination of the Tulloch–Kingussie route[37] – perhaps in response to Moffatt's excursion, perhaps thinking to head off Forman's latest activities in the Great Glen, as he and Andrew Dougall had done in 1893, by once more mooting a Spean-and-Laggan, West Highland-to-Highland, connection. There is no evidence that Conacher and Dougall had reached a fresh understanding, and the latter's many years of service were about to end in controversy. Nevertheless William Roberts, who would succeed Murdoch Paterson as the Highland's engineer, paid his own visit to Lochaber a few weeks later, on the heels of the Great North of Scotland officers, and he was accompanied by the Highland's goods manager. They too returned by Kingussie; and in November press reports of a Badenoch public meeting would hint that the Highland besides the Great North were interested in a Spey-to-Spean line. Meanwhile Conacher had instructed William Arnott, the North British superintendent at Fort William, to be alert for any news of surveying parties along Loch Laggan.[38]

The Great North "officials", heading homeward, had obtained a short interview with Badenoch proprietor Cluny MacPherson, besides meeting with David McCall of Formans & McCall at Kingussie or Newtonmore – so Arnott discovered; and he would report a chance encounter with Forman and an unidentified companion (surely David Reid of Keyden, Strang & Girvan?) at Tulloch on 8th October – i.e. the day after their interview with Moffatt (above). The engineer's luggage labels showed that he had come via Forres and Kingussie (surely from Aberdeen?). At Kingussie the two travellers had hired a coach; and the coachman, when interrogated, recounted how they paused at Kinlochlaggan, where Forman had consulted a bundle of plans.[39] Together with MacPherson of Glen Truim, Cluny would go on to organise a local petition to the Great North board, repeating their appeal of 1894.[40] The two large landowners of the Laggan district took no part. Sir John Ramsden of Ardverikie, though friendly to the West Highland Company, had always been unwilling to have a railway pass too close. The Mackintosh, one of the figurehead directors displaced from the West Highland board by the North British, showed no appetite thereafter for more involvement, and the war of words whereby Inverlair station became Tulloch had been conducted largely by his factor.

West Highland Secretary George Wieland had thought it advisable at first to keep open the possibility of a Strathspey link to barter against whatever might be afoot in the Great Glen, but he correctly concluded that the Great North would await events on both fronts.[41] The Highland directors, whose suspicions had brought on the crisis of 1894-5, seem to have been sufficiently convinced a year later that no hostile conspiracy was being hatched. Highland and North British, trusting to their re-written Great Glen treaty, would fight the Invergarry & Fort Augustus in wary unison. They were not to be inveigled a second time into supporting a compromise Spean-and-Spey promotion; and, if Forman's hopes had fixed on Moffatt, he was in the end to be disappointed.

References

J. McGregor, *The West Highland Railway: Plans, Politics and People*, Birlinn (John Donald), 2005, cited as PPP.

Keyden, Strang & Girvan abbreviated to KSG.

1. PPP, chapters 4-6.
2. NRS/BR/PYB(S)/1/342, Joseph Chamberlain, evidence, West Highland Railway Bill, Lords, 3 April 1889. PPP, pp.82-3.
3. *Glasgow Herald*, 9 August 1894.
4. PPP, pp.129-35.
5. NRS/BR/NBR/8/1764/Box 4, general manager's files relating to West Highland Railway, letters and telegrams, John Conacher to James Thompson and Thompson to Conacher, 23 May-8 July 1895. Ibid., Benjamin Hall-Blyth to Conacher, 6 August 1895. Ibid., William Arnott, report on prospective traffic at Ballachulish, 24 September 1895. NRS/BR/NBR/1/42, North British Railway minutes, 20 June and 18 July 1895. PPP, p.149.
6. NRS/BR/PYB(S)/1/385, Conacher, evidence, Charles Forman, evidence, and Hall-Blyth, evidence, West Highland Railway Ballachulish Extension Bill, Lords, 12-3 May 1896. NRS/BR/PYB(S)/1/380, Thompson, evidence, John Wolfe-Barry, evidence, Callander & Oban Railway Ballachulish Branch Bill, Lords, 14-5 May 1896. (The two bills were taken together.)
7. NRS/BR/PYB(S)/1/394, omnibus Callander & Oban Railway Bill, session 1896-7 including Ballachulish Ferry-Ballachulish extension.
8. NRS/BR/NBR/8/1764/Box 4, Conacher to Forman, 25 October 1895, and Forman to Conacher, 29 October 1895. Ibid., Arnott to Conacher 29 November and 14, 16 and 19 December 1895. *Glasgow Herald*, letter by "Bi Faicilleach", 7 December 1895. NRS/PYB(S)/1/385, Fort William burgh commissioners' hostile petition (subsequently withdrawn).
9. NRS/BR/PYB(S)/1/385, Conacher, preliminary Proof for West Highland Railway Ballachulish Extension Bill, cf. evidence, Lords, 12 May 1895.
10. SRPS24457BARR, Scottish Railway Preservation Society Archive, Thomas Barr to John Anderson, undated. J. McGregor, Railway to Ardnamurchan?, *West Highland News*, 2016-7.
11. NRS/BR/PYB(S)/1/386, speeches (counsel for promoters) and evidence (various witnesses) Invergarry & Fort Augustus Railway Bill, Lords, May 1896.
12. Ibid.
13. NRS/BR/IFA/4/1, KSG to George Malcolm, 3 December 1895, and various telegrams seeking Lord Abinger's whereabouts, 21 December 1895. NRS/BR/IFA/1/1, Invergarry & Fort Augustus Railway minutes, 16 January, 25 March, 16 April and 22 July 1896 – the promoters' only formal meetings (thrice in London, once in Glasgow) prior to Parliament's authorising their scheme.
14. NRS/BR/IFA/4/1, KSG to Captain John Walker, 12 December 1895.
15. NRS/BR/IFA/4/1, KSG to Malcolm, with copy of letter from Nigel MacKenzie (In his capacity as secretary, Glenfintaig Trust), 9 January 1896, and to MacKenzie, 11 March 1896. NRS/BR/IFA/1/1, Invergarry & Fort Augustus Railway minutes, 16 January 1896.
16. NRS/BR/IFA/4/1, KSG to Forman and to Lachlan MacKintosh, 12 December 1895. NRS/BR/LNE/8/468, timber extraction on Invergarry & Fort Augustus line, under NBR and LNER ownership, 1913-27.
17. NRS/BR/IFA/4/1 KSG to John C. Brodie & Sons, 7 and 10 January 1896, to Edward Ellice, 17 January 1896, and to George Malcolm, 22 February 1896. Ibid., David Reid (KSG) to Sir Donald Matheson, 24 February 1896.
18. NRS/BR/PYB/(S)/1/376, protection clause for Glengarry Trustees.
19. NRS/BR/IFA/4/1, KSG to Malcolm, 3 and 26 December 1895, and to Innes & MacKay, 31 December 1895 and 27 February 1896. NRS/BR/PYB/(S)/1/376, protection clause for Lord Lovat and tenant, Inchnacardoch.
20. NRS/BR/IFA/4/1, KSG to K. Angelo and to Charles Innes, 17 December 1895, to John Kennedy, 23 January, 10 February and 16 March 1896, to Innes, 27 February 1896, and to Innes and Malcolm, 7 March 1896.
21. NRS/BR/PYB(S)/1/376, Forman, evidence, and Charles Steel, evidence, Invergarry & Fort Augustus Railway Bill, Lords, 8 and 11 May 1896, and Conacher, evidence, Invergarry & Fort Augustus Railway Bill, Commons, 27, 28 and 29 July 1896.
22. NRS/BR/PYB(S)/1/376, Malcolm, evidence, Invergarry & Fort Augustus Railway Bill, Lords, 7 May 1896. NBR/BR/NBR/8/1764/Box 6, general manager's files relating to West Highland Railway, Arnott to Conacher, 8 October 1895.
23. NRS/BR/PYB(S)/1/376, Malcolm, evidence, and Forman, evidence, Invergarry & Fort Augustus Railway Bill, Lords, 7 and 8 May 1896.

24. NRS/BR/IFA/4/1, G. Strang-Watkins (KSG) to Edward Ellice, 16 December 1895, to Brodie & Sons, 7 January 1896, and to Emmanuel Restori, 13 February 1896.
25. NRS/BR/IFA/4/1, KSG to Malcolm, 7 January 1896, and Strang-Watkins to Lord Burton, 9 January 1896.
26. NRS/BR/IFA/4/1, Strang-Watkins to Innes, 19 June 1896, and Reid to Malcolm 31 December 1896. (These letters make explicit the hints in other correspondence earlier in the year.)
27. NRS/BR/IFAR/1/1, Invergarry & Fort Augustus Railway minutes, 25 March 1896. NRS/BR/IFA/4/1, Reid to Kennedy, 23 January 1896 and 4 March 1896.
28. NRS/BR/IFA/4/1, Reid to John Cunninghame, 27 February and 2 March 1896, to Sir Donald Matheson, 28 February 1896, to Malcolm, 5 and 7 March 1896, and to Charles Innes, 2, 7 and 10 March 1896.
29. NRS/BR/IFA/4/1, Strang-Watkins to MacKenzie (telegram), to Malcolm (telegram), and to William MacLennan, factor, Inverlochy, (telegram and letter), 7 March 1896.
30. NRS/BR/IFA/4/1, KSG to MacKenzie, 12 and 16 March 1896, and to Duncan MacNiven, 19 March 1896.
31. NRS/BR/IFA/4/1, KSG to MacLennan and to Thomas Wilkinson, 11 April 1896.
32. NRS/BR/IFA/4/1, Strang-Watkins to Malcolm, 1 April 1896.
33. NRS/BR/IFA/4/1, KSG to Innes, 7 March 1895 and to Malcolm, 9 March 1895, and Reid to Reverend Donald Cameron, with notes on Cameron's prospective evidence, 11 April 1896; also KSG to Innes, 9 October 1896, and to Gordon & Whitelaw, 23 February 1897 – the later letters touch on Cameron's "unreliable" performance.
34. NRS/BR/GNS/1/13, Great North of Scotland Railway minutes, special board meetings, 25 September and 23 October 1895, and parliamentary committee meetings, 16 October and 13 November 1895.
35. NRS/BR/GNS/1/13, Great North of Scotland Railway minutes, finance committee meeting, 9 January 1895, noting resolution of public meeting (December 1894) at Laggan.
36. NRS/BR/NBR/8/1764/Box 6, Arnott to Conacher, 5 October 1896
37. NRS/BR/NBR/8/1764/Box 6, Conacher to Arnott, 5 October 1895.
38. NRS/BR/NBR/8/1764/Box 6, Conacher to Arnott, 5 October 1895, and Arnott to Conacher (two letters), 8 October 1895. Ibid., Arnott to Conacher, 25 November 1895, citing *Northern Chronicle*, 20 November.
39. NRS/BR/NBR/8/1764/Box 6, Arnott to Conacher, 8 October 1895.
40. NRS/BR/GNS/1/13, Great North of Scotland minutes (finance committee meeting), 27 November 1895.
41. NRS/BR/NBR/8/1764/Box 6, George Wieland to Conacher, 4, 7 and 13 October 1895, and Conacher to Wieland, 5, 9 and 15 October 1895.

Mallaig harbour's combined breakwater-and-pier under construction. In the name of economy, the outer breakwater first intended was not built. A campaign to enlarge and better protect the harbour would continue intermittently from 1905 until the 1930s.

(Courtesy Science Museum Group)

CHAPTER FIVE

A NEW PLAYER, THE INVERGARRY & FORT AUGUSTUS RAILWAY, 1896-97

The Invergarry & Fort Augustus promoters faced a more rigorous parliamentary contest than some among them had anticipated and Strang-Watkins had urged that they keep a confident demeanour while the situation developed. The resolve of Highland and North British to justify and maintain the Great Glen truce would be tested, while Caledonian and Great North of Scotland might yet take a hand:

> After we see the attitude of the different…Companies in the first House, we will be better able to decide on a policy. Meanwhile we are ignorant of the exact relationship between the Highland and the West Highland [under the restored Agreement].[1]

Nevertheless, Strang-Watkins looked to an eventual bargain with the North British and recognition of the proposed railway as, de facto, a West Highland branch. Provision for agreement with other companies was deleted before the Invergarry & Fort Augustus Bill came to Committee (House of Lords) in May 1896. In like fashion, the promoters of the Glasgow & North Western Railway had decided to treat the North British as their main hope, narrowing down the facilities and running powers which initially they proffered wholesale (see Chapter 1).

The Highland Company's petition asserted that the state-aided "extension" lines to Kyle of Lochalsh and Mallaig had been government priorities. Other schemes could not be achieved all at once and, on mature consideration, might not be needed for many years. Parliament had recognised as much, thereby implicitly endorsing the Great Glen Agreement. Because the Aviemore cut-off and the Kyle extension were heavy burdens, despite the assistance which the latter had obtained, the Highland more than ever deserved Parliament's protection. Though variously disguised, the Invergarry & Fort Augustus project was a "partial renewal of defeated attempts to promote a new line to Inverness". The North British and West Highland petitions struck a similar note. West Highland resources were not elastic and the revenue generated in the first eighteen months of operation was less than expected. In these circumstances, it would be "irresponsible" to introduce an independent company into West Highland territory, and the interlopers' proposals for exchange of traffic with the Caledonian Canal were likely to harm the newly opened Banavie branch. The West Highland Ballachulish Extension Bill, also before Parliament, exemplified "judicious expansion" within the confines of Lochaber – if powers were obtained, construction would follow when the time was ripe – but a Fort Augustus line was by any test premature.[2]

George Malcolm's evidence set out the promoters' version of events. The Great Glen, and especially its southern half, had looked with confidence to the West Highland Inverness Extension, only to be betrayed by the North British. Nothing could be expected of the Highland Company. The local communities, thrown back on their own resources, now looked to achieve a local railway, modestly viable and sure to be bolstered by the seasonal traffic of several sporting estates.[3] Charles Forman, cultivating a cautious and realistic tone, provided more detail. Construction along Loch Ness, inevitably expensive, did not arise. The country south of Fort Augustus was easier, but he had erred on the safe side, fixing cost-per-mile at £700 more than the final figure for the West Highland between Craigendoran and Fort William. Nevertheless, three or four of the promoters could together fund the scheme themselves. Tourist business, already buoyant, would grow once a railway complemented the waterway. The sporting tenants and sub-lessees who had welcomed their new West Highland railhead at Spean Bridge wanted even better facilities for themselves and their guests.[4]

The Highland and North British, said Forman, must eventually find the means of co-existence in the Great Glen; but only in North British hands could a through route to Inverness become a paying proposition. Though the Highland, in self-defence, might demand shared ownership, neither local traffic to and from Inverness nor traffic fed to their Perth route could justify a large outlay on their part. They might plead that all Great Glen schemes should be postponed until the results of the company's financial overhaul following Andrew Dougall's retirement could be thoroughly assessed. However, like their plea that other lines had to be finished, this was beside the point, and the Highland's only real interest was to bar the way. The North British, for their part, had been too impatient, too pessimistic, and they ought to welcome the Invergarry & Fort Augustus. They were not doing enough to boost West Highland earnings, which nonetheless promised to grow. In 1888-9 his projections had included a share of Oban traffic, but the West Highland's Crianlarich spur to the Callander & Oban lay unopened (it would do so into 1897), while the additional construction costs of which the North British now complained were attributable to their own requirements. Forman denied that the Invergarry & Fort Augustus syndicate had behaved covertly. In helping to fashion the West Highland Ballachulish Extension Bill, he had not concealed his other activities from North British general manager John Conacher. Honest dealing had been, in any case, a matter of self-interest, because he looked to further commissions – the West Highland Company's Inverness Extension might yet be revived, perhaps absorbing the Invergarry & Fort Augustus, or Highland and North

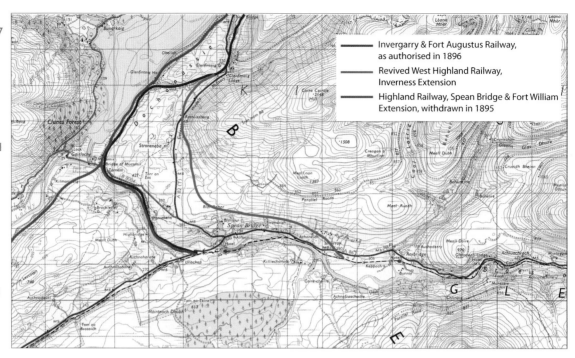

Competing lines at Spean Bridge, 1896-7 superimposed on the 1956 Ordnance Survey map which shows the West Highland line as built. The North British-cum-West Highland Bill claimed running powers from Invergloy over the Invergarry & Fort Augustus Railway; purely West Highland construction would have resumed along Loch Ness. Cf. the Highland Company's Great Glen scheme of 1894-5, also shown here.

British might decide after all that they wanted a Spean-to-Spey connection. As for the Great Glen crisis of 1894-5, Forman absolved the North British Company; they had turned to him when the Highland Company tore up the 1889 Agreement and threatened the West Highland with an Inverness–Fort William line.[5]

Conacher, while not excusing Forman, attacked Malcolm as all too eager to encourage an unwise independent promotion. The factor had sought a promise of North British support equivalent to their West Highland guarantee, with the intention of attracting "outside" investors. That pledge Conacher could not have given, but he had not refused to listen. Though bound to consult the Highland Company, whose opposition was only to be expected, the North British might have entertained an unprofitable Great Glen branch, on condition that the loss was borne by the landowners and "sportsmen" who were said to want it. He suspected, too, that Malcolm had made a similar approach to the Highland Company, calculating how they would be tempted to adopt the Invergarry & Fort Augustus as a "block" line.[6] Charles Steel, who had become the Highland's general manager on Dougall's departure, neither denied nor confirmed this charge; but he echoed Conacher's resolve to uphold the reconstituted Great Glen pact against any "forcing scheme". The Highland, Steel implied, now accepted that the North British had been fellow victims of Forman's earlier speculative ventures, and the two companies stood ready to resist any repetition.[7] But who had encouraged Forman's Great Glen surveys in 1893, if not Burton, Innes and Malcolm? The culprits were described opaquely as private individuals "friendly to the West Highland". All concerned now preferred, it seems, not to explain or explore further. And neither Malcolm nor Forman revealed that in December of 1895 Burton had sounded his son-in-law, James Baillie of Dochfour, as to the likely attitude of the main landowners between Fort Augustus and Inverness if a through line to Inverness were independently promoted. When Baillie was discouraging, Forman had framed

the Invergarry & Fort Augustus as an "interim", "half-way" scheme, in the hope of winning over Lord Lovat, Mrs Ellice and all the other proprietors south of Fort Augustus.[8]

* * *

Battle intensified in the House of Commons (July), where the Highland attacked the Invergarry & Fort Augustus as "the first move towards a new line to Inverness", no matter how disguised.[9] The North British-cum-West Highland petition (jointly submitted to secure a North British locus) was explicit:

> *The real Promoters…are the Engineer, Mr Forman, and the Solicitors. It is not a genuine scheme…but a purely speculative Bill for powers which [they] hope…to dispose of on favourable terms…The majority of the ostensible Promoters have no direct…interest in the district [but intend], if the Bill be passed, to promote an extension to Inverness, so [as] to hawk their powers between the Highland…and [us]…*[10]

In reply, counsel for the promoters denied that any next move had been planned and roundly condemned both Highland and North British:

> *[We] are only doing what landowners have done before… [That] is what these…Railway Companies are here to prevent…They neither of them care that the other should make the [Great Glen] line; they neither of them want to make it at present; they want to lock up the country…*[11]

Forman once more expounded the Invergarry & Fort Augustus case and parried the assaults of cross-examining counsel. A fresh initiative was needed to break the Highland–North British deadlock. Scotland's railway map had been largely fashioned by local lines subsequently absorbed by the principal companies, whose seeming resistance was often tactical. He portrayed the North British as protesting too much. Though they affected to be overburdened, they had exercised control of the West Highland from the outset, discouraging a larger stake on the part of landowners and private investors; and now they stood to acquire an entirely viable branch line.

They would admit as much sooner or later, but meanwhile the backers of the Invergarry & Fort Augustus needed neither working agreement nor guarantee and the little railway could be worked independently on a one-engine-in-steam basis, perhaps for a period of years. Spean Bridge was the obvious and most useful junction for a local line, with reversal of Fort William– Fort Augustus trains a minor inconvenience which need not be addressed until a through route to Inverness came back into the reckoning. If the West Highland Inverness Extension of 1894-5 had been approved, a Glasgow–Inverness service would have become the prime concern of the North British, and they might well have settled on Roy Bridge as the point of exchange for local traffic, postponing a "direct" Achindaul–Stronaba spur indefinitely. In this and other matters, their pretended solicitude for the district should not go unquestioned.[12]

The West Highland had most to gain, but the Invergarry & Fort Augustus and its steamer subsidiary must generate an increase in Great Glen traffic to and through Inverness, from which both the Highland Company and, more remotely, the Great North of Scotland were bound to benefit. His negotiations with the Great North, said Forman, were thus entirely explicable, and the promoters remained at pains to convince the Highland that there was nothing to fear. The Mallaig Extension, though vital to the West Highland's financial well-being, would not greatly enhance Fort William's market-town pretensions. However, better connection with Ballachulish Ferry in one direction and with Fort Augustus in the other was sure to do so, and the latter, with its own railway, would grow into a thriving "watering place". Replete with special pleading and not altogether consistent, Forman's was nevertheless a skilful performance. In the end, he implied, Glasgow–Inverness and Oban–Inverness rail routes would assuredly come into being. Neither Highland nor North British wanted to explore this eventuality, and he was not pressed to explain how or when.[13]

In reply, Conacher reiterated that revenue in the West Highland's first year of traffic had been "exceedingly disappointing" with working expenses barely met. This had clinched the postponement of an Inverness extension. Livestock earnings, besides passenger business, fell short of expectations and siding accommodation at Spean Bridge and Banavie had proved over-generous. The North British, who were open to all realistic proposals, had encouraged an experimental coach service between Spean Bridge and Fort Augustus (initiated by hotelier Thomas Wilkinson). They would continue to honour their West Highland guarantee. However, they were not bound by the over-optimistic calculations of Conacher's predecessor, John Walker; and abandonment of the Banavie branch, with train-and-steamer exchange relocated to a new Banavie station on the Mallaig Extension, might yet prove a necessary economy. Working the Invergarry & Fort Augustus at the West Highland figure (50% of gross revenue) was unthinkable. Income, Conacher admitted, showed peaks and troughs. The annual shed and wintering of sheep, summer tourism and the sporting season all counted; fish traffic on the Mallaig Extension, despite seasonal fluctuation, would count a great deal. But the fundamental disadvantage was a scanty year-round population, and West Highland solvency rested on "the broader back of the North British shareholders".[14]

Conacher had kept up Walker's pretence of West Highland independence and did not wish to advertise how completely the North British were paymasters – which had provided a partial defence against the last-ditch opponents of subsidy for the Mallaig Extension. But, in denouncing the Invergarry & Fort Augustus promotion, the North British were disadvantaged by their pose of semi-detachment. What if Parliament ignored the bigger picture and scrutinised only the immediate practicalities of the proposed Spean Bridge to Fort Augustus line – considered as simply a 20-mile adjunct of the West Highland and solely that company's concern? That the North British might be refused a hearing in their own right was not just the wishful thinking of the promoters' agents (see Chapter 4); and indeed North British and West Highland together were restricted to a limited locus in the Lords, though the Commons Committee chose to be more indulgent. The Highland, by contrast, enjoyed a full liberty to present their case in both Houses.[15] These uncertainties may explain why Conacher, usually measured and urbane, did not show to best advantage. Prevarication tinged his detailed defence of the North British record and his irritation showed clearly. Here was a speculative promotion, doubly dishonest in that Forman's Invergarry & Fort Augustus plans derived from "[those] deposited by the West Highland Company in 1894… for which the Engineer…was paid…with money provided by the North British Company under their guarantee…for future use…". All involved hoped to be bought off; they expected "to go out with something".[16]

Charles Steel gave a laboured explanation of his company's opposition, bewailing "Mr Forman's tendency to project lines". In 1894-5 the Highland had abrogated the Great Glen Agreement and reluctantly promoted their extension to Fort William "entirely for protective purposes". With the Aviemore and Kyle lines in hand, and a light railway from Forsinard to Gills Bay on the north coast under consideration, they could not afford to be pressured into any unproductive scheme. Moreover, one or two of the "north of Strome" lines assessed by the Lothian Commission would take on a different complexion once the Light Railways Act was in place, and these were more needed than a branch (sic) down the Great Glen from Inverness. The Invergarry & Fort Augustus was an ill-considered, even cynical, distraction:

> It is [promoted] purely with a view of asking either the Highland or the North British Company or some other… to take it over…It is not reasonable that an independent Company should come in…and practically force…other Companies to make this line…[17]

The Highland, said Steel, had been justified in resisting both the West Highland Railway and its Mallaig Extension, and they would resist a West Highland presence, covert or other, in the Great Glen; but he acknowledged that the North British were now established at Fort William and had the right to set the pace of further development within Lochaber. His own company, he submitted, deserved at least a breathing space. The Highland's finances were being reordered, to distinguish income from reserves (where Dougall's practice had been ambiguous); and an interval would be needed after the Aviemore cut-off opened for traffic to measure the success of their shortened Perth– Inverness main line against the cost of retaining the original

CHEAP DAY EXCURSIONS

FROM
GLASGOW, DUMBARTON, CRAIGENDORAN,
HELENSBURGH UPPER, ROW, SHANDON, AND
GARELOCHHEAD TO FORT WILLIAM OR
FORT AUGUSTUS.

Return Fare—Third Class, { FORT WILLIAM \
FORT AUGUSTUS } 7s. 6d.

☞ Tickets available on day of issue only ☜

Going.					a.m.	B a.m.	
Glasgow (College)	...	...	...	depart	...	10 1	...
„ (Queen Street High Level)		„			7 13	...	...
„ („ Low Level)		„			...	10 10	...
„ (Charing Cross)		„			...	10 13	...
„ (Partick)	...	...	...	„	...	10 18	...
Cowlairs	...	...	...	„	7 25	...	...
Dumbarton	...	...	...	„	7 48	10 35	...
Craigendoran	...	...	...	„	7 57	10 47	...
Helensburgh (Upper)	...	...	..	„	8 4	...	..
Row	...	...	...	„	8 9	...	...
Shandon	...	...	...	..	„	8 15	11 0	...
Garelochhead	...	...	...	..	„	8 21	11 6	...
Fort Augustus	...	...	...	arrive	12 55 pm	p.m.	...
Fort William	...	...	...	„	11 48 am	2 12	...

Returning.					B p.m.	p.m.	p.m.
Fort William	...	...	...	depart	12 55	3 45	5 5
Fort Augustus	...	...	...	„			3 35
Garelochhead	..	...	...	arrive	4 4	6 59	8 15
Shandon	...	...	...	„	4 10	7 5	8 20
Row	...	...	...	„	4 15	7 10	¶
Helensburgh (Upper)	...	...	..	4 19	7 14	8 30
Craigendoran	...	...	...	„	4 23	7 18	8 34
Dumbarton	...	...	...	„	4 37	7 30	8 45
Cowlairs	...	...	..	„	5 12	7 57	9 12
Glasgow (Queen Street High Level	..	5 20	8 5	9 20

College, Charing Cross, and Partick Passengers return to Queen Street High
Level Station.
¶ Calls when required, on notice being given to the Guard.
B Ceases after 17th September.

Tickets will also be issued from Glasgow (Queen Street) by 5-50 a m. and
from Arrochar and Tarbet by 7-4 a.m train (Mondays, Wednesdays, and Fridays
only after 14th September), valid on day of issue only, going to Fort Augustus
by Rail, David MacBrayne, Ltd., Steamer to Banavie, and thence Rail to
destination.   Fare—3rd Class and Steerage, **10s.**

Local Tours from Fort William.

Caledonian Canal, Fort Augustus, and Invergarry.

Going via Banavie and Fort Augustus, returning via Invergarry and
Spean Bridge or vice-versa.

	First Class and Cabin.	Third Class and *Steerage.
FARES.	**13s. 6d.**	**6s. 3d.**

Passengers may break their journey at any place on the route.
* Holders can travel in Cabin of the Steamers of David MacBrayne,
Limited, on payment of 4s. 6d. extra to purser on board.

N.B. Tour, 24 F.

From 1907 the North British Company's summer excursion
programme embraced the Invergarry & Fort Augustus Railway. See
also page 109.   (Scottish Railway Preservation Society archive)

route over Dava. He trusted in the restored Great Glen treaty;
but authorisation of the Invergarry & Fort Augustus must
tempt the North British to make terms with the new company,
whereupon the crisis of 1894-5 would be repeated, with no
better chance of a lasting resolution.[18]

As consulting engineer for the North British, Benjamin
Hall-Blyth had adjusted Forman's estimates both for the
West Highland Inverness Extension in 1894-5 and for the
West Highland Ballachulish Extension during the latest
parliamentary round. Retained in the same capacity by the Great
North of Scotland Company, he had acquired some knowledge
of William Moffatt's negotiations with the Invergarry & Fort
Augustus activists (see Chapter 4). In his evidence, Hall-Blyth
favoured a shared North British-and–Highland line all through
the Great Glen – which a "half-way" scheme would only delay.
The conditions of the mid-1880s, he reminded the Commons
Committee, no longer applied. Then the Glasgow & North
Western promoters had before them a largely empty map; but
the West Highland now existed, wandering across Rannoch

into Glen Spean, where any northward extension towards
Inverness must begin. Forman's layout of 1894-5, "direct" from
Roy Bridge to Invergloy, should be preferred, and Parliament, if
disposed to indulge the Invergarry & Fort Augustus promoters,
ought to insist that their line conformed. To detour by the
lower Spean valley, with an otherwise unnecessary viaduct
at Highbridge, was pointless and might never be remedied.
There was little call for additional local provision, but a hillside
station opposite Spean Bridge, if desired, could serve the whole
district around Gairlochy. Exchange between train and steamer
at Fort Augustus, in addition to West Highland Banavie, would
suffice. It was an exaggeration that the Caledonian Canal had
created a busy series of traffic "concentration points", which a
railway must inherit.[19]

The North British general manager had paid a "between
Houses" visit to Lochaber (tracked by the Invergarry & Fort
Augustus party, who tried to guess his purpose). He investigated
Forman's Spean Bridge–Invergloy layout – and this no doubt
influenced Hall-Blyth's evidence.[20] Conacher's hope was that
entry to the Great Glen from Roy Bridge would be preserved
in all eventualities, and with it the West Highland's pretensions
ultimately to control the whole valley. The Invergarry & Fort
Augustus promoters, said Hall-Blyth, might be sincere in
pledging that their line, once approved, would be built; but to
secure a working agreement with the North British, adjusting
their plans to North British wishes, was their obvious course.
By angling for an unrealistic guarantee, they had revealed their
speculative purpose; he feared that they intended to auction
whatever powers they might acquire, when the asking price
would reflect the strategic value of their little railway, not its
own meagre prospects. In sum, his testimony reinforced the
complaints of Conacher and Steel and gave some colour to
the dubious claim that the North British "owned" Forman's
plans. On any alternative scheme for a Laggan link and the
Great North's possible involvement, Hall-Blyth had nothing
to say or chose to remain silent. However, he confirmed how
Malcolm had made an early appeal, before the Invergarry &
Fort Augustus promotion took firm shape, for intervention in
the Great Glen by the Aberdeen company.[21]

* * *

Authorisation of the Invergarry & Fort Augustus on 14th
August 1896 constituted one more step towards a through
Oban–Inverness route, in which the Caledonian were sure to
claim a share, on behalf of the Callander & Oban. The North
British were refused running powers and the Caledonian did
not intervene, as they might otherwise have done, to demand
balancing rights. Reciprocal claims were a dimension of the
regular sparring between Caledonian and North British – a lesser
level of warfare, kept within bounds by the Peace Agreement –
and this partially accounts for the delayed opening of the West
Highland Crianlarich spur; there were other reasons, including
the resistance of the landowner immediately involved. Alerted
by Callander & Oban tactics over the Mallaig Extension, the
North British were wary. If exchange at Crianlarich were
begun, would the Caledonian bid for access to Fort William,
Mallaig and Fort Augustus, as a rejoinder to earlier North
British designs on Oban?[22] And Sir Donald Matheson, during

Gondolier at Banavie, c.1925, with a luggage van in attendance as passengers seek the footpath to Banavie Pier station (see also page 36). The line rose steeply to the canal bank, with a back shunt to the pier-side.

(J L Stevenson collection, courtesy Hamish Stevenson)

his evidence for the Invergarry & Fort Augustus Bill, touched on the soon-to-take-effect agreement, by which the Lanarkshire & Dumbartonshire Company and their Caledonian patron were to become part-owners of the Vale of Leven line and the Loch Lomond steamers plying between Balloch and Ardlui. Beyond the latter point, Matheson suggested, they might claim an interest in general traffic on the West Highland, including the local traffic of the Great Glen which he and his fellow-promoters looked to bring to Spean Bridge.[23]

When the North British took up the West Highland project in 1888-9, securing their north-of-Clyde preserves had been a large part of their purpose (see Chapter 1). But the Glasgow Central Railway and its Lanarkshire & Dumbartonshire extension (which opened in stages between 1894 and 1896) constituted a serious Caledonian invasion. Here was one more reason why John Conacher and Lord Tweeddale had come to look ruefully on their company's West Highland obligations, as lacking any compensating rewards – and it had not sweetened their relations with Charles Forman that both these Caledonian subsidiaries were engineered by Formans & McCall. Establishment of the Dumbarton & Balloch Joint Railway in 1892 had been a notable North British surrender, offsetting their gains in Aberdeen and Inverness traffic after the opening of the Forth Bridge.[24] Their confidence had been dented, along with their finances, and escape from entanglement in the western Highlands was impossible. In 1896 these anxieties probably tinged Conacher's Great Glen testimony. On the other hand, by the year's end the North British could find a good deal in which to take satisfaction. Their exclusive possession of the West Highland Mallaig Extension had met with no further challenge, and the Treasury Guarantee was at last in place – construction would begin in January 1897 when the "first sod" was cut at Corpach. Parliament had approved the two Ballachulish schemes in a fashion which would exclude Callander & Oban and Caledonian from Lochaber, at least for the time being. The Invergarry & Fort Augustus Company were as yet an unknown

quantity, but they must, in some measure, look to the North British – which meant that the Highland had more to fear.

*   *   *

The Commons Committee had indicated that running powers between Spean Bridge and Fort Augustus for both Highland and North British should be re-investigated if a railway all through the Great Glen were seriously in prospect;[25] and at once it became a question how events would develop. The Invergarry & Fort Augustus directors might be content to tout their assets (i.e. their powers to build), but they might construct their line. If Spean Bridge were to become a junction, the North British must sooner or later take a position – and it seems that George Malcolm sought an early decision. He resumed his earlier correspondence with John Conacher, glossing over their mutual accusations in Parliament. Did the North British contemplate new measures in the next session, whether on their own account or in the name of the West Highland? Would they seek to subsume the authorised Spean Bridge–Fort Augustus line in an updated version of the West Highland Inverness Extension? Conacher refused to be drawn. What, he asked, would be the attitude of the principal landowners along Loch Ness to any new Fort Augustus–Inverness promotion? Malcolm replied that he could not say – first the North British must bring forward a definite scheme. It was, for the moment, an impasse.[26]

In June 1896, after the Invergarry & Fort Augustus scheme had carried the day in the House of Lords, Sir Donald Matheson made an unexplained journey to Inverness. He met several officers of the Highland Company, who told him that their directors were prepared to tolerate a Spean Bridge to Fort Augustus line – but not in North British hands and only if it went no further. Pre-emptive action and occupation of the northern half of the Great Glen was a surer course, and the Highland board so resolved within a few weeks of the outcome in the Commons. Early in September 1896 the press reported that a line

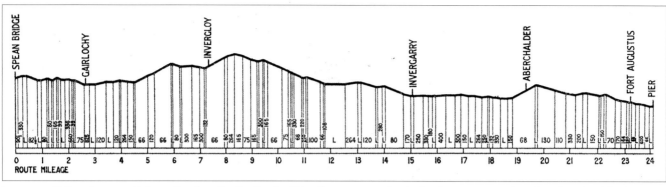

Invergarry & Fort Augustus Railway Gradient Profile: On the 2½ mile descent to Gairlochy there was one short length at 1 in 75. On either side of Letterfinlay summit, beyond Invergloy, the ruling gradient was 1 in 66. At the northern end of Loch Oich, the line climbed for just under a mile at 1 in 68 through Aberchalder then dropped steadily to Fort Augustus and Loch Ness.

"joining" the Invergarry & Fort Augustus was being discussed – and in fact general manager Steel had already written formally to Conacher, as the restored Great Glen Agreement required, that a "half way" scheme (i.e. Inverness–to–Fort Augustus) would go forward (see panel below).[27] Something more was secretly afoot, recorded by Charles Forman in a memorandum of 10th September. On that day Steel visited the Glasgow offices of Formans & McCall and posed two questions. Would Forman become consulting engineer for the Highland's "half-way" line? Would he advise the Invergarry & Fort Augustus directors to merge their company into the Highland system? Steel emphasised that, although a shared line through the Glen might be acceptable, his directors demanded absolute control north of Fort Augustus. They would abandon their bill at the first sign that the North British, or any other company, might obtain running powers. Stipulating that Invergarry & Fort Augustus interests must be "fully secured", Forman made counter-proposals. If the Highland bill proved successful, he would recommend amalgamation, to be speedily followed by the completion of a through line from Spean Bridge to Inverness. The alternative was joint ownership of the through line, in which case the Invergarry & Fort Augustus would remain nominally independent – but a 3% or 3½% guarantee would secure for the Highland the same measure of control as the North British exercised over the West Highland. Agreeing to a further meeting, he warned that the Invergarry & Fort Augustus, if menaced by Highland or North British, would feel entitled to pursue their own extension to Inverness.[28]

Lord Burton was now at Glenquoich for the season and out

of touch with Matheson, the designated company chairman. Captain Ellice, spending some time in Scotland, insisted that any new financial commitments be very clearly a company and not an individual matter. Lord Abinger held back – it was February 1897 before he agreed to remain a director by taking up his modest £500 of shares. Emmanuel Ristori of the British Aluminium Company, who had not been much involved during the parliamentary tussle of 1896, entertained hopes that the Highland would take their proposed line through Foyers. Averse to any promotion using Forman's earlier surveys by Invermoriston and Glen Urquhart on the opposite shore of Loch Ness, he was soon to distance himself entirely from the Invergarry & Fort Augustus.[29] Meanwhile, Keyden, Strang & Girvan had been confirmed as company solicitors, with Innes & MacKay as local agents; and Charles Innes had begun to seek potential witnesses against the possibility of a Fort Augustus–Inverness extension bill. Letters and telegrams multiplied, while Strang-Watkins and David Reid struggled to maintain a single strategy – they urged caution "in our communications with all parties".[30] Nevertheless, Strang-Watkins exuded confidence ("Parliament will protect us."). He believed that the Great Glen Agreement, if not already dead, would inevitably be rewritten to accommodate the Invergarry & Fort Augustus:

The Highland has more to fear from us than we from them [and] a Highland-NB alliance could not be complete without us.[31]

To emphasise that the company would keep faith with the people of the Great Glen, Strang-Watkins proposed that the next board be held at Invergarry; but Burton "grudged losing a day's stalking". A quorum met instead in Glasgow, on 10th October (conveniently for Burton on his end-of-season way south).[32] Forman's second interview with Steel had been inconclusive and the Highland had begun to re-survey in earnest between Inverness and Fort Augustus. To demonstrate that the Invergarry & Fort Augustus would not be overborne, it was resolved that the authorised Spean Bridge–Fort Augustus line should be staked out as soon as possible, with a view to inviting tenders. Meanwhile Forman would make another survey to Inverness. But further negotiations were not ruled out, provided that the Highland conceded a fixed guarantee.[33] Meeting Steel at Perth on 17th October, Reid raised Forman's figure to 4% and afterwards wrote to Malcolm that a take-it-or-leave-it stance should be maintained in any dealings with the Highland Company's landowner-directors or their agents.[34]

The traditional summer sailings on the Caledonian Canal did not resume after the 1939-45 War and all traffic on the West Highland Banavie branch ceased from 1951. Banavie Pier station building fell quickly into sad disrepair, but by 1969, when this photograph was taken, it had become a private dwelling. It has since been further altered and thoroughly refurbished.

(Keith Fenwick)

The Highland directors did not ponder long. In the hope of a decisive result, they pressed for a conference in Glasgow, which took place less than a week later (23rd October) at the offices of Keyden, Strang & Girvan. Sir George MacPherson-Grant, the Highland chairman, attended, together with Baillie of Dochfour and the company's solicitor, William Burns (of Stewart, Rule & Burns, Inverness). Matheson and Lord Burton, with Forman, Malcolm and Strang-Watkins, represented the Invergarry & Fort Augustus. (It is unclear whether Burton continued his journey only to return to Scotland.) They insisted on a guarantee of at least 3½% and a meaningful degree of independence. Construction from Spean Bridge to Inverness must be left in the hands of the lesser company, who would undertake to protect the Highland's interests:

> *The negotiations on our part were… to the effect that the line to Inverness must… not become a block… in the hands of the Highland [and] that they must give an absolute guarantee… [Both] lines would have to be proceeded with by us with all despatch.*[35]

To such conditions, endorsed in absentia by Ellice, Cunninghame and Neilson, the Highland delegates could not agree.

* * *

By late 1896 another Great Glen confrontation loomed, with the newly established Invergarry & Fort Augustus Company a third belligerent, somehow to be accommodated if a settlement were once again patched up. In response to Steel's formal letter the North British directors had challenged the Highland's unilateral action, while offering a conciliatory meeting whereby the Great Glen Agreement might again be repaired or rewritten. Concealing his negotiations with Forman, Steel replied (14th September) that the truce as restored in 1895 had been designed to ward off rogue "half-way" projects. It did not rule out Highland or North British promotions after due notice, which the Highland had given; and a defensive scheme linking Inverness with Fort Augustus was solely the Highland's business.[36]

From mid-October the North British moved unwillingly towards another Great Glen contest. To ensure a locus, they would lodge a bill jointly with the West Highland. In any negotiations with the Highland Company, Conacher looked to avoid including the Invergarry & Fort Augustus as a third party; and he assumed that they would be reduced to dependency or bought out on North British terms if the North British–West Highland Bill succeeded. Hall-Blyth drew plans for new construction between Roy Bridge and Invergloy and between Fort Augustus and Inverness (c.35 miles in total), on the basis that the Invergarry & Fort Augustus would surrender

---

NORTH BRITISH RAILWAY, MINUTE OF SPECIAL COMMITTEE, 12 OCTOBER 1896

[The] West Highland Company should deposit a Bill…to be jointly promoted by them and the North British Company, for the construction of a Railway from Roy Bridge to the point on the authorised Invergarry & Fort Augustus Railway where it diverges from the route adopted [by the West Highland Company] in 1894, with running powers from there to Fort Augustus, and a Railway from Fort Augustus to Inverness, with a separate station there, and a Junction with the Highland Railway. The Bill also to contain powers for running over the Highland Railway into [their] station at Inverness, and for contributing to the cost of enlarging that station, as also, if found desirable, for carrying [our] Railway along the bank of the Caledonian Canal… and for scheduling the land believed to have been acquired by the Highland Company for the construction of a new passenger station at Inverness. [Mr] Hall Blyth should be the engineer for the Scheme [and be given] instructions for a survey of the line to be made at once.

NRS/BR/NBR/1/42

at once. If instead they persisted in precarious independence and built their authorised line, the North British would claim running powers to close the Invergloy–Fort Augustus gap. The Spean Bridge–Invergloy "detour" might be abandoned later or modified to establish a connection in the Fort William direction. In sum, the intention was to recreate the West Highland Inverness Extension more-or-less in its 1894-5 guise (see panel on previous page).[37]

Approaching Inverness, the Invergarry & Fort Augustus and North British-cum-West Highland schemes, which alike derived from Forman's previous surveys, differed only in detail. Adding to the tangle, the Highland Company likewise elected to follow the Caledonian Canal, discarding the layout by Millburn, Culduthel and Bona Ferry which Murdoch Paterson had chosen for his Spean Bridge & Fort William Extension two years earlier. When competing lines intertwined, exchange of plans beforehand was the usual practice, whereby reconcilable differences might be identified; and into early 1897 it remained Conacher's hope that from these routine preliminaries a larger compromise might follow, leading to the withdrawal of all three bills. Steel likewise had not given up, and he made one last approach to the Invergarry & Fort Augustus proposing immediate amalgamation.[38] But neither Highland nor North British would concede the Invergarry & Fort Augustus Company's sine qua non – construction without delay of an end-to-end Great Glen railway.

The Invergarry & Fort Augustus directors had achieved their declared goal, approval for an "interim" local project, and Lord Burton had stated that "what was done north of Fort Augustus" need not be their concern.[39] In so rapidly promoting their extension to Inverness, they faced an inevitable charge of deceit, but Strang-Watkins confidently framed a plea of altered circumstances and public interest. The Highland had courted a new battle. If it were fought out, Parliament this time might well insist on the winner's committing to a through line, and thus the completion of a second rail route from the Central Belt to the North was probably within sight. Though the Highland Company, who had always resisted it, and the North British, who had proved ambivalent, might be compelled to end their stand-off, they would evade, if they could, any unwelcome parliamentary prescription. The Invergarry & Fort Augustus Company, whose well-being and the well-being of the Great Glen were identical, could be trusted. Should they emerge victorious, they would possess Spean Bridge-to-Inverness powers. These they would use without delay, or part with only on the strict condition that a line equivalent to the West Highland-cum-Great Glen route to Inverness, lost in 1895, was commenced at once. Bad faith apart, Highland and North British, with "many interests to serve, totally apart from [our] District", could never be single-minded. Now that "local gentlemen" (sic), in sympathy with "the people of the country" and its "trading interest", had forced them into action by promoting the Invergarry & Fort Augustus, it would risk more obfuscation and delay to close prematurely with the terms on offer, Highland or North British. The two were equally likely to renege, falling back on the excuse that an inter-company balance across northern Scotland ought to be preserved.[40]

Strang-Watkins assured Lord Burton that "our Invergarry (sic) should be able to hold its own". To other correspondents he wrote that it would be "amusing" to hear the North British explain in Parliament why they were now eager for a line to Inverness, after Conacher had emphatically asserted that this could only be a long-term objective. The public must be persuaded that the Invergarry & Fort Augustus would not give in. When an honourable settlement finally came, they would bequeath to Highland or North British the best railway for local and regional needs; and in the interval – perhaps a period of years – they were ready to make their own working arrangements. But the fact remained that local, along-the-route investment remained relatively slender (if arguably better than the West Highland Company could show), and there was danger, as Strang-Watkins admitted, in "false impressions".[41] Allegations were circulating that Matheson and Cunninghame had gained substantially from their involvement with the Lanarkshire & Dumbartonshire and the Lanarkshire & Ayrshire Companies, encouraging them to enlarge their gamblers' stake in the Great Glen by endorsing, along with Neilson, a continuing line to Inverness. Beginning a new round of public meetings along the valley, Innes and Malcolm encountered rumours that the Highland Company were to buy out the Invergarry & Fort Augustus directors at £10,000 a head.[42]

At every meeting the Invergarry & Fort Augustus spokesmen received a hearty vote of confidence, and they reported that hostile misinformation had made little impact. However, they could not win over the key proprietors north of Fort Augustus. Though Charles Forman promised to adjust his detail plans, satisfying every landowner's demands, Grant of Glenmoriston and Lady Seafield eventually declared for the Highland Company. Baillie of Dochfour remained at heart a Highland director, though his personal ties with Lord Burton entered too and he could not altogether ignore the wishes of his constituents in North British Lochaber. Stressing the advantages of a westerly through route to Glasgow, Edinburgh and England, Innes canvassed town councils, merchant associations and chambers of commerce all over the Northern Counties.[43] His efforts, ranging east to Forres and north to Wick and Pultneytown, recalled the catch-all methods of the Glasgow & North Western promoters in 1882-3, and Forman warned that this should not be overdone. From long experience, the engineer wanted a disciplined presentation, not an indiscriminate round-up of witnesses who might contradict themselves or turn half-hearted under cross-examination. Some who were eager at first to air their grievances would succumb in the end to the argument that the region could not afford the downfall of the Highland Company. Strang-Watkins urged that all recruits "be educated up (sic) to tell practically the same story" – a litany of the Highland's misdeeds, which competition alone could remedy. Prospective witnesses who looked for reimbursement should be reminded how the Invergarry & Fort Augustus directors were public-spirited "private gentlemen", whose resources were entirely adequate but still finite.[44]

To emphasise the board's resolve, bids were invited for construction of the authorised line. On Forman's recommendation, the contract was quickly awarded to James Young of Glasgow, whose figure of £172,000 was second lowest. Lucas & Aird, builders of the West Highland proper,

Double-headed by two ex-LNER K2 class 2-6-0s and composed of ex-LNER coaches, a west bound Mallaig train c.1950 quits Glen Finnan viaduct on the steep ascent through Glenfinnan station. Rock cuttings abound in the 30 miles between Kinlocheil and Mallaig (not to mention the eleven tunnels), and construction of the Highland Company's 10-mile Kyle of Lochalsh extension had been similarly exacting.

(J L Stevenson collection, courtesy Hamish Stevenson)

and Robert McAlpine & Sons, contractors for the Mallaig Extension, both submitted tenders. (John Aird, influenced no doubt by his West Highland experience, prudently offered "cost plus 5%".)[45] Young's formal contract had not been signed when on 2nd March 1897 two "first sods" were cut, at either end of the route, after Lord Abinger and Lord Lovat had given their respective permissions to break ground. At Spean Bridge Mrs Ellice wielded the ceremonial spade. At Fort Augustus the directors, who could not easily choose between Abbot Linse and his Free Church ally, looked at first to Angelo of Culachy but fixed instead on the mother of Forman's senior subordinate, J. E. Harrison. David MacBrayne provided a special sailing from Gairlochy, along the Caledonian Canal, connecting the two events. The Fort Augustus ceremony included a controlled explosion shattering a boulder.[46]

Conacher suspected a sham performance, calculated to influence Highland and North British; but Young was indeed under instruction to make a serious start as soon as possible, before the three competing Great Glen Bills of 1896-7 came to Committee.[47] Though the day passed off well, Strang-Watkins's belief that one or two weighty "names" would now identify with the Invergarry & Fort Augustus went unfulfilled. Lovat's cooperation had been encouraging, but he firmly refused to join the board. Ristori, it was suspected, had advised him to hold back, arguing meanwhile that the Highland Company would do well to reconsider – their line should take the "superior" route through Foyers and Lovat ought to exert his influence to that end. Might The Mackintosh prove friendly? Dissatisfied still at the slow progress of the Aviemore cut-off and its disruptive impact on his Moy estate, he was not well-disposed to the Highland board; and his shooting tenants in Glen Spean, whose sport would be hampered by the revived Roy Bridge–Invergloy cut-off, were believed to dislike the North British-cum-West Highland Bill. However, soundings produced nothing useful.[48] Bolstering the company's local credentials, George Malcolm had become an Invergarry & Fort Augustus director – he would

be better able, Strang-Watkins assured him, to exploit his long experience and many contacts across the North. But Malcolm could find no means of inducing the Ellice family or their sporting lessees to take a larger part. He achieved one small success, persuading Sir John Stirling-Maxwell to oppose the North British-cum-West Highland Great Glen Bill.[49]

Matheson had been chosen to head the Invergarry & Fort Augustus campaign in Inverness. With an exploratory meeting scheduled for 16th December 1896, Strang-Watkins sought to orchestrate the occasion at long range; he bombarded Innes, whose instincts he was prone to ignore or override, with a volley of anxious admonitions (see panel below), including the surely superfluous warning not to use the Highland Railway's Station Hotel. Matheson, showing his businessman's temperament, would have preferred an intimate dinner with "three or four of the most influential gentlemen" in the town, who in this way might be won over. However, Malcolm feared "jealousies" among those not invited while Innes objected that "secretive" arrangements would encourage rumours of surrender to the Highland and discourage other waverers who might have been

---

G. STRANG-WATKINS TO CHARLES INNES, 10TH AND 12TH DECEMBER 1896.

[We] put it as a meeting of gentlemen who are in favour of the immediate extension of [our] Line to Inverness, and we presume you will not ask... any who are lukewarm... or decidedly in favour of the Highland or NB Companies... It would be a mistake to have the meeting a public one. In view of the number you are inviting, however, it will practically amount to this. [Full] short-hand notes should be taken [but] we require to consider carefully what is to appear in the Newspapers [and] you should [not] have any Reporters present whom you cannot control...

NRS/BR/IFA/4/1

converted. The idea was abandoned and Matheson, briefed by Innes on the questions of greatest concern for Inverness, presided at the more-or-less open meeting (in the Caledonian Hotel) with Cunninghame and Malcolm in support.[50]

Inverness Harbour Board expected to drive down railway charges for the future by playing off the competing companies one against the others; but Forman's layout was generally well-received. It promised new rail access both to Kessock Ferry and to Thornbush Quay, which accommodated larger vessels than could use the inner harbour. The town council inclined to the Invergarry & Fort Augustus – until Provost William McBean recalled how Perth had seen the locomotive works of the Scottish North Eastern Railway reduced to repair shops and paint shops, following the amalgamations of the 1860s, when the enlarged Caledonian Company concentrated their new construction in Glasgow. Railway employment in Inverness would be forfeit if the Highland were fatally weakened and forced into amalgamation:

> The benefits conferred upon the North of Scotland by the Company deserve at least this much gratitude, that [we] should not come to a hasty decision…[They provide] for the maintenance, if [we take] the workmen and their families and dependants, of not less than 3,000 souls. [51]

Though Matheson's endeavours caused Charles Steel some alarm, only a few prominent citizens (among them "Mr Guild, the brewer at Thornbush") showed any readiness to commit.[52] There was gratitude that Lord Burton and his allies had forced the issue, but friendly declarations were muted and tinged with doubt. The Invergarry & Fort Augustus might win entire possession of the Great Glen, but could they remain independent, and did they genuinely mean to persevere? In the end Matheson found not one Inverness "name" willing to become a director.[53]

The little company's Act had bestowed capital powers of £240,000, and by March of 1897 the allocation of shares read thus:- Matheson, £100,000; Burton, £50,000; Neilson, £50,000; Forman, £20,000, Cunninghame, £10,000; Watkins, £2,000; Ellice, £1,000; Malcolm, £1,000; Abinger, £500. Matheson's holding was divided equally with his associate, Alexander Wylie, MP for Dunbartonshire.[54] Cunninghame was ready to take a larger holding, but the balance had been reserved for the British Aluminium Company and for lesser contributors in Inverness and in every other northern town where support was to be found. Strang-Watkins impressed on Innes and Malcolm that even the smallest amounts would help to cultivate a picture of broad-based good-will, which must be advantageous when their Bill came to Committee.[55] Though evidence of this stamp often made little impact, these were exceptional circumstances. Three schemes, indistinguishable for most of their length, were to be assessed – and anything might turn the scales. To Strang-Watkins's disappointment, few subscribers came forward; and Ristori, who refused any contribution, made his disenchantment utterly clear:

> "He …would like the three…Bills thrown out [this year] with one of the Companies giving him a definite promise that they will make a line up the east side [of Loch Ness].[56]

* * *

Meanwhile, the Great North of Scotland Company had deposited their latest Bill for running powers to Inverness and Muirton, with an engine depot and sidings at Longman.* To overcome any "differences and difficulties", they proposed to fund double-tracking along the Highland Railway between Elgin and Dalcross. In 1895-6, judging that to associate with a line which terminated at Fort Augustus was pointless, the Great North had refrained from asserting an interest in the Great Glen. In 1896-7 they sought powers to enter into agreement with "any Company authorised under any Act to construct Railways to or near Inverness", a form of words which covered a partnership in due course with the Invergarry & Fort Augustus or with the North British, and also the possibility that the latter would soon absorb or control the former.[57] At Inverness, both Hall-Blyth's plans (North British–West Highland Bill) and Forman's (Invergarry & For Augustus Bill) could have been adjusted with little difficulty so as to join hands with the Great North.

In November 1896 Innes recorded, after an "interview with Great North officials", that they were eager for an overt agreement. With competing Fort Augustus–Inverness schemes in preparation, the Aberdeen Company could not but recognise an exceptional opportunity to clothe their ambitions in the language of public advantage. A through Great Glen line would multiply the routes available to passengers and traders far and wide (cf. the case for a West Highland link into Strathspey), and the Great North could claim quite plausibly that they had a part to play. Moreover, double tracking east of Inverness in anticipation of increased traffic was a fair and straightforward expedient by comparison with their earlier and obviously calculated offers to encourage the promoters of a Black Isle line, to assist the Garve & Ullapool Company, or to take up another of the "Lothian lines". On Strang-Watkins's instructions, Innes trod warily – it was enough to keep discussion open, which might make the Highland and North British more amenable. In February 1897, by which time all three Great Glen Bills had gone forward, and the Great North Bill too, Strang-Watkins proposed that negotiations move to Westminster. The Invergarry & Fort Augustus and the Great North should grant discretion to their respective parliamentary agents, then await events. Compromise at Committee stage was not unusual, and a four-sided situation – five if the Caledonian were included – must generate unpredictable opportunities.[58] Forman's visit to Aberdeen a week later is unexplained.[59] Nothing indicates that his Lochaber–Strathspey link-line was once again under consideration. The Great North, if earlier receptive to his second string project (see Chapter 4), now meant to concentrate on their own Elgin–Inverness bid. And it bears remembering (see panel, page 71) that their calculations were in some degree defensive.

References

J. McGregor, *The West Highland Railway: Plans, Politics and People*, Birlinn (John Donald), 2005, cited as PPP.

Keyden, Strang & Girvan abbreviated to KSG.

Note 8 – the Cameron of Lochiel Papers (Lochaber Archive) include

---

* Presumably the purpose of a very short branch, to be owned purely by the Great North.

the Glenquoich estate Letter Books, which contain much of George Malcolm's correspondence.

1. NRS/BR/IFA/4/1 KSG to George Malcolm, 9 March 1896.
2. NRS/BR/PYB(S)/1/386, Highland Railway petition, North British Railway petition and West Highland Railway petition, Invergarry & Fort Augustus Railway Bill, Lords, May 1896.
3. NRS/BR/PYB(S)/1/386, Malcolm, evidence, Invergarry & Fort Augustus Railway Bill, Lords, 7 May 1896.
4. NRS/BR/PYB(S)/1/386, Charles Forman, evidence, Invergarry & Fort Augustus Railway Bill, Lords, 8 May 1896.
5. Ibid.
6. NRS/BR/PYB(S)/1/386, John Conacher, evidence, Invergarry & Fort Augustus Railway Bill, Lords,13 May 1896.
7. NRS/BR/PYB(S)/1/386, Charles Steel, evidence, Invergarry & Fort Augustus Railway Bill, Lords, 11 May 1896.
8. Lochiel Papers, Lochaber Archive, CL/A/12/1/Glenquoich letter books, Malcolm to Lord Burton, 1 December 1895.
9. NRS/BR/PYB(S)/1/386, Highland Railway petition, Invergarry & Fort Augustus Railway Bill, Commons, July 1896.
10. NRS/BR/PYB(S)/1/386, combined North British Railway and West Highland Railway petition, Invergarry & Fort Augustus Railway Bill, Commons, July 1896.
11. NRS/BR/PYB(S)/1/386, introductory speech, counsel for promoters, Invergarry & Fort Augustus Railway Bill, Commons, 23 July 1896.
12. NRS/BR/PYB(S)/1/386, Forman, evidence, Invergarry & Fort Augustus Railway Bill, Commons, 24 July 1896.
13. Ibid.
14. NRS/BR/PYB(S)/1/386, Conacher, evidence, Invergarry & Fort Augustus Railway Bill, Commons, 27, 28 and 29 July 1896.
15. NRS/BR/PYB(S)/1/386, Invergarry & Fort Augustus Railway Bill, Lords and Commons.
16. NRS/BR/PYB(S)/1/386, Conacher, evidence, Invergarry & Fort Augustus Railway Bill, Commons 27July 1896.
17. NRS/BR/PYB(S)/1/386, Steel, evidence, Invergarry & Fort Augustus Railway Bill, Lords, 11 May 1896.
18. Ibid.
19. NRS/BR/PYB(S)/1/386, Benjamin Hall-Blyth, evidence, Invergarry & Fort Augustus Railway Bill, Commons, 27 July 1896.
20. NRS/BR/IFA/4/1, KSG to Malcolm, 1 April 1896 and to Charles Innes 10 April 1896.
21. NRS/BR/PYB(S)/1/386, Hall-Blyth, evidence, Invergarry & Fort Augustus Railway Bill, Commons, 27 July 1896.
22. PPP, pp.150-1 and 169-70.
23. NRS/BR/PYB(S)/1/386, Sir Donald Matheson, evidence, Invergarry & Fort Augustus Railway Bill, Lords, 8 May 1896.
24. PPP, p.35. D. Ross, *The North British Railway*, pp.148 and 164.
25. NRS/BR/PYB(S)/1/386, Invergarry & Fort Augustus Railway Bill, Commons, August 1896.
26. NRS/BR/NBR/8/1764/Box 6, general manager's files relating to West Highland Railway, Malcolm to Conacher, 17 August and 15 September 1896, and Conacher to Malcolm, 4 September 1896.
27. NRS/BR/IFA/4/1, KSG to Malcolm, 2 June and 4 September 1896. NRS/BR/NBR/8/1764/Box 6, Steel to Conacher, 28 August 1896.
28. NRS/BR/CAL/1/152, minutes of meetings between Caledonian Railway and North British Railway general managers, memorandum of Forman-Steel discussion, 10 September 1896. [I cannot explain why this memorandum is to be found in a Caledonian Company source.]
29. NRS/BR/IFA/4/1 G. Strang-Watkins to Edward Ellice, 7 December 1896 and to John Kennedy, 13 January 1897. NRS/BR/IFA/1/1 Invergarry & Fort Augustus Railway minutes, 19 February 1897.
30. NRS/BR/IFA/4/1, KSG to Malcolm, 14 September 1896.
31. NRS/BR/IFA/4/1, Strang-Watkins to Kennedy, 16 September 1896.
32. NRS/BR/IFA/4/1, Strang-Watkins to Malcolm 14 and 25 September

1896 and Malcolm to Strang-Watkins (telegram), 14 September 1896.
33. NRS/BR/IFA/1/1, Invergarry & Fort Augustus Railway minutes, 10 October 1896.
34. NRS/BR/IFA/4/1, David Reid to Malcolm, 20 October 1896.
35. NRS/BR/IFA/4/1, KSG to Charles Innes, 27 October 1896.
36. NRS/BR/NBR/1/42, North British Railway minutes, 10 September 1896, with minutes of special committee of directors, 29 September and 12 and 22 October 1896. NRS/BR/NBR/8/1764/ Box 6, Conacher to Steel, 10 September, and Steel to Conacher, 14 September 1896.
37. NRS/BR/NBR/1/42, North British Railway minutes, 5 November 1896, cf. minutes of special committee of directors, 12 October 1896.
38. NRS/BR/IFA/4/1, KSG to Malcolm and to Ellice, 26 November 1896, and to Innes, 9 February 1897.
39. NRS/BR/CAL/1/152, memorandum of Forman-Steel meeting, 10 September 1896.
40. NRS/BR/IFA/4/1, Strang-Watkins to Innes 30 October 1896.
41. NRS/BR/IFA/4/1, Strang-Watkins to Burton, 15 October 1896, to Kennedy, 30 October 1896 and to Ellice, 7 December 1896.
42. NRS/BR/NBR/8/1764 Box 6, undated press report of public meeting at Fort Augustus, addressed by Charles Innes. NRS/BR/ IFA/4/1, KSG to Innes, 9 February 1897.
43. NRS/BR/IFA/1/1, Invergarry & Fort Augustus Railway minutes, 16 December 1896, and 14 January and 3 February 1897.
44. NRS/BR/IFA/4/1, Strang-Watkins to Innes, 23 November 1896 and 7 February 1897.
45. NRS/BR/IFA/1/1, Invergarry & Fort Augustus Railway minutes, 16 and 19 February 1897.
46. NRS/BR/IFA/1/1, Invergarry & Fort Augustus Railway minutes, 19 February 1897. NRS/BR/IFA/4/1, Reid to James Young, 20 February 1897; KSG to MacDonald & Graham, 22 February 1897; and Strang-Watkins to Malcolm, 22 February 1897, and to Innes, 23 February 1897.
47. NRS/BR/IFA/4/1, Reid to various Scottish newspapers, announcing decision to build and let contract, 19 February 1897.
48. NRS/BR/IFA/4/1, Strang-Watkins to Innes, 26 and 27 December 1896, and to Kennedy, 13 January 1897; and KSG to Forman, 23 January 1897, and to Malcolm, 15 February 1897.
49. NRS/BR/IFA/1/1 Invergarry & Fort Augustus Railway minutes, 10 October 1896. NRS/BR/IFA/4/1, Strang-Watkins to Malcolm, 17 November 1896 and 15 February 1897, and Reid to Malcolm, 31 December 1896.
50. NRS/BR/IFA/1/4 KSG to Innes & MacKay, 2,3,4,7,8,10 and 12 December 1896.
51. NRS/BR/PYB(S)1/501, Great Glen Bills, 1896-7, provost McBean's warning quoted in evidence.
52. NRS/BR/IFA/4/1, Strang-Watkins to Innes, 4 December 1896; and KSG to Innes, 7 December 1896, and to Malcolm, 8 January 1897. NRS/BR/IFA/1/1, Invergarry & Fort Augustus Railway minutes, 3 and 19 February 1897.
53. NRS/BR/IFA/4/1, Strang-Watkins to Innes, 9 February 1897.
54. NRS/BR/IFA/1/1, Invergarry & Fort Augustus Railway minutes, 23 December 1896 and 14 January 1897.NRS/BR/IFA/4/1, KSG to Malcolm, 22 January 1897.
55. NRS/BR/IFA/4/1, KSG to Innes & MacKay, 25 December 1896, and to British Aluminium Company, 9 January 18906; and Reid to Malcolm, 31 December 1896, and to Lord Abinger, 7 January 1897.
56. NRS/BR/IFA/4/1, Strang-Watkins to Kennedy, 13 January 1897.
57. NRS/BR/PYB(S)/1/391, Great North of Scotland Railway Bill, 1896-7.
58. NRS/BR/IFA/4/1, Strang-Watkins to Innes, 19 November 1896, and KSG to Kennedy, 13 and 20 February 1897.
59. NRS/BR/IFA/4/1, KSG to Kennedy, 20 February 1897.

Ballachulish station, terminus of the Callander & Oban branch from Connel Ferry. The traffic of the slate quarries in the background, won from coastal shipping, was a mainstay, as were summer tourists visiting Glen Coe. The British Aluminium Company's smelter at Kinlochleven became a customer from 1909 (LGRP)

The railway pier at Kyle (see also p.16), more generously proportioned than Mallaig's compromise pier-cum-breakwater, is wide enough to hold the "island" station building. It points due south into Loch Alsh, thereby obtaining a sufficient depth of water for flexible operation. In this photograph the paddle steamer Lovedale lies at the west side. (Highland Railway Society collection)

CHAPTER SIX

A SEVERAL-SIDED CONTEST, 1896-97

"We must prepare to fight both the Highland and the North British." (G. Strang-Watkins, agent-cum-secretary, Invergarry & Fort Augustus Railway, October 1896)

"This time the matter ought to be settled." (Counsel for the Invergarry & Fort Augustus Railway, House of Commons, March 1897)

"No railway should be permitted between Inverness and Fort Augustus, unless powers are conferred upon your Petitioners to run over the Highland Railway to Inverness and so to have the same rights with respect to the Invergarry & Fort Augustus Railway…as are sought by the Highland Company." (Great North of Scotland Railway petition, House of Commons, March 1897)

"The Great North might come to Inverness and we might enter into arrangements with them. We might tap the Caledonian…" (Lord Burton, director, Invergarry & Fort Augustus Railway, evidence, House of Commons, March 1897)

"If it is in the public interest that this line should be made, then it is in the public interest that every company south of Perth should have the fullest opportunity of using it. What we want is the same protection as is given between ourselves and the North British at Perth and Aberdeen." (Counsel for the Caledonian Railway, House of Lords, July 1897)

"No small company can possibly live in the Highlands." (John Conacher, general manager, North British Railway, evidence, House of Commons, March 1897)

"We want a strong competing line…While the people have much sympathy with the Invergarry Company [who have] compelled the strong Companies…to initiate their own Bills, at the same time the fear is…that [they] would not be able to continue this competitive element…" (Alexander McLannan, merchant and town councillor, Inverness, evidence, House of Commons, March 1897.)

"The Caledonian are afraid of the North British and the Invergarry are afraid of the North British; the North British are afraid of the Caledonian; and the whole matter is [being] fought out in the interest of the Highland, by reason of the jealousies of these three opponents." (Counsel for the Highland Railway, House of Lords, July 1897)

"The Highland Company shall be bound to work in full efficiency the West Highland and Fort Augustus route to Inverness and to run…a sufficient number of trains conveniently timed." (Proposed protection clause for the North British Railway and the West Highland Railway, House of Commons and House of Lords, March and July 1897).

In 1897 Parliament was to hear the arguments of 1896 all over again, albeit with some shifts of position by the principal protagonists. In both Houses, the Committees endured wearisome repetition. The Highland, Invergarry & Fort Augustus and North British-cum-West Highland plans were almost identical, and attention fastened disproportionally on detail variations – for example, at Temple pier on Loch Ness (Glenurquhart bay) or at the River Moriston, where Grant of Glenmoriston initially rejected all three versions of an unavoidable viaduct.[1] The history of the Great Glen Agreement was rehearsed once more, and both Highland and North British chose a submissive tone. Believing, under correction, that Parliament had endorsed their treaty, they acknowledged that Parliament alone must decide whether the time had come to complete a westerly rail route to Inverness.[2] In the Commons, where the three Bills began, the chairman strove to be even-handed, noting how "certain points…have been already threshed out…almost to the last degree".[3] The crux, he intimated, was the real feeling of proprietors along Loch Ness:

If a landowner…is not opposing one railway and is opposing the [other] two, we want to hear from…cross-examination why it is that these two work any injustice to him that the other one [does] not…[4]

Any landlord or sporting lessee who objected to one line must logically object to all three or admit that he was partisan; and Strang-Watkins hoped that this would deter opposition to the Invergarry & Fort Augustus.

The Highland Company, refreshing a familiar argument, declared that defensive measures had been forced upon them. Against the charge of conservatism and self-interest, the landed proprietors on the Highland board were furnished with a model answer, in all probability drafted by Charles Steel:

[It] may be said to be a duty in a…landowner…to become a director and to take a share in promoting the development of railways in the Highlands, as the best means of ameliorating the condition of the people and advancing their prosperity, and not to get large returns in the way of dividend. The shareholders continue to place upon the board [representatives of the] class…who originated [our] lines and administered them all along.[5]

Inverness, the draft continued, was the natural centre of an *"agricultural, pastoral and sporting country"*, which made it necessary *"to have gentlemen on the board who can conveniently attend [there]"*. The Highland did not neglect to attack the Great North of Scotland Bill (see Chapter 5), which portended an alliance with *"companies whose proposed lines to Inverness have not been authorised and are heavily opposed".* Such a vague and open-ended proposition was unprecedented, and in the crises of 1882-3 and 1894-5 the Great North had not intervened so blatantly. Elgin-to-Inverness running powers should be treated as a separate question – until the Great North obtained these, the partnerships which they projected could have no meaning.[6]

The Caledonian Company offered their support, predictably asserting that the Highland's well-being (and their own as well) hung on the volume of traffic exchanged at Perth. The impending contest might leave the Invergarry & Fort Augustus in thrall to the North British and bring the West Highland to Inverness. Thereafter the shorter through route via the West Highland and the Great Glen, though inferior in journey time and general usefulness, would set fares and rates under Railway Clearing House rules, to the Highland's severe injury. The Caledonian petition also complained that the existing patterns of exchange at Aberdeen would be altered to their particular disadvantage, should North British and Great North of Scotland come together at Inverness to offer a new westerly service between Glasgow and all the districts east of Elgin. In short, North British intrusion spelt all-round robbery. If Caledonian fears materialised, they intended to seek compensatory running powers, north from Crianlarich and onwards from Spean Bridge. On the assumption that one day the Callander & Oban and West Highland would be linked at Ballachulish, they reserved the right to share, by running powers or other means, in the Oban–Fort William–Inverness route which might result.[7]

North British general manager John Conacher had made his own off-the-record estimates, which suggested that, with due allowance for single-line operation and at least one change of locomotive, the Glasgow–Craigendoran–Roy Bridge–Inverness journey would require a minimum of 5 hours 40 minutes, though express trains might win back 30-40 minutes These telling calculations, in Conacher's unmistakable hand and preserved among his correspondence, were literally "back of an envelope".[8] To schedule regular passenger workings, with intermediate stops, at just over 5 hours would require additional passing places along some ninety miles of the West Highland proper – easing the worst curves would not suffice. While a through line via Roy Bridge and Fort Augustus would retain a mileage advantage, completion of the Aviemore cut-off could only confirm the primacy of the Glasgow–Perth–Inverness route. The Forth Bridge-and-Perth route, in being since 1890, would remain superior for Edinburgh to Inverness traffic – where already the Highland Company's dependence on the Caledonian had been satisfactorily reduced and the North British had won a larger share.

In 1895 the Highland and the North British, recognising how exchange at Perth must remain a common interest, had backed away from a Great Glen confrontation – and inevitably the West Highland Company had conformed (see Chapter 3). But it was a different matter to contrive a settlement binding three parties, Highland, North British and Invergarry & Fort Augustus, when the West Highland made a nominal fourth and two others, Great North of Scotland and Caledonian, were prepared to demand their say. By January 1897 the North British board had concluded that battle must be joined.

As the triangular parliamentary contest loomed closer, most observers judged that either Highland or Invergarry & Fort Augustus would prevail – a prediction which did not entirely displease Conacher and his chairman Lord Tweeddale, who contemplated with some misgivings the consequences and, above all, the cost of West Highland (i.e. North British) victory. Cameron of Lochiel, writing to the West Highland secretary, George Wieland, in December 1896, had warned that Great Glen opinion could not be won over. He advised against meeting the public at Fort Augustus. Abbot Linse was unwilling to chair any occasion sponsored by the North British, and an embarrassing resolution, condemning earlier deceits, was the only likely result:

> There is a not unnatural feeling…that the District has not met with fair play from the two rival Companies (i.e. Highland and North British) and gratitude to the Invergarry & Fort Augustus Company has led the inhabitants almost to a man…to support [them].[9]

Lochiel no longer feared that the distractions of a Great Glen contest would endanger the West Highland Mallaig Extension (where construction would soon begin) but he thought brinkmanship very risky:

> Whoever gets Parliamentary authority to construct the [Inverness] Railway will have to do it [and] procrastination will hardly be possible [this time].[10]

Pressing his point, he argued, as he had done two years earlier, that the Great Glen should be left to the Highland Company. They must bring goods and passengers to Spean Bridge – a bonus for the West Highland, at no cost to the North British. It would be *"the very best thing that can happen"* if the approaching parliamentary tussle were to result in *"the Highland's occupation of the District between [Glen] Spean and Inverness".* (Lochiel assumed that, if the Highland were victorious, the Invergarry & Fort Augustus directors would come to terms with them at once.)

*   *   *

Highland and North British could not easily explain away their previous postures, and the stated objectives of all the embattled companies made a formidable coil. While the North British proposed to subsume the Invergarry & Fort Augustus in a revived Roy Bridge–Inverness line, the Highland wanted their own Inverness–Fort Augustus line and supplementary running powers to Spean Bridge. For the Invergarry & Fort Augustus, Sir Donald Matheson and his fellow directors would declare themselves ready to operate a Spean Bridge to Inverness line – which implied the acquisition of plant and equipment on a scale much beyond the provision of one-engine-in-steam for a Spean Bridge–Fort Augustus shuttle. Nonetheless their vaunted independence was qualified; their Bill provided for a working and maintenance agreement, sooner or later, with any ready bidder, Highland or North British, Great North of Scotland or Caledonian. If the Highland Bill gained Parliament's approval, the Great North were pledged to seek facilities at Fort Augustus, whereby to ensure the free flow of through traffic between their own system and the West Highland. And the Caledonian had served notice that they could not be indifferent to Parliament's decision. A rival Glasgow–Inverness trunk line would be thoroughly objectionable, and they would oppose it strongly. However, a complementary through route traversing the western Highlands might be justified, and to be "optimum" it ought to follow the Callander & Oban, from Crianlarich by Connel Ferry and Ballachulish, and not the West Highland across empty Rannoch Moor – an argument which made the North British all the more determined to preserve a definite frontier at Loch Leven.

On 24th March 1897 the Highland Company's Great Glen Bill would pass the Commons but running powers to Spean Bridge were not granted. Both the Invergarry & Fort Augustus and the North British, refusing to give in, mounted a stubborn opposition before the Lords Committee, who on 8th July would decline to approve a line which the Highland had so loudly complained was forced upon them. The Great North of Scotland Bill was defeated in the Commons on 6th April. There follows a summary of the principal testimony, chiefly in the first House.

For the Invergarry & Fort Augustus Railway

Lord Burton again attacked the original Great Glen Agreement. He alleged that in 1889 the then North British general manager, John Walker, alarmed at the loss of the Roshven extension in the House of Lords, had made hasty overtures to the Highland's Andrew Dougall before the West Highland Bill came to the Commons Committee (see Chapter 1). In fact Walker's reaction had been more calculated than panicky; but, by Burton's account, he had gained Fort William for his company by promising not to mount an early assault on Inverness – which condemned the Great Glen to many rail-less years. There had been no consultation, and the West Highland party could only submit, though both Lochiel and the late Lord Abinger were known to have been embarrassed by accusations of betrayal. (They had found consolation and excuse, said Burton, in the certainty that the Glen would have a new railhead at Spean Bridge.) Worse had followed, when in 1895 the North British broke faith completely by repairing the redundant Agreement, after the Highland had renounced it.[11] In their evidence, George Malcolm and Charles Forman had already seized the opportunity to paint a picture similar to Burton's, flattering the Invergarry & Fort Augustus promoters as intrepid giant-killers intent on righting wrongs.[12] Malcolm reiterated, to good effect, his anger and disillusionment at North British double-dealing. Forman's version of history was subtly persuasive. Dougall and Walker, he suggested, had moved from the Great Glen Agreement to a general review of Highland–North British relations. Their discussions had included interchange at Perth and concessions for the Highland's through traffic by the Forth Bridge – and from that moment North British interest in the western Highlands had begun to wane.

John Conacher, in Forman's not inaccurate portrayal, had been dismissive of the West Highland's prospects when he succeeded Walker, wanting only the best bargain with the Treasury and completion, as soon as possible, of the traffic-boosting Mallaig Extension (see Chapter 2). At Stirling-Maxwell's Corrour and elsewhere along the West Highland, the North British had evaded earlier promises; and the long delay in opening the Crianlarich spur showed that both

Conacher and Lord Tweeddale lacked the appetite to confront the Caledonian and push for a worthwhile share of Oban traffic. Charles Steel, the Highland general manager, was an advocate of retrenchment who wished the Caledonian and the North British to follow the Highland's example, consolidating their own preserves and practising live-and-let live. Such all-round collusion, disregarding local wishes, threatened to leave the Great Glen for ever a railway no-man's land. But the gaps in the Scottish network would be closed eventually – in that the engineer's faith was undimmed. Local promotions, exemplified by the Invergarry & Fort Augustus, must set the pace and awaken the established companies to their duty.[13]

Locking up the Great Glen for years ahead was inadmissible. Local transport needed fostering – a task best left to the Invergarry & Fort Augustus, whose authorised railway and associated steamer service on Loch Ness, serving both shores, would stimulate economic growth and expand tourism. For the moment, a Fort Augustus–Inverness rail link was less needed; in the short term it might even do harm, competing with the steamers for a still limited traffic. In any case, if Parliament decided otherwise, they should award the line to the local company. Beyond Fort Augustus there were additional sporting estates to serve; and from the districts westward to the coast sheep would be driven to every "concentration point" between Gairlochy and Drumnadrochit (Glen Urquhart). The Invergarry & Fort Augustus could be trusted to develop their entire catchment; and, when the time came, they would hand on a healthy package of passenger and general business. Either Highland or North British might eventually take over; but both would benefit, and in the end the Highland would be compensated more than sufficiently for any shift of livestock traffic from their Dingwall & Skye route to new railheads along the Great Glen.[14]

The Highland Company and the North British, Forman continued, were rushing in to undertake what neither really wanted to do, impelled by mutual distrust. He warned that they would introduce inadequate and distorted timetables, the one favouring Inverness and the Inverness–Perth route, the other favouring Fort William and the West Highland route to Glasgow. No matter what conditions were imposed, they would conspire to hinder shared workings. If Parliament ruled in favour of a through line, much the most desirable outcome for the immediate future was that it be built and operated by the Invergarry & Fort Augustus. In that happy event, temporary tolls should be imposed on Highland and North British, in proportion to the traffic exchanged at either end of the Great Glen – the proceeds would subsidise additional local trains and thereby new business would develop. The Caledonian could be confident that their traffic would receive fair treatment, and Caledonian vigilance would deter both Highland and North British from starving the westerly through route. Once assured of unfettered entry to Inverness, and likewise of access to Fort William, the Invergarry & Fort Augustus would deal indifferently with both neighbours. They would deal in the same spirit, if events so developed, with Caledonian and Great North of Scotland.[15]

Forman's depiction of traffic patiently nurtured over several years mirrored the Highland's plea that traffic north

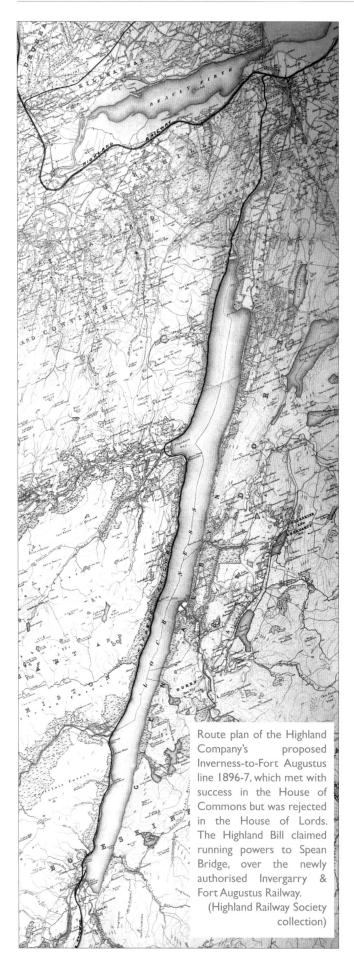

Route plan of the Highland Company's proposed Inverness-to-Fort Augustus line 1896-7, which met with success in the House of Commons but was rejected in the House of Lords. The Highland Bill claimed running powers to Spean Bridge, over the newly authorised Invergarry & Fort Augustus Railway.

(Highland Railway Society collection)

of Inverness was of necessity gathered "in driblets". Thus he turned to advantage the earlier assertions of Highland and North British that any Great Glen scheme was premature. That geography had bequeathed western feeder valleys all along the Glen was an old argument, first employed to justify building the Caledonian Canal and then updated by the promoters of the Glasgow & North Western Railway; and witnesses friendly to the Invergarry & Fort Augustus (notably Lord Burton's neighbour, Birkbeck of Loch Hourn) were ready to expound the same theme.[16] However, Burton and his fellow-directors could not deny that they had joined in discussions which aimed at amalgamation and the speedy completion of a through line, with no suggestion that local traffic must first be nursed into more vigorous life. Burton, under cross-examination, was combative. If the Invergarry & Fort Augustus board had not promoted their own Inverness extension, they would have been "sandwiched" between the Highland Company and the North British, and inevitably ignored or overridden. In 1895-6 he would have preferred an unambiguous partnership with the West Highland; but the North British, who held the whip hand, had been unresponsive. Tweeddale and Conacher, he suspected, would have reduced the Invergarry & Fort Augustus to clientage then abandoned the little company's authorised line, in favour of a new edition of the execrable Ten Years Truce. As for the Highland, they had not *"come to close quarters"* (i.e. they had refused a firm promise not to "block" the Great Glen).[17] Abbot Linse shared Burton's suspicions – the North British had forfeited all trust and he was now *"heart and soul"* for the Invergarry & Fort Augustus. The Reverend John McKay concurred, adding that the Highland, if they won, must be compelled to build their Inverness to Fort Augustus line – because they would back out if they could. Opinion in the Great Glen, he insisted, overwhelmingly favoured a second victory for "the local company".[18]

Sir Donald Matheson repeated Forman's call for local enterprise, citing the promoters of the Lanarkshire & Dumbartonshire. By winning Caledonian patronage, they had expedited the extension of the Glasgow Central Railway to the Vale of Leven and Loch Lomond, despite North British resistance. In a not dissimilar fashion, the Invergarry & Fort Augustus Railway had compelled Highland and North British to address the needs of the Great Glen. This parallel, though plausible, was forced: on north Clydeside the enmity of Caledonian and North British could be counted on, but in the Great Glen Highland and North British were at bottom reluctant adversaries, as they had proved in 1894-5 and in 1895-6. The Invergarry & Fort Augustus Company, said Matheson, possessed both substance and staying power. The promoter-directors, uniting local patriotism with "Glasgow money", were together making a large and honest investment. It was irrelevant to make comparison with the finances of the West Highland, whose landed supporters had been ready in 1888-9 to contribute as generously as they could, besides arranging to tap the City. Their input had been much less, but only because the North British preferred to keep control and had discouraged or bought out other subscribers.[19] On this heated question Forman had already clashed with Conacher.

For the Highland Railway

General manager Charles Steel briskly updated the Highland's well-worn case. Neither the Aviemore cut-off nor the Kyle of Lochalsh extension was ready, and the impact of the two schemes on the company's long-term fortunes had yet to be tested; but provision was being made for the enlargement of Inverness station, in anticipation of increased traffic. Thanks to the Light Railways Act, new branches were in prospect and at least one "Lothian line" might be reassessed for light construction. All would be jeopardised if the Highland's finite resources were allocated elsewhere. Little revenue could be earned between Fort Augustus and Inverness, whether from local or long-distance traffic, and his directors remained of opinion that no railway was needed. Nevertheless, the Highland would build their Great Glen line, should Parliament empower them to do so – it was the only answer to recurring controversy. If a continuous Spean Bridge–Inverness line were created, through traffic would be divided thereafter between the Perth and Great Glen routes. The Highland need not own but must control, by whatever means, the entire 50 miles. Only thus could they protect themselves. As to exchange with the North British at Spean Bridge, the Railway & Canal Commission would enforce Parliament's prescription and investigate all complaints. Making what they could of the Great Glen route, his company would have no reason to "block" and their ability to do so had always been exaggerated.[20] The adjacent panel shows the Up passenger trains in Steel's conjectural Highland timetable.

Sir George MacPherson-Grant emphatically ruled out any return to the difficult and barely adequate methods which had sustained the penurious Dingwall & Skye and financed the piecemeal route to Wick and Thurso. Light lines were the best hope for Scotland's remoter rail-less districts and more than 200 route miles might eventually be added to the Highland system. He dismissed the "show" which the Invergarry & Fort Augustus had staged a few weeks earlier by commencing to build their line – they had *"cut two sods and blown up a rock"* but would they continue? It was all *"for the purpose of selling"*. A guarantee of 3% or 4%, on which negotiations had foundered, was wildly unreasonable – to build from Spean Bridge to Inverness would cost nearly £1,000,000, for a return of perhaps 1%. He had not been surprised when Lord Burton and his associates sought an Inverness extension. Their dishonest statements in 1896, that they looked no further than Fort Augustus, were at one with the West Highland promoters' fraudulent plea, back in 1888-9, that they did look beyond Fort William – and Charles Forman's had been throughout the guiding hand.[21] Lord Lovat added his own accusations of bad faith, alleging that, before agreeing a year earlier to part with the land required for access to the new Loch Ness pier, he had obtained Forman's absolute word that an Inverness scheme was not intended.[22] Lord Colville, who represented the East Coast alliance on the Highland board, complained that the North British were being disingenuous. The Great Northern Company and the North Eastern had

CHARLES STEEL'S CONJECTURAL GREAT GLEN TIMETABLE

Steel assumed that the Highland Company would obtain running powers to Spean Bridge. He allowed for two through goods trains daily in each direction via the West Highland and the Great Glen.

		1.	2.	3.	4.
Inverness	d.	5.35 am	11.10 am	2.45 pm	5.00 pm
Glenurquhart		6.10	11.45		5.38
Invermoriston		6.38	12.13 pm		6.06
Fort Augustus	a.	6.50	12.25	3.40	6.17
Fort Augustus	d.	6.55	12.30	3.45	6.30
Invergarry		7.15	12.50		6.51
Spean Bridge	a.	7.48	1.25	4.30	7.30
Spean Bridge	d.	7.54	1.35	4.39	
Glasgow	a.	12.20 pm	5.45	8.50	
Edinburgh	a.	3.30	7.16	10.05	
London King's Cross	a.	10.45	5.40 am*	7.35 am*	
London Euston	a.	10.45	3.50 am*	7.10 am*	

*Next day –

1. Through coaches via West Highland to Glasgow/Edinburgh
2. Through coaches via West Highland to Glasgow/Edinburgh
3. Express, through coaches via West Highland to Glasgow/Edinburgh and London King's Cross
4. Through coaches to Fort William

Comparison, after completion of Aviemore cut-off:
Best time, Inverness-Glasgow via Perth, estimate 5 hours 25 minutes
Best time, Inverness-Edinburgh, via Perth, estimate 5 hours 7 minutes
Best time, Inverness-London via Perth, estimate 15 hours 45 minutes (same day), 13 hours 10 minutes (overnight).

every reason to believe that their Anglo-Scottish business would be penalised if a West Highland-cum-Great Glen route were indeed achieved. They feared that their wayward North British partner had seen the opportunity to filch a larger share of northern Scotland's through traffic, though in itself a westerly line to Inverness was a very dubious proposition. The two East Coast companies were, as ever, wary that the North British would draw closer to the Midland Railway and favour the Midland-Scottish route via Carlisle.[23] Did memories persist of the rumoured Midland interest in the Glasgow & North Western scheme some fifteen years previously (see Chapter 1)?

Henry Munro, an Inverness corn merchant and town councillor, harked back to the short-lived "half-way" scheme of 1893 (see Chapter 2). He described how Inverness solicitors Anderson & Shaw* had made it known to prospective subscribers in the North that Forman could find additional "outside" capital for a local promotion designed to disrupt the Great Glen Agreement. Though several Inverness businessmen were recruited, they soon withdrew, and Munro himself had not participated. He surmised that Forman had been more successful two years later in commending the Invergarry & Fort Augustus promotion to his Glasgow contacts. (*"He is the steam tug…and Sir Donald Matheson and his followers are the*

---
* Innes & MacKay had been the local agents for the West Highland Inverness Extension in 1894-5 but afterwards Charles Innes had identified with the Invergarry & Fort Augustus. Anderson & Shaw handled the North British-cum-West Highland Bill in 1896-7.

barges.") In Munro's opinion, although discontent with the Highland Railway was intermittent across Ross-shire, Sutherland and Caithness and never absent from Inverness, enthusiasm for a competing company always proved shallow.[24] His testimony chimed with the arguments of the Highland's counsel, who reworked the old theme of justified monopoly while roundly condemning the North British:

> The modern disposition of Parliament is not to give competition for competition's sake. [A] regulated monopoly need not be contrary to the interests of the public. There are dozens of districts [across Britain] which are now lamenting [that] Parliament listened to the cry of competition and are landed in (sic) two bad services rather than one good one…The North British own the West Highland, and a *damnosa hereditas* it is…[They intend] to supply the [West Highland] deficiency …from the revenue of somebody else…[25]

For the North British Railway

John Conacher claimed that the original Great Glen Agreement had been concluded with the full consent of the West Highland promoters, who looked to occupy the ground in the fullness of time but had never intended an early advance on Inverness. He denied that the Highland might now legitimately reach south to Spean Bridge. The existence of the Invergarry & Fort Augustus Company was a fact to be accepted, and their line when completed, be it 20 miles long (as already authorised) or 50 (if extended to Inverness), should be recognised as belonging within the ambit of the North British, who would offer facilities satisfactory to the Railway & Canal Commissioners or, if desired, honourable terms of amalgamation. Neither the Invergarry & Fort Augustus directors nor the inhabitants of the Great Glen need fear that local traffic would be neglected, because the North British record spoke for itself. Besides hastening fish to the cities, the Mallaig line, now building, would carry short-distance goods and passenger traffic, while the West Highland Ballachulish Extension, which had been designed to meet local needs south of Fort William, would provide a railhead for the districts across the Corran–Ardgour ferry. The North British fully intended that the latter railway should be built and, if necessary, the West Highland Company would apply for renewed powers.[26]

Conacher's was a coherent but carefully selective defence of his company's behaviour. He argued that the North British, in backing the short-lived West Highland Inverness Extension Bill of 1894-5, had aimed to test Parliament's attitude to the Great Glen treaty, after the Highland had refused to abide by it. Along with his chairman, he had seized the first opportunity to repair the rift, with no thought of deceiving the public. If in 1895 the Roy Bridge–Inverness scheme had proceeded,

The coach service between Fort William and Kingussie gave connection at Tulloch after the West Highland Railway opened. Stables and a turning circle were provided at the station. A traditional horse-drawn mail coach remained in use until the 1920s.   (Author's collection)

winning Parliament's approval, the North British would have seen the line completed, though they believed it to be ahead of its time. Postponement and a modified Agreement was the better option. Postponement but not abandonment – here the Invergarry & Fort Augustus party had misrepresented the facts, in order to exploit the ensuing disappointment. (Counsel for the North British, more bluntly patronising, spoke of "credulous Highlanders", their minds "poisoned" by Forman and his associates.) Conacher reiterated how the North British, despite well-justified reservations, had been prepared in 1895-6 to evaluate the Spean Bridge to Fort Augustus project as a West Highland feeder – until the promoters' speculative purpose was laid bare by their demand for an inflated guarantee. If the Invergarry & Fort Augustus Company again won the day and attempted to complete and operate a through line to Inverness, hard realities would quickly overtake them. They could not hope to remain independent. "Your troubles", warned Conacher, in a prophetic aside to Malcolm, "are only beginning".[27]

Benjamin Hall-Blyth, cross-examined on the details of his plans, undertook to satisfy any landowner north of Fort Augustus who preferred Forman's amenity arrangements. He also reinforced Conacher's testimony by explaining the "generous" intentions of the North British. If the West Highland-cum-North British Bill succeeded, ownership of the Roy Bridge–Invergloy cut-off might be transferred to the Invergarry & Fort Augustus Company, who would then possess the entire southern half of the through route. Forman's Spean Bridge–Invergloy "detour" ought to be deleted, and the North British must be assured of running powers between Roy Bridge and Fort Augustus, whence their own tracks would reach to Inverness. Subject only to these conditions, this arrangement might endure for some time, but absorption of the Invergarry & Fort Augustus into the West Highland or the North British, a distinction which had almost ceased to matter, would surely come – there would be nothing to prevent an amicable and orderly buy-out at a reasonable figure. Hall-Blyth confirmed that, besides providing a new terminus at Inverness, the North British would share the cost of doubling the Ness viaduct for entry to the Highland station. And this, though it went unstated, would have facilitated exchange of traffic with the Great North of Scotland had the Aberdeen company's Bill succeeded.[28]

Invited to state his personal view, Hall-Blyth agreed in principle that the North British had earned the right to share in a Great Glen line (though he offered no opinion on the rewards which they might expect). Their presence at Inverness need hurt the Highland no more than the West Highland had hurt the Callander & Oban. Whether he genuinely thought so is a different matter, but he did not cast doubt on Conacher's declared belief, at odds with the general manager's private calculations (above), that Perth route and West Highland-cum-Great Glen route would settle down to compete on approximately equal terms after the Aviemore cut-off was completed. In tones of saving the misguided Highland directors from themselves (the same style as Conacher had adopted), he recalled the Callander & Oban Company's Glen Falloch "block" scheme of 1888-9.* What the Highland contemplated now was an expensive and probably futile "block". Instead, let them develop their northern hinterland, as they claimed they wished to do.[29]

For the Caledonian Railway

The Caledonian Company obtained a locus in the House of Commons, where general manager James Thompson forcefully expressed his misgivings – echoed by their counsel in an unsuccessful appeal to be heard in the Lords.

Thompson reminded the Committee how Caledonian and North British had emerged evenly matched from the amalgamations of the 1860s. Their respective English partners, and the Board of Trade also, had come to regard a "Scottish equilibrium" as desirable. Parliament had shown a resolve to maintain it and it was enshrined, albeit precariously, in the New Lines Agreement of 1891, which had laid down that certain districts should belong exclusively to one company while other districts might be shared. The North British, he conceded, had been hampered throughout the 1870s and 1880s by a ramshackle system, but they were no longer penalised by geography and yet their "aggression" persisted. Their "Bridges route" across Forth and Tay had reshaped both internal Scottish traffic and Anglo-Scottish traffic very much to his company's loss. Under protest, the Caledonian directors had bowed to Parliament's approval of the West Highland and the West Highland Extension, and before long North British Mallaig would "balance" Caledonian Oban. A compromise boundary had been found at Ballachulish (Loch Leven). Moreover, the Caledonian were ready to see the Crianlarich spur opened, for the better integration of the Callander & Oban and West Highland routes – any further delay must be laid at the North British door.[30]

Enough was enough, said Thompson (though he made no mention of the Caledonian's own aggression and compensating gains north-of-Clyde). That the North British might prevail unchecked in the Great Glen was unthinkable and his directors were determined to make a stand. In his opinion, compensatory running powers for the Highland, to Fort Augustus or to Spean Bridge, did not meet the case, while a Highland victory with safeguards for the North British would be no better. Promises had been made that in either situation a shared through service to Inverness would come into being. Whatever form this took, it must loosen Caledonian–Highland ties and encourage North British theft. Matters had so developed over the previous twelve months that he would prefer to see the entire Great Glen awarded to the Invergarry & Fort Augustus,

with sufficient sureties for their continued independence. On that basis, the little company could prioritise local traffic while meeting impartially with both Highland and North British. The Caledonian had no desire to take a hand, but might be forced to do so:

If no powers are given, either to the North British or the Highland…give [none] to the Caledonian: we are content… But if powers are given…we ought to get similar powers…[31]

Thompson's underlying threat was clear. If the North British came to share in a completed westerly route to Inverness, the Caledonian would demand to become a party to the arrangement – and they were ready to invoke the 1891 treaty, appealing once again to Lord Watson. Arbitration under the so-called Peace Agreement had made the Mallaig Extension exclusively North British, but Lord Watson had not pronounced explicitly against Caledonian intervention in the Great Glen – which rendered uncertain any North British "right" to bar the Callander & Oban at Ballachulish. And a Caledonian claim for running powers north from Crianlarich over the West Highland had not yet been put to the test. (Despite an extravagant hint from Lord Burton that the Invergarry & Fort Augustus would seek running powers to Crianlarich, and connection there with the Callander & Oban, it is more likely that he hoped to see the Caledonian at Spean Bridge.)

* * *

In 1896-7, as on previous occasions, the Great North of Scotland Company's bid to advance from Elgin to Inverness ultimately rested on their original powers of 1846 – powers which had been set aside (or, arguably, nullified?) by the negotiations in 1854-5 whereby the Inverness & Aberdeen Junction Railway had extended east to Keith. This time the Great North Bill was framed to ensure through running beyond Inverness, into the Great Glen (see Chapter 5), but it fared no better. Would the outcome have been different if, in the previous month, the Commons Committee had approved either the Invergarry & Fort Augustus Bill or the North British-cum-West Highland Bill? In that event, no doubt the Highland would have fought on in the House of Lords. Whether they would have seen off the double assault on Inverness is impossible to say but, if defeated, no doubt they would have demanded (and surely obtained?) substantial protection clauses in the enemy Acts. Few witnesses were out-and-out supporters of the Great North; few were utterly hostile to the Highland; and most admitted that the latter faced a daunting two-fronts assault. Indeed, unqualified support for any of the three schemes to fill the Fort Augustus–Inverness gap was hard to seek. Cross-examination brought out the reservations of ostensibly committed witnesses. There was much praise for the promoter-directors of the Invergarry & Fort Augustus. Highland and North British, who would have consigned any Great Glen railway to the indefinite future, had been compelled to think again; and it must be the little company's interest to develop both local and long-distance traffic. But the general belief remained that the Invergarry & Fort Augustus would capitulate in the end – and probably to the North British, whose record was suspect. A better service eastward might well result if the Great North gained access to Inverness; but only a Great Glen line joined with the West

---

* The Glen Falloch Railway of 1887-8, originally a local project with Hall-Blyth as engineer, had been blighted by the mutual suspicions of Caledonian and North British. It was revived the following year in a hurried Caledonian attempt to frustrate the West Highland promotion.

Highland could challenge the Highland to any purpose – and only if the North British chose to make the challenge real.[32]

Inverness merchant Alexander McLannan, like Henry Munro (above), held that the Highland Company's critics invariably lacked staying power. An underlying pride in the native company of the North and an instinct to settle for the known against the unknown always resurfaced. In 1882-3, as he freely admitted, McLannan's own initial enthusiasm for the Glasgow & North Western promotion had turned before long into opposition.[33] Thomas Wedderspoon, director of a large dealership in livestock and wool, presented himself as a disinterested witness; he was unconvinced that the Highland main line could ever be superseded. Caledonian and North British had always fought over the through traffic which they handled at Perth, and this already amounted to a large proportion of all that the North of Scotland could yield. Some part of the existing whole might be diverted if another route were created, but more could not be generated unless the Highland Company were freed from Great Glen distractions and encouraged to pursue new feeder lines beyond Inverness.[34] John MacLeod, Crofter-Liberal MP for Sutherland and owner of the *Highland News*, claimed that the English market, best reached via Inverness, Perth and Carlisle (i.e. by the Highland Railway, the Caledonian and the London & North Western) was key for his fishermen-constituents. Demand in Glasgow and the west of Scotland counted for less, and a West Highland-cum-Great Glen route would offer them little. To combat depopulation, MacLeod advocated that one or more of the "Lothian lines" be re-surveyed for light construction (understandably, he favoured the Lochinver and Laxford Bridge options), and to this end the Highland Company must be able to reckon their resources with confidence.[35] Ross-shire county councillor Andrew Maitland of Tain (an architect with distillery interests) entertained similar hopes. The Highland, once set free, ought to consider light lines to Garve and Aultbea, besides others on the east coast.[36]

* * *

In consequence, the parliamentary process turned into something of a debate over the obligations of Highland and North British, now that the Light Railways Act was in place, and James Baillie of Dochfour seized the opportunity to show that the Highland had not been backward. As Inverness-shire's MP, he had consulted with the committee established by the County Council to investigate narrow-gauge light railways for the Isle of Skye. From his private resources, he had contributed to a preliminary examination of several routes; and the Highland board, who saw merit in at least one feeder to the Dingwall & Skye, which would open to Kyle of Lochalsh in November 1897, had agreed to meet the cost of a more thorough survey between Portree and Kyleakin Ferry.[37] The thrust of Baillie's testimony could not be missed. In 1890 the Lothian Commission had recommended that the practicalities of light railways both in Lewis and Skye should be further examined, as the concomitant of one or more subsidised lines to the Atlantic coast. This, he suggested, laid a moral duty on Highland and West Highland alike, now that both companies were recipients of government aid; and it was within his knowledge that West Highland secretary George Wieland, who could promise nothing without

North British consent, had rebuffed the County Council's "Skye committee" when they sought support for a light railway commencing at Armadale or Isleornsay in connection with the Mallaig Extension.[38]

Speaking as an MP, Baillie held that the benefits of any conventional railway through the Great Glen ought to be measured dispassionately against what light lines might achieve north and west of Inverness, but he admitted that he was in the end a Highland director and in sympathy with their Bill. At a personal level, he denied that the Highland's plans (drawn up by company engineer William Roberts) would do unnecessary damage at Dochfour. Charles Forman, who offered an "amenity tunnel" or "covered way", claimed that Baillie was sacrificing his own interests; and it seems that both the Invergarry & Fort Augustus engineer and their secretary-agent Strang-Watkins had entertained hopes of winning him over.[39] Whether Lord Burton exerted family pressure does not appear. Baillie, for his part, did not expect to influence the Invergarry & Fort Augustus board through Burton – he possessed "very little power" over his father-in-law.

These are uncertainties; but the emphatic Unionist victory of 1895 had removed Baillie's electoral anxieties. Having disposed of his obligations to Cameron of Lochiel by supporting the Treasury's Mallaig Extension Guarantee, he clearly felt free to attack the North British; and his calculated reproach struck home. Nonplussed at first, John Conacher could only detail anew the large sums which his company had devoted to the West Highland without hope of early reward. To soften Wieland's flinty response, he undertook that any project nominated by Inverness-shire County Council would be fully considered before the opening of the Mallaig line, and he pointed out that the North British intended to help finance the Loch Fyne Light Railway (from West Highland Arrochar & Tarbet to St Catherine's Ferry).

Mounting a counterattack, Conacher ridiculed any idea that the Highland board would entertain an aggregate 200 miles of light construction. The Forsinard–Port Skerra scheme had progressed, under pressure from the Duke of Sutherland, but would others follow? What of the proposed Cromarty line (engineered by Forman), which they had discouraged? It was notorious that the Highland directors had met every threat to their monopoly at Inverness with overblown promises of imminent improvement. They might enthuse over the new Light Railways Act, but they were behaving just as they had always done.[40] Counsel for the Invergarry & Fort Augustus, taking Conacher's cue, badgering Charles Steel and Sir George MacPherson-Grant to concede that any Highland contribution to light promotions would be circumscribed and selective.[41] Nevertheless, the subject was a delicate one for the North British – they had required that Forman's original West Highland plans, which leant towards a light railway, be modified to create a more conventional, more expensive railway; and the West Highland Extension would be built to more-or-less the same, relatively costly, standard (which they justified as operationally necessary). Board of Trade conservatism had enabled the North British to repel all suggestion that the subsidised Mallaig line made an obvious candidate for light, economical construction – though in the end footbridges were dispensed with at intermediate stations, while the elaborate signalling which guarded Banavie swing bridge on the Caledonian Canal was simplified several years after traffic had begun.[42]

In cool reason, the case for a light line all along the Great Glen deserved serious attention – given all-round acceptance that the westerly route to Inverness, in whatever form it might be achieved, must remain of secondary character. But there was no such consensus. Ever since the promotion of the Glasgow & North Western Railway in 1882-3, Great Glen conflicts had set in a grander, ultimately self-defeating, mould. As later chapters will explore, the proposed Lochend Light Railway (1897-8) and the half-hearted attempts to convert the Invergarry & Fort Augustus to light working (after 1910) are the only pointers to what might have been.

References

J. McGregor, *The West Highland Railway: Plans, Politics and People*, Birlinn (John Donald), 2005, cited as PPP.

Keyden, Strang & Girvan abbreviated to KSG.

NRS/BR/PYB(S)/1/501, Great Glen Bills 1896-7 (Invergarry & Fort Augustus Railway, Highland Railway and North British Railway with West Highland Railway) abbreviated to GGB97,

1. GGB97, Commons and Lords.
2. Ibid., opening speeches by counsel, Commons, 9 March 1897.
3. Ibid., intervention by chairman, Commons, 15 March 1897.
4. Ibid., intervention by chairman, Commons, 12 March 1897.
5. Ibid., Highland Railway notes for their witnesses and counsel.
6. NRS/BR/PYB(S)/1/391, Great North of Scotland Railway Bill, 1896-7, petition against by Highland Railway.
7. GGB97, opening speech by counsel for Caledonian Railway, Commons, 9 March 1897.
8. NRS/BR/NBR/8/1764/Box 2, North British Railway, general manager's files relating to West Highland Railway, undated.
9. NRS/BR/NBR/8/1764/Box 6, North British Railway, general manager's files relating to West Highland Railway, Cameron of Lochiel to George Wieland, 28 December 1896 (with cutting from *Inverness Courier*).
10. Ibid.
11. GGB97, Lord Burton, evidence, Commons, 15 March 1897.
12. GGB97, Charles Forman and George Malcolm, evidence, Commons, 11 and 12 March 1897. (Malcolm's evidence was completed on 11 March.)
13. GGB97, Forman, evidence, Commons, 11 March 1897.
14. Ibid.
15. Ibid.
16. GGB97, Birkbeck of Loch Hourn, Commons, 12 March 1897.
17. GGB97, Burton, evidence, Commons, 15 March 1897.
18. GGB97, Abbot Leo Linse and Reverend John McKay, evidence, Commons, 15 March 1897.
19. GGB97, Sir Donald Matheson, evidence, Commons, 16 March 1897. Also intervention by Committee, querying Invergarry & Fort Augustus finances.
20. GGB97, Charles Steel, evidence, Commons, 10 March 1897, and Lords, 6 July 1897.
21. GGB97, Sir George MacPherson-Grant, evidence, Commons, 10 March 1897, and Lords, 7 July 1897.
22. GGB97, Lord Lovat, evidence, Great Glen Bills 1896-7, Commons, 22 March 1897.
23. GGB97, Lord Colville, evidence, Commons, 10 March 1897.
24. GGB97, Henry Munro, evidence, Lords, 7 July 1897.
25. GGB97, counsel for Highland Railway, concluding speech, Commons, 11 March 1897.
26. GGB97, John Conacher, evidence, Commons, 18 and 19 March 1897 and Lords, 7 and 8 July 1897.
27. Ibid. Also GGB97, speech by counsel for North British Railway and West Highland Railway, Commons, 17 March 1897.
28. GGB97, Benjamin Hall-Blyth, evidence, 19 March 1897.
29. Ibid.
30. GGB97, James Thompson, evidence, 22 March 1897.
31. Ibid.
32. For example, GGB97, Reverend John Campbell, John Gordon, Donald Grant, and William Smith, evidence, Commons, March 1897.
33. GGB97, Alexander MacLannan, evidence, Commons, 19 March 1897.
34. GGB97, Thomas Wedderspoon, evidence, Commons, 19 March 1897.
35. GGB97, John MacLeod, evidence, Lords, 7 July 1897.
36. GGB97, Andrew Maitland, evidence, Lords, 7 July 1897.
37. GGB97, James Baillie MP, evidence, Commons, 19 and 22 March 1897, and Lords, 7 July 1897.
38. GGB97, George Wieland to Light Railways Committee (date uncertain), quoted in Baillie's evidence, Commons, March 1897.
39. GGB97, Forman to Baillie, 19 January 1897 and Baillie to KSG, 18 February 1897, quoted in Baillie's evidence, Commons and Lords, 7 and 8 July 1897. NRS/BR/IFA/4/1, KSG to Baillie, 13, 17 and 20 February 1897.
40. GGB97, Conacher, evidence, Lords, 7 and 8 July 1897.
41. GGB97, Steel and MacPherson-Grant, evidence, Lords, 6 and 7 July 1897.
42. PPP, passim.

New Inverlochy Castle, Torlundy, Scottish seat of the Abinger family, who purchased the Lochaber estate of Inverlochy, north of Fort William, c.1840. William Scarlett, 3rd Baron Abinger, (d.1892), an enthusiastic supporter of the Glasgow & North Western Railway, subsequently became a promoter of the West Highland Railway and was the West Highland's first chairman.

(Gillespie collection)

The Lovat Arms Hotel at Fort Augustus proved a very dubious investment for the Invergarry & Fort Augustus Company, while "and Station" made a clumsy addition. Earnings did not improve.

(Valentine postcard)

Gondolier, on passage from Muirton at Inverness to Banavie, eases into the lowest lock at Fort Augustus. The Oich viaduct, its masonry piers new and unweathered, appears at middle right.

(John Penny collection, courtesy D Carmichael)

CHAPTER SEVEN

INTERLUDE, 1897-99

[All] three promotions were equally activated by selfish motives. It was for the Committee to determine whose selfishness would do most good for the public.

So *Engineering* had concluded in a pawky summary of the background history (see panel below), after the Highland Company's Great Glen Bill passed the House of Commons in March 1897. A line which three warring contenders sought to build, only 30 miles long and estimated at less than £500,000, had engaged "the foremost Parliamentary Queen's Counsel", whose committee-room jousts were widely reported. Behind this extraordinary situation lay repeated "foraying" in the Great Glen and the stubborn ambitions of the Great North of Scotland, whereby the Highland had "woken up" at last:

Fort Augustus, like Elgin in the east, has become…the outpost of an advancing enemy.[1]

It remained to be seen whether the House of Lords would confirm the Highland's success, and about that *Engineering* had mixed feelings:

The expenses they have…incurred are urged as a reason why a competitive line should not get into Inverness, but their quickened enterprise might have been an argument on the other side. More competition would do a world of good.[2]

The Invergarry & Fort Augustus had "coquetted" for a guarantee and would now come under renewed pressure to sell, both from the Highland and from the North British, whatever the outcome in the Lords. Local support for the little company was incontrovertible. However, their likely revenues had been overstated and could not be sufficiently developed in the foreseeable future to maintain a genuine independence. With their own line to Inverness, the directors would have commanded "*a good price*"; held at Fort Augustus, they would find themselves "*between the upper and the nether millstone*". Because the concern of both Highland and North British was through traffic, "*the people of the Great Glen were likely to come off worst*".

Judging that the Invergarry & Fort Augustus had made the best case, the *Railway Times* pronounced more strongly – the Commons Committee had granted the Highland a "block" line, demonstrating how much the landed interested, so strongly represented on that company's board, still influenced the Lower House. An efficient additional rail route to the North, if this was Parliament's genuine desire, required that the North British gain access to Inverness or the Highland access to Spean Bridge. The latter ought to have accompanied the Highland's victory, and an early treaty to unite the two "half-way" lines would almost certainly have followed. Instead, the Invergarry & Fort Augustus would remain "*a hapless enterprise*", at the mercy of their larger neighbours.[3]

In the second House, both the West Highland Company and the Invergarry & Fort Augustus submitted remodelled protection clauses, for inclusion in the ensuing Act if the Highland prevailed.[4] By this means the North British looked to secure their full share of all possible traffic when a through westerly route was completed. They had little choice, *Engineering* declared, because their West Highland protégé, now three years in being, had not met working expenses. Pending the

---

Engineering, 2nd April 1897

The Highland Railway have a monopoly of the North of Scotland…Envious eyes have…been cast…and in 1883 the Glasgow & North Western [proposed] to run a line up the west country…but the Highland Company triumphed. However, in 1889 Mr Charles Forman, on the principle that half a loaf is better than nothing, promoted a scheme to Fort William…and the West Highland is practically now part of the North British system. This success was in some measure due to an agreement…that neither [the West Highland Company nor the Highland Company] should for ten years seek powers for a line between Fort William and Inverness.

Notwithstanding the agreement, the West Highland was closely watched…As soon as Mr Forman's skirmishers were found making surveys, an opposition scheme was promoted. Thus the whole case was soon before Parliament again, largely because the dwellers in the Great Glen were dissatisfied. [And] Mr Forman was induced a year ago to formulate a scheme branching off the West Highland at Spean Bridge and extending…to Fort Augustus, whence steamers were to be run to Inverness. This railway was sanctioned, and Parliament refused running powers either to the [North British] or to the Highland.

[The Highland Company] decided to construct their own line over the intervening space. Upon this becoming known in the autumn of 1896, there was a rush of the conflicting clans: the local proprietors of the Spean Bridge and Fort Augustus line determined to continue to Inverness; the West Highland, which is practically the North British, joined with the latter to seek running powers over the Fort Augustus line and reach on to Inverness; and to complete the case the Caledonian and the Great North of Scotland saw a danger of competition by the North British in this new field.

hoped-for benefits of the Mallaig Extension, no boost to income could be neglected. Even the slender earnings of the lines north and west of Inverness need not be despised – every mile, on the Highland's own figures, contributed £600 per annum in through traffic via the Perth route. Though only stunted competition might be expected from the West Highland-cum-Great Glen alternative under three quarrelsome owners (i.e. North British, Invergarry & Fort Augustus and Highland), perhaps £120,000 out of an annual total of circa £175,000 was at stake. As for the Highland's core business, generated in Inverness, completion of the Aviemore cut-off must strengthen their position. Nevertheless, the shorter distance via the Great Glen would rule fares and rates, and the North British could not fail to make inroads in some measure. Much would depend on the Highland's ability to starve the shared route:

> They will not be disposed to encourage traffic over their thirty miles of the opposition [line] when they may take it 144 miles [via Forres] to Perth.[5]

But the Highland Bill was rejected. General manager Charles Steel and the other witnesses for his company had harped repeatedly on the unfair burden of self-defence. Steel had "threatened" (as one report put it) that several light railways beyond Inverness might be sacrificed (see Chapter 6). It was illogical, the Lords Committee concluded, to confer powers which would be used unwillingly or retained only for "blocking" purposes, and better to declare what amounted to an open verdict, so that all parties might come back to Parliament at some future date.[6] The *Railway Times*, modifying their previous view, saw in this fudged result a victory of sorts after all for the Invergarry & Fort Augustus, who could hope anew either to sell advantageously or to fight another day for Inverness.[7]

* * *

The Invergarry & Fort Augustus board reacted with a fresh show of confidence, even bombast. The company's full "territorial rights" would be maintained. Against the possibility of another battle in Parliament, funds would be set aside to retain Henry Worsley-Taylor, the high-priced parliamentary counsel whom they had employed in 1896 and again in 1897. Meanwhile they meant to continue the construction of their authorised line, hastily begun six months earlier, and to investigate the lease of a steamer for Loch Ness, as they were pledged to do.[8]

The fatal decision to continue building – as in retrospect it must appear – drew applause for some time thereafter from those convinced that railway expansion in the western Highlands was gathering pace. In a wide-ranging overview, the *Financial News* (7th June 1898) recalled the Caledonian Company's decision, almost a quarter-of-a-century earlier, to complete the faltering Callander & Oban Railway. From that, the West Highland had followed – the product of Caledonian and North British rivalry – after the failure of the too-ambitious Glasgow & North Western.* Next had come competing schemes for the Great Glen and Ballachulish, and the process would only accelerate:

> The ball, once set a-rolling, has gathered size and force…

---
*   See also Chapter 1 which presents a not dissimilar argument.

and now the Highlands, from Cantyre (sic) up to Ullapool, appear to have been mapped out by the railway engineer…It is impossible to believe that the [Connel Ferry – Ballachulish line] is being constructed merely for the sake of…granite and slate and…holiday-makers, whose season is…of four months duration; [and] it is no secret…that the ultimate object of the West Highland is Inverness… In three years…it may be anticipated that the Caledonian and North British, through their subsidiary companies, will have made connection in Fort William…Then heigh-ho for Inverness, up the green banks of the Caledonian Canal! [The Invergarry & Fort Augustus Railway] is even now begun…and it is difficult to see how Parliament can refuse [next time] to sanction the connecting link…[9]

Some three months later, *Railway News* would enthuse that trains on the Dingwall & Skye were running to Kyle of Lochalsh, which had proved a great improvement on Stromeferry, while the Highland Company's Aviemore cut-off was at last almost ready to open. (It would do so that November.) The West Highland Mallaig Extension was well begun and the Invergarry & Fort Augustus directors, in choosing to complete their line, had refuted every allegation of a scheme "only made to sell".[10] South Argyll, meanwhile, could entertain hopes of at least a Loch Fyne railhead in compensation for the collapse of the Clyde, Ardrishaig & Crinan Company in 1892. And there is indeed evidence of a wide-spread optimism, not least among the rising generation. Appin-born Duncan Kennedy began his engineering career on the Connel Ferry–Ballachulish line (and would live to see the branch closed in 1966). He has recorded how in certain weather conditions the sound of distant blasting on the Mallaig and Great Glen contracts carried to the navvy gangs under his supervision on the Linnhe shore – and in this the young Kennedy found exhilarating proof of a general awakening across the western Highlands.[11]

Preferring the drama of the Great Glen, popular histories have neglected the Callander & Oban Bill of 1896-7, which comprised station and pier improvements at Oban, a short extension to Ballachulish village (see Chapter 4), and a sixteen-mile line to Inveraray.[12] A branch south by Loch Awe, diverging at Dalmally, together with a branch from Connel Ferry into Lochaber, had been among the first ambitions of the Callander & Oban promoters, who were soon to find challenge enough in the long-drawn-out completion of their main line. The company's latter-day Dalmally–Inveraray branch, by Claddich and Glen Aray, was designed to prevent a West Highland probe from Ardlui or Arrochar. Endorsed by the Caledonian and engineered by the ever-ready Charles Forman, it was pushed energetically by secretary-manager John Anderson – and one notable supporter was George Malcolm, who tendered his "expert" advice on agricultural and sporting traffic.[13] (He also proclaimed his disenchantment with the North British.) In the parliamentary set-piece which followed, the Callander & Oban met with defeat. Forman's plans invaded the policies of Inveraray Castle and this the Duke of Argyll adamantly resisted, rejecting Anderson's appeals. The ducal family made known their preference for the Loch Fyne Light Railway, which Benjamin Hall-Blyth had surveyed on North British instructions from Arrochar & Tarbet over Rest-and-be-

OTHER LIGHT RAILWAY SCHEMES

The Cromarty & Dingwall Light Railway was authorised in 1902, but difficulties ensued; only partially constructed, it was abandoned during the 1914-18 War. The Dormoch Light Railway opened in 1902, the Wick & Lybster in 1903. Examples elsewhere in Scotland include the light lines to Carmyllie, Lauder, Moniave and St Combs.

Thankful to St Catherine's.[14] (See Chapter 6) This contest and its aftermath added to the sense of quickening activity and demonstrated the expectations invested in the Light Railways Act. Forman, in laying out his line, had envisaged a continuing chain of light projects down Loch Fyne and into Kintyre. Argyll County Council would press instead for a light railway along Loch Awe (Dalmally – Ardrishaig). There were suggestions, too, that the Arrochar & Tarbet – St. Catherine's line might be extended south to Strachur and Dunoon.[15]

But doubts would multiply. Save for the isolated narrow-gauge Campbeltown & Macrahanish line (1906), South Argyll would remain rail-less. The Loch Fyne Light Railway and the Forsinard, Melvich & Port Skerra Railway shared the same fate – though authorised, with powerful landed support, they would not be built. (See panel above for other light railways and how they fared.) Awareness grew that promotions under the 1896 Act, though relatively cheap and simple, were not always easy. Local energies and enthusiasm might persist, but it was more difficult to keep wavering landowners up to the mark, while county councils, wary of financial commitment to schemes which might or might not proceed, were prone to prioritise instead their annually recurring statutory expenditure. As for the West Highland Ballachulish Extension, authorised as a conventional railway, North British intentions had already fallen under suspicion, despite repeated assurances. And it became an uncomfortable possibility that stalemate in the Great Glen might prove acceptable to both Highland and North British, as a substitute for their shattered Ten Years Truce. In October 1898, without fanfare, they would reach a new and simple pact – potentially renewable, it had no set term and involved no other company – to abstain from any new promotion north of Fort Augustus.[16]

* * *

From the last months of 1897 into 1899 the practical business of construction dominates the minutes and letter books of the Invergarry & Fort Augustus. (See, for example, panel below.) By April 1898 Formans & McCall could report that all the land required was in the hands of contractor James Young, who had completed 40% of the formation and installed 18 miles of telegraph wire. A third of the permanent way materials had been delivered. Work had commenced on the masonry piers of the Spean (Highbridge) and Oich (Fort Augustus) viaducts; and the public roads had been realigned, for over-bridges and under-bridges, to the satisfaction of Inverness-shire County Council. The equivalent report a year later would record that 54% of the permanent way had been laid, while work on the Spean and Calder Burn viaducts was proceeding steadily. The solitary tunnel on Lochoichside had posed no difficulty but the Invergloy and Oich viaducts and the swing bridge on the Caledonian Canal at Fort Augustus, were behind schedule. Station plans were in preparation – "islands" for Gairlochy and Invergarry; a terminal layout at Fort Augustus with one through road, i.e. the Loch Ness "extension" spanning waterway and river. The chalet-style buildings along the West Highland influenced station design.[17]

During four years of building, no exceptional problems would be encountered. Severance claims were troublesome, and Miller of Corriegour proved stubbornly demanding. A few accommodation works were cheapened by agreement – for example, Henry Bellairs of Altrua settled for £100 and a bracken sling over the railway. Near Gairlochy the Post Office required that the public telegraph line be re-routed. The Canal Commissioners

Invergarry & Fort Augustus Railway Minutes, 18th June 1897

Land taken, proprietors' and tenants' claims

Lord Abinger, Inverlochy	£1,108 2 0	Settled for £800
Captain Walker, Tirindrish	£356 17 6	Agreed
Glenfintaig Trustees	Awaited	
Glebe, Muccomir Free Church	Awaited	
Major Bailey, Invergloy	£3,106 13 6	Offer £1,250
Mr Cameron, Glenfintaig	Awaited	
Mr Bellairs, Altrua	£1,000 0 0	Offer £380
Mr McKintosh, Letterfinlay	Awaited	
Mr Miller, Corriegour	£5,891 17 2	Growing timber to be valued
Ellice Trustees	£9,000 0 0	Offer £7,000
Mr Angelo, Culachy	£6,012 5 0	Under negotiation
Caledonian Canal Commissioners	Awaited	
Lord Lovat, Fort Augustus	£3,849 0 0	Offer £1,300
Mr Davey, Spean Bridge*	£73 14 1	Agreed
Mr Wilkinson, Abinger Arms, Spean Bridge	£130 17 0	Offer £100
Mr Cameron, Aberchalder#	£1,000 0 0	Under negotiation
Mr McGregor, Cullochy#	£10 0 0	Under negotiation

George Malcolm to settle outstanding claims of less than £100 at his own discretion.
Certain accommodation works not yet agreed.
£900 already paid to Lord Lovat for immediate possession, in order to have "first sod" ceremony at Fort Augustus.
*Inverlochy (Abinger) and Glenfintaig shooting tenant, and an early supporter of the West Highland Railway.
#Ellice tenants

NRS/BR/IFA/1/1

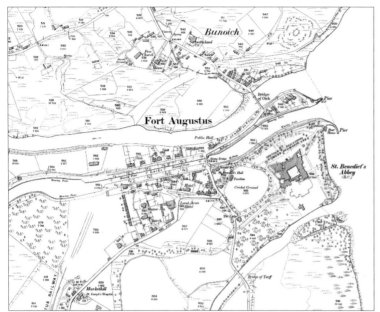

feared for the stability of their embankments at Fort Augustus locks, on either side of the new swing bridge. They were to receive £750 for lengthening their wharf, and this was raised to £1,000 on condition that water be supplied on a permanent basis for locomotive servicing and other railway needs. (The canal engineer, J. G. Davidson, proved a vigilant negotiator.) Lord Lovat stipulated that his Inchnacardoch woodlands be specially insured. There were complaints of disturbance to deer in Culachy forest and allegations that Young's carts had subjected the highways to excessive wear and tear. As usual, the county authorities required that the railway company bear the cost of additional police provision to restrain unruly navvies. Mis-measurement on the Glengarry estate, which resulted in damage to standing timber, meant supplementary compensation. (George Malcolm's son was the surveyor responsible – which occasioned some embarrassment.) Mrs Ellice insisted that the Loch Oich embankments be sown with grass, as earlier agreed. The directors had decided in 1897 to purchase the Lovat Arms Hotel at Fort Augustus, and the sale took some time to complete. When Young's firm became a limited company, they refused his request for a renegotiated contract.[18]

In April 1898 the board met in Glasgow and recorded with

appropriate regrets the death of Strang-Watkins. Now in full charge of Keyden, Strang & Girvan, David Reid was confirmed as agent-cum-secretary of the Invergarry & Fort Augustus Company.[19] At the next board – in London just a month later – Sir Donald Matheson would resign the chairmanship, to be succeeded by John Neilson. For some time, Matheson and his intimate ally Alexander Wylie had ignored the "calls" proportional to their shareholdings. It now emerged that they were together £40,000 in arrears and at risk of bankruptcy. But the two troubled businessmen escaped this fate. By January 1899 both had been formally released. Their shares were resold (for the most part at half the original value) and largely taken up by the other directors.[20]

To all appearances, the Invergarry & Fort Augustus board continued to exude confidence that events must eventually play into their hands. Nonetheless, John Conacher of the North British was for several months unconvinced that they genuinely meant to complete their railway, and thereafter he bided his time, anticipating an appeal for fresh negotiations before long. Reid, like the deceased Strang-Watkins, favoured a bold, unbending front. His directors, however, came to think otherwise – and it may be that Matheson's downfall gave them pause. Well placed to choose the right moment, Malcolm was once more their intermediary. In his factor's capacity he dealt frequently with the North British, routinely arranging the journeys of Mrs Ellice, Lord Burton and their guests, over the West Highland to and from Spean Bridge; and he had continued to pursue better facilities at Corrour for Sir John Stirling-Maxwell.[21] His first step, in early August 1898, was to seek a "private interview" with Conacher.[22] It is probable that Lord Tweeddale, the North British chairman, looked to make the Invergarry & Fort Augustus a simple West Highland

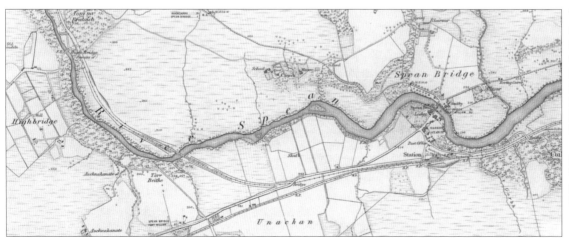

branch, tolerated as such by the Highland Company. In 1895-6, when the little railway was first proposed, a settlement on that basis had been out of reach. Might it now be achieved?

Prior to Malcolm's interview, which took place in Edinburgh on 9th August, Conacher revisited his earlier estimates of the feeder traffic which the West Highland Company could expect to gain; and he instructed the North British accountant to examine these figures more thoroughly. Afterwards, having reported to his directors, the general manager was empowered to confer with other representatives of the Invergarry & Fort Augustus, "on the ground" in the Great Glen – with a view to a working and maintenance agreement.[23] On 18th August Lord Burton wrote from Glenquoich:

> Mr Malcolm tells me you propose to inspect our "Great
> Central"* about the middle of next month. My wife and I
> should be delighted if you could interpose a little trip here.
> On leaving us we could send you by a lovely route via Loch
> Hourn in our little yacht either to Kyle [of Lochalsh] or to
> Mallaig…It might perhaps suit you to see your new [Mallaig]
> line.[24]

Presumably, Neilson and Reid had encouraged the invitation, and it was Burton's hope that terms acceptable to his colleagues could be thrashed out ahead of Conacher's visit. If all went well, he anticipated a positive outcome by October.[25]

Conacher's expedition was arranged as Burton suggested, but in reverse. From an inspection of the West Highland Mallaig Extension – like the Invergarry & Fort Augustus now some eighteen months begun – he spent a Saturday-to-Monday (10th-12th September) at Glenquoich lodge:

> The…yacht should be at Mallaig at 12 o'clock. We dine at
> 8.15. Four hours should easily bring you here [and] the
> carriage will be waiting…at Lochhournhead. It is about 2½
> hours…to Invergarry [and] we will send you off on Monday
> morning [for Spean Bridge]. I am asking Mr Malcolm to
> come…Saturday night.[26]

The weekend proved fruitful in that negotiations went forward – though less speedily than Burton had calculated and without a clear decision. After several letters had passed to and fro during December 1898 and January 1899, the North British indicated that sufficient facilities would be given, on terms yet to be settled, if the Invergarry & Fort Augustus directors choose to work their line themselves. They now inclined, it seems, to this course. Forman undertook to seek out the best price for new or second-hand rolling stock, and his plans for the junction at Spean Bridge were submitted to the North British engineer.[27] But the situation would be utterly transformed in the following months by the downfall of Tweeddale and Conacher (below).

* * *

Hints of a local scheme at the extreme northern end of the Great Glen had begun to circulate immediately after the defeat of the Highland Company's 1896-7 Bill. In June 1898 the Lochend Light Railway was announced, just over seven miles in length, from Inverness by Craigdunain to Dochfour and Loch Ness, terminating at a new pier opposite Aldourie. It was laid

out to diverge west of the Ness viaduct, taking approximately the route which the Highland Company's lost Inverness–Fort Augustus line would have followed, with a swing bridge over the Caledonian Canal at Kinmylies and a very brief tunnel near Craig Phadrig. The plans showed one intermediate station (Dochfour) and two "platforms" (Craigdunain Gate and Dochgarroch). Prominent among the promoters were James Baillie of Dochfour, Sir Kenneth Matheson of Lochalsh and provost William McBean. Their agent was Inverness solicitor Donald Grant.[28] As Inverness-shire's MP and a Caledonian Canal Commissioner, Baillie could take a public interest stance while still avowing his Highland Railway directorship, and his ties with Lord Burton occasioned little remark. He expected to benefit personally, as did those promoters who owned various properties in Inverness. Matheson was the son of Sir Alexander Matheson, the Highland Railway's first chairman (who had been made a baronet in 1882). His motives are uncertain, but the previous Great Glen battles may have alerted him to the possibility of profitable speculation – he would have been a large beneficiary of compulsory purchase, had Charles Forman's layout within the town materialised. (There was no family connection with Sir Donald Matheson of the Invergarry & Fort Augustus.) McBean, a forceful figure in local government, had a long record of pushing "improvement" in and around Inverness.

At this very moment Charles Steel departed the Highland Railway, to be succeeded as general manager by Thomas Wilson. That Highland and North British were to reach a loose treaty three months later (above) suggests that Wilson and Conacher,

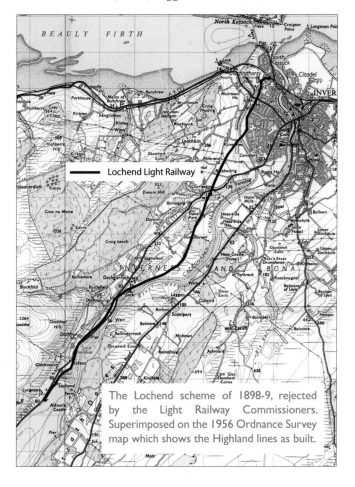

The Lochend scheme of 1898-9, rejected by the Light Railway Commissioners. Superimposed on the 1956 Ordnance Survey map which shows the Highland lines as built.

---

*   A jocular description of the 20-mile Spean Bridge–Fort Augustus line. The Great Central Company's London Extension, Britain's "last main line", was then under construction.

warily of one mind, wanted their two companies to move towards more relaxed and pragmatic relations in the Great Glen; and the Highland board were aware – they remained, it seems, untroubled – that Conacher had commenced discussions with the Invergarry & Fort Augustus. But the Lochend promotion (a formal application to the Light Railway Commissioners was lodged with the Board of Trade in November 1898) ran counter, making for renewed antagonism. Perhaps prompted by Conacher, the Invergarry & Fort Augustus directors chose to test the Highland Company's intentions. To their request for clarification, Wilson replied that it had not yet been decided whether to resist the Lochend project, adding that he excluded a local light railway and its possible merits from any Highland "understanding" with the North British.[29] Conacher, to whom David Reid copied both his formal letter of enquiry and Wilson's response, had indicated already that the North British would oppose. Urging that the Invergarry & Fort Augustus do the same, he warned Reid how the Highland, though perhaps not complicit, would welcome what was practically a "block" scheme, obstructing the way to Inverness for West Highland and Invergarry & Fort Augustus alike.[30]

Though all the Lochend syndicate had ties, more-or-less close, with the Highland Company, they asserted that theirs was an independent venture, to be assessed on its own modest merits. With capital fixed at £60,000 in £5 shares, they expected to raise the necessary funds very easily. Together with a "fast steamer", the line would bring Fort Augustus within two hours of Inverness, supplementing the Loch Ness mail service out of Muirton. The Invergarry & Fort Augustus Company, suffering no injury, would be left to connect the southern half of the Great Glen with the West Highland, as had been their original intention. At Inverness the Great North of Scotland would be offered the same facilities as already applied west of Elgin, to which the Highland could not reasonably object. All the communities along the Glen should be realistic – their need was adequate local transport, with better access to Inverness or Fort William. The inconclusive parliamentary battle of 1896-7 had shut up the northern half of the valley indefinitely, and a through railway, desirable or otherwise, might well be unattainable.[31]

The Highland's Muirton branch, like the West Highland Banavie branch sixty miles to the south, already gave connection with MacBrayne's Caledonian Canal steamers. Interchange at Lochend, slightly shortening the Inverness–Fort William journey for summer tourists, was a minor consideration, and the promoters looked primarily to the districts bordering on Loch Ness, where Charles Forman had conceded that a "premature" line between Fort Augustus and Inverness might do more harm than good (see Chapter 6). Their fast steamer, like David MacBrayne's vessels, would call along both shores, while a railway must follow one side, leaving the other disadvantaged – and, indeed, worse-provided, if competition led to fewer sailings. This was a hoary plea – it had been employed to resist the earliest railways planned along Loch Lomond, and the Glasgow & North Western scheme had been similarly attacked in 1882-3. However, with a greater emphasis on rail-and-water co-ordination all along the Great Glen, the Lochend scheme would have been more convincing and a compromise

agreement with the Invergarry & Fort Augustus Company was surely indicated. But the promoters' arguments challenged the by now familiar Invergarry & Fort Augustus position that traffic could be patiently built up, making a through railway entirely viable in the longer term.

For the hearing before the Light Railway Commissioners on 18th May 1899 friendly witnesses were recruited all around Loch Ness. The Glen Urquhart and Glen Moriston spokesmen, when pressed, would admit that they wanted their own railway sooner or later, and they confessed to some anxiety that it might be forfeit if the Lochend line succeeded – at which the promoters' case faltered. The Great North of Scotland Company, the Highland, the Invergarry & Fort Augustus and the North British were all represented – and the North British sent their solicitor James Watson, who protested without finesse that the West Highland and the Invergarry & Fort Augustus faced a "blocking" conspiracy. The Commissioners did not indulge him. Parliament's latest intention, as they construed it, was to keep the Great Glen "open" for future projects, which they thought sufficient insurance for any complainant. Nonetheless, this prejudged the Lochend party's contention that a line along Loch Ness was now unlikely ever to be built. The promoters were further handicapped by the revelation that "Mr Gordon", their engineer, (not otherwise identified) lacked railway experience. In fact, Gordon's estimates were reasonable. Contrary to Conacher's suspicions, it was apparent that the Highland's declared neutrality verged on hostility – and negotiations for access to Inverness station had paused. Inverness-shire County Council and the Caledonian Canal management were tepid supporters, while MacBrayne, though not an out-and-out opponent, thought the proposed pier at Lochend too exposed. Opinion on Inverness Town Council and on the Chamber of Commerce was divided. When the Commissioners gave their adverse verdict, the Lochend Light Railway died.[32]

* * *

From mid-1898 the North British and the Invergarry & Fort Augustus had moved some way towards cooperation, and by early 1899 an arrangement at West Highland Spean Bridge seemed in the making – from which a working and maintenance agreement might yet have followed. During the Lochend hearing four months later, solicitor Watson was content to reinforce the objections which counsel for the little company presented (in particular, their shared suspicions of a "blocking" scheme). But upheaval in the North British boardroom supervened. The half-yearly shareholders' meeting in March 1899 had seen Lord Tweeddale overthrown. In June John Conacher would resign, having found his position impossible. The assault on chairman and general manager was carried out by a self-serving faction who had orchestrated disquiet among the shareholders. Too much control, these malcontents alleged, was passing to the company's officers, for whom efficient operation counted more than dividends. Although the reputation of the North British under Tweeddale and Conacher stood distinctly higher than before, their unconcealed partnership in setting policy had disgruntled several directors and fed into the unease which the conspirators exploited. Sir William Laird made a malleable

West Highland Spean Bridge, looking towards Achindaul and Fort William. The alterations to accommodate the Invergarry & Fort Augustus Railway were such as would have served a trunk line to Inverness – note the double turnout junction; the extended up platform and additional bay; and the new "Junction" signal cabin, its roof just visible. The sign on the platform announces the Invergarry and Fort Augustus Railway.

(Highland Railway Society collection)

new chairman. William Jackson, the new general manager, was a competent and conscientious company loyalist, with no ambition to shape policy.[33]

Rancour persisted. The incoming regime, whose own behaviour scarcely bore scrutiny, proved more ruthless (or less principled) than those who fought back on Tweeddale's behalf. Conacher preferred to seek a new path in the business world, quitting the railway industry. Head-hunted by the Caledonian, he would decline their offer. During 1900 George Wieland, who had been elected to the board in 1892, increasingly took control. He would succeed Laird in May 1901, a month after traffic began (with scant ceremony) on the West Highland Extension. In command until his death in 1905, Wieland made a virtue of strict economy. As a result, the North British lagged in the turn-of-the-century shift to modern rolling stock and more powerful locomotives, so that the shareholders in the end gained little. Under his successors, until 1914 the board would undertake a concentrated and expensive programme of replacement. It was certainly prudent to resist any early expansion of Mallaig harbour without additional government aid on a substantial scale; but the pursuit of petty savings blighted the first years of the Mallaig line. Wieland's own record was questionable. On what terms, to what personal advantage, had he remained secretary of several subsidiary companies, the West Highland

included, after resigning his main post with the North British? However, he had judged shrewdly in identifying with the 1899 boardroom coup.[34]

During the building of the Craigendoran–Fort William line, Wieland had been the sole executive figurehead of the West Highland Company. Abrasive and not over-scrupulous, he roused complaints in several quarters; and the Marquess of Breadalbane, who well knew that authority ultimately lay with the North British, was not the only proprietor who protested.[35] When the railway opened in a barely completed condition, the remedial work of 1894-6 made for recurring friction between Conacher and the West Highland secretary. Those North British directors and shareholders who now roundly condemned entanglement with the West Highland (which some of them had supported earlier) were not appeased by Conacher's solid achievement. With the North British commitment of 1889 redefined and the hard-won West Highland Extension soon to yield additional revenue, an end was in sight – arguably the best outcome available; but the general manager's critics were irreconcilable. They harked back to the New Lines Agreement with the Caledonian in 1891, claiming that an accommodation might have been reached more speedily. This, they argued, would have adequately protected North British interests in the Dunbartonshire and Loch Lomond districts, obviating the ill-considered West Highland adventure.[36] It was a thin charge. Conacher was then newly appointed in John Walker's stead, while Wieland, who evaded blame, had been intimately associated with Walker during 1887-8 in encouraging the West Highland promoters (see Chapters 1 and 2).

How matters would have developed had Tweeddale and Conacher remained in command can only be guessed. Everything suggests that their goal was to bring the Invergarry & Fort Augustus Company firmly under North British control before the new railway opened. In a letter despatched during his final weeks in office Conacher asked that Reid obtain Forman's latest assessment. Might the line be finished during 1900 and ready for inspection by the Board of Trade?[37] There was at the very least the possibility of a durable Great Glen settlement; but his recent doings, including his visit to Burton's Glenquoich, were used against him – evidence, said the opposition faction, that the company risked committing to another over-generous guarantee for another penurious dependant. North British policy under Laird and Wieland would leave Reid and his directors with no easy way forward, no means of retreat without ruin, and the Invergarry & Fort Augustus would be driven into the less than welcoming arms of the Highland Company.

References

J. McGregor, *The West Highland Railway: Plans, Politics and People*, Birlinn (John Donald), 2005, cited as PPP.

Note 21 – the Cameron of Lochiel Papers (Lochaber Archive) include the Glenquoich estate Letter Books, which contain much of George Malcolm's correspondence.

1. *Engineering*, 2 April 1897.
2. Ibid.
3. *Railway Times*, 27 March 1897.
4. NRS/PYB(S)/1/501, Great Glen Bills 1896-7, Commons and Lords.
5. *Engineering*, 2 April 1897.
6. *Railway Times*, 10 July 1897. NRS/BR/PYB(S)/1/501, Great Glen Bills, Lords, 8 July 1897.
7. *Railway Times*, 10 July 1897.
8. NRS/BR/IFA/1/1, Invergarry & Fort Augustus Railway minutes, 8 July and 6 August 1897.
9. *Financial News*, 7 June 1898.
10. *Railway News*, 10 September 1898.
11. Duncan Kennedy, *The Birth and Death of a Highland Railway*, John Murray, 1971
12. NRS/BR/PYB(S)/1/394, Callander & Oban Railway Bill, 1896-7.
13. NRS/BR/PYB(S)/1/394, John Anderson, evidence, and George Malcolm, evidence, Callander & Oban Railway Bill, Commons, 30 March 1897.
14. NRS/BR/PYB(S)/1/394, Callander & Oban Railway Bill, Duke of Argyll, petition against; also Marquess of Lorne, evidence, and Duke of Argyll, evidence, Commons, 31 March 1897. NRS/BR/WEH/1/1, West Highland Railway minutes, 6 May 1897 ("Arrochar & Loch Fyne" Light Railway Order).
15. PPP, pp.157-8. NRS/BR/PYB(S)/1/394, Benjamin Hall-Blyth, evidence, Callander & Oban Railway Bill, Commons, 30 March 1897. NRS/BR/COB/1/5, Callander & Oban Railway minutes, 19 October 1897.
16. NRS/BR/IFA/1/2 Invergarry & Fort Augustus Railway Minutes, 16 December 1898 and 11 January 1899.
17. NRS/BR/IFA/1/1, Invergarry & Fort Augustus Railway minutes, 18 August, 9 October and 27 November 1897, and 23 February, 29 April 1898 and 23 June 1898. NRS/BR/IFA/1/2, Invergarry & Fort Augustus Railway minutes, 16 December 1898 and 20 April, 15 June and 17 August 1899.
18. Ibid. (all references cited in 17).
19. NRS/BR/IFA/1/1, Invergarry & Fort Augustus Railway minutes, 19 April 1898.
20. NRS/BR/IFA/1/1, Invergarry & Fort Augustus Railway minutes, 23 June and 16 November 1898. NRS/BR/IFA/1/2, Invergarry & Fort Augustus Railway minutes, 16 December 1898, and 17 June and 17 August 1899.
21. For example:- Lochaber Archive, Lochiel Papers, CLA/12/1/ Glenquoich letter books, passim (Lord Burton's travel arrangements). See also NRS/BR/NBR/8/1764 Box 7, general manager's files relating to West Highland Railway, Malcolm to John Conacher, 13 July 1897 (urgent need for passenger shelter at Corrour).
22. NRS/BR/NBR/8/1401, North British Railway, files relating to Invergarry & Fort Augustus Railway (1898-1903), Malcolm to Conacher 3 August 1898.
23. NRS/BR/NBR/8/1401, estimates of costs and revenues; also Conacher to Malcolm, 11 August 1898.
24. NRS/BR/NBR/8/1401, Lord Burton to Conacher, 18 August 1898.
25. NRS/BR/NBR/8/1401, Burton to Conacher 29 (or 30) August 1898.
26. Ibid.
27. NRS/BR/IFA/1/2, Invergarry & Fort Augustus Railway minutes, 16 December 1898 and 27 January 1899.
28. C. Gair, "Inverness & Lochend Light Railway", *Highland Railway Journal*, Nos. 53 and 54 (Spring and Summer, 2000). *Inverness Courier*, 29 November 1898.
29. NRS/BR/IFA/1/2, Invergarry & Fort Augustus Railway minutes, 16 December 1898 and 11 January 1999, the latter quoting Wilson's reply.
30. NRS/BR/IFA/1/2, Invergarry & Fort Augustus Railway minutes, 16 December 1898 and 11 January 1899, the latter noting Conacher's warning.
31. C. Gair, op.cit.
32. C. Gair, op.cit. *The Scotsman*, 22 May 1899.
33. NRS/BR/SPC/9/2, Conacher Papers, including press reports of Tweeddale's defeat, 23 March 1899; letter to newspapers by Conacher's chief opponent, 19 June 1899, and Conacher's circular in reply (undated).
34. PPP. p.178. NRS/SPC/9/2, Conacher Papers, letter re possible "counter-revolution" in favour of Tweeddale and Conacher, 10 August 1899. D. Cattanach, unpublished monograph on George Bradley Wieland.
35. PPP, pp. 182 and 221.
36. Cattanach, op. cit.
37. NRS/BR/IFA/1/2, Invergarry & Fort Augustus Railway minutes, 17 August 1899, noting Conacher's letter some two months earlier.

CHAPTER EIGHT

FINDING A SAVIOUR, 1899-1902

Whether George Malcolm brought definite proposals to his "interview" with John Conacher in August 1898 is uncertain, but the North British general manager went to Glenquoich a month later ready to state the terms which he might recommend to his directors. In the ensuing correspondence the North British offered to work the Invergarry & Fort Augustus for 60% of gross revenue, meeting all administrative costs. A small allowance would be made for directorial expenses; a joint committee of the two companies would set fares and monitor traffic; and the owning company might be credited on a mileage basis for any measurable increase in West Highland loadings between Crianlarich and Spean Bridge.[1] One condition was inescapable, against the day when completion of a railway through the Great Glen might be fought out again at Westminster – the Invergarry & Fort Augustus must forgo their independence:

"[They] shall use their best endeavours to assist [the North British Company] to obtain Parliamentary powers to construct a line from Fort Augustus to Inverness if called upon to do so."[2]

Burton had hoped for something more akin to an equal partnership, in which the Invergarry & Fort Augustus would retain a free hand for the future, and his resolve was stiffened by company secretary David Reid. With some bravado, Malcolm and Reid both dismissed Conacher's proposals. They needed no financial aid to complete their railway; and a working arrangement with the North British afterwards was no more than a matter of mutual advantage and mutual convenience.[3] Conacher, bending to this rebuff, accepted that negotiations should deal instead with terms of access to West Highland Spean Bridge, on the assumption that the little company would work their line themselves.[4] Nevertheless, he expected

Spean Bridge station, looking up Glen Spean, during the Highland Company's "occupation" of the Invergarry & Fort Augustus (1903-7). Their Yankee Tank with three coaches stands at the up platform and it seems that a down West Highland train is expected though not yet signalled.. A taller signal box has succeeded the original dwarf cabin. Note the cattle trucks in the siding behind. The West Highland Inverness Extension, diverging west of Roy Bridge, would have climbed the hillside on the far left.   (Highland Railway Society collection)

Looking north through the short tunnel beside Loch Oich, between Invergarry and Aberchalder. The signal wire (left) was part of the warning system if rock falls occurred. (LGRP)

a humbler appeal in due course and prepared accordingly. When the Invergarry & Fort Augustus fell to the North British, the West Highland Banavie branch might be closed. Fort Augustus would become the principal point of exchange with the Caledonian Canal steamers and local needs at the southern end of the Great Glen might be met by transfer between rail and steamer at the new Banavie station on the Mallaig Extension.[5] But Conacher's strategy was confounded when in March 1899 Lord Tweeddale was driven from the North British chairmanship – and his own resignation followed three months later.

With John Neilson in interim command, after the resignation of Sir Donald Matheson, the Invergarry & Fort Augustus had opposed the Lochend Light Railway in edgy amity with the North British. (The hearing which saw the scheme rejected took place betwixt Tweeddale's overthrow and Conacher's departure.) On 15th June 1899 Lord Burton was elected chairman (and thereafter the board often met at his London residence, Chesterfield House). As a member of the South Eastern & Chatham Management Committee,* Burton did not lack experience and he had been for many years an active shareholder in the Midland Railway – though a 20-mile line in the Scottish Highlands was a very different proposition. John Ratcliff, son of Burton's sometime business partner, had taken up a large block of Sir Donald Matheson's forfeited shares. When Neilson now resigned too, James Lambrick, secretary of brewers Bass, Ratcliff & Gretton and the new chairman's nominee, would join the Invergarry & Fort Augustus board.[6]

The installation of William Jackson as North British general manager went unremarked, and it was agreed that Charles Forman should continue to seek arrangements for entry to Spean Bridge, in consultation with the North British district engineer. But October 1899 brought an unexpected North British offer to operate the Invergarry & Fort Augustus at cost (as the Caledonian worked the Callander & Oban). Burton and his fellow-directors refused – to accept would have been a gamble that their railway could pay its way at once – but the door seemed ajar for more discussion and a percentage working agreement perhaps more generous than Conacher had envisaged twelve months earlier.[7] It soon appeared that any optimism was misplaced. A new round of meetings, left

for the most part to Forman, made little headway. Striving over several months to soften the terms presented by North British solicitor James Watson, the engineer also encountered the unyielding George Wieland. By mid-February 1900, a prospective treaty had been shaped, though it was not to Forman's liking. Wieland and Watson looked to an agreement in perpetuity – after six years, there would be one opportunity to withdraw. For 60% of gross revenue, which might reduce to 55% when traffic grew to £12 per mile per week, the North British would run four trains in each direction on weekdays and carry out "ordinary maintenance". Burton's plea, that the working company undertake all "extraordinary maintenance", was ignored. The owning company must take responsibility for any faults in construction and bear the risk of "landslides and the like".[8]

Though reluctant to terminate these discussions, the Invergarry & Fort Augustus directors refused outright to consider the North British demand for a guaranteed minimum payment of £6,000 per annum, while Reid complained that *"[the] fixed minimum would create an inducement to your Company not to do their best."*[9] If finalised quickly, the agreement could be included in the North British general bill of 1899-1900, and Watson applied pressure to this end, hinting at compensatory relaxations when the minimum had been accepted. (*"You will have only yourselves to blame if no practical result ensues."*) By resort to debentures, the Invergarry & Fort Augustus directors expected to cover the remaining costs of construction; and the North British indicated that they might take up most of the debenture stock – easing the way but increasing their grip for the future. Testy who-said-what exchanges sputtered on into June. Had Forman undertaken to recommend the North British package to Burton? Had he warned Wieland that any minimum was likely to be rejected? The North British, Watson flatly

*   The South Eastern Railway and the London, Chatham & Dover Railway were jointly managed from 1899.

declared, had shown generosity enough by settling on £6,000, a reduction from the (unspecified) amount first contemplated. What was there to fear? With average earnings of £8-£10 per mile per week (a lower figure, he alleged, than Forman had projected in 1896) and the gross amount split 60:40, the North British would receive between £5,000 and £7,000, at which figure the minimum need not come into play.[10]

Burton had recruited Alfred Willis, general manager of the South Eastern & Chatham, as a possible mediator – whose efforts Wieland sarcastically dismissed:

> [He described] the incomparable advantages of the railway to [my] Company but, as he had not been there and I had, our conversation did not last many minutes.[11]

On one question, both Jackson and Wieland were of Conacher's mind. When the Mallaig Extension opened, the Banavie branch would be truncated to a mere half-mile and it might be abandoned entirely if the Invergarry & Fort Augustus were gathered in. But by May 1900 a decision whether to remodel the new Banavie station for exchange traffic had become urgent, while North British officers continued to debate the economies which could be achieved. Wieland was unconvinced that these justified more concessions to Lord Burton,[12] and the negotiations tailed away, after Reid had protested that the North British, once in control, could compel total surrender. (*"[It would be] in your power to stand greatly in the way of the development of traffic on [our] line."*)[13]

* * *

Meanwhile, construction of the Invergarry & Fort Augustus had continued, and the company's minutes are rich in detail – how North British charges for rails and other materials brought to Spean Bridge were queried to no avail; how a delivery of sleepers was left unloaded, incurring demurrage; how a "steam digger" was employed to speed the earthworks near Aberchalder... Among their correspondence, is a letter from R. F. Yorke, engineer and managing director of the recently established Fort William Electric Lighting Company, who had been commissioned by the North British to equip their old-fort engine shed and goods yard; the Invergarry & Fort Augustus should adopt electricity too, employing an "electric vessel" on Loch Ness. Also recorded is Lord Burton's gift to Reid – an impressively antlered stag's head. (The secretary's thanks, promising "urgent preservation", do not read as altogether

(Above) The tunnel, looking south, with Loch Oich on the right. Note again the signal wire (right), which ran through the bore. Nearer the tunnel portal, a steeply-inclined drainage trough spans the line. The prominent post (centre left) is another part of the warning system in case of rock falls.
(Highland Railway Society collection)

(Left) A similar view in June 2021 shows how the trackbed is now part of the Great Glen Way. a popular long-distance footpath. The trough is still in place.

(Keith Fenwick)

William Jackson (named, bottom right) became general manager of the North British Railway in 1899 and thus the description of the West Highland line as "newly opened" is misleading. This poster of c. 1900, though not be interpreted too "politically", surely proclaims that Lochaber belonged to the North British. The West Highland Mallaig Extension (which would open in 1901) and the West Highland Ballachulish Extension (authorised in 1896 but not commenced) are both shown, while the Callander & Oban Ballachulish branch (likewise approved in 1896 and under construction) is conspicuously absent. The poster also includes the Invergarry & Fort Augustus Railway – where by 1900 construction was well advanced, amid North British manoeuvres to take control. Further south, the Loch Fyne Light Railway appears (from West Highland Arrochar & Tarbet to St Catherine's); though authorised in 1897, it would not be built. Several summer-season coach routes are featured (faint dotted lines) – for example from Bridge of Orchy to Ballachulish, for connection with MacBrayne's steamers, with the option of a side excursion to Glen Etive. Extended tours by rail, road and water remained popular, alongside the growing demand for day trips.

(Paul Telway collection)

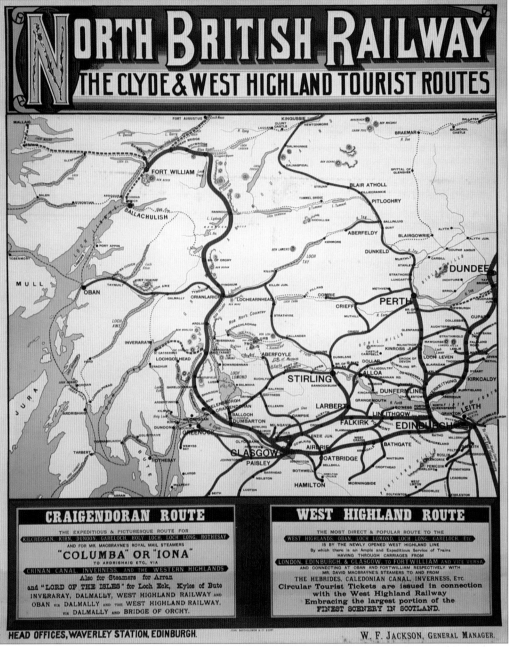

sincere.) In the manner of many small companies, the directors gave much attention to matters relatively trivial, like the design of their seal. Would the public think it tasteless, they wondered, to feature Invergarry's Well of the Seven Heads, which commemorated a bloody seventeenth century feud?[14]

More weighty concerns, of course, appear too. Work on the Loch Ness "extension" was hindered by the Caledonian Canal Commissioners, who objected to a temporary bridge at Fort Augustus; and their engineer claimed that the piers of the Oich viaduct had already altered the river currents, endangering the canal embankments to the south. On a more positive note, the several proprietors on the former Letterfinlay estate all sought railway facilities. In response, Forman planned a basic platform and siding at Invergloy, where Major Bailey had provided encouraging estimates of his personal traffic. The company's cumulative commitments to landowners and tenants along the route were potentially burdensome. However, the directors

were not the naive spendthrifts that they have sometimes been painted. In accordance with standard practice, contractor James Young received payment by instalment, after his periodic claims had been certificated by Formans & McCall. The several disputes over Young's entitlement to further reimbursement, after unexpected difficulties, were not unusual. It was normal too, and quite legitimate, that Forman and Reid took shares in lieu of payment. The final cost of accommodation works, always uncertain, was kept in view, with £2,000 reluctantly set aside towards a negotiated settlement when Miller of Corriegour threatened to raise an action in the sheriff court. Small parcels of land were always disproportionally expensive, and Reid pressed the Glenfintaig Trustees for the simplest possible conveyance of an additional plot at Gairlochy, required for the stationmaster's house. On second thoughts, a smaller, cheaper station building was substituted at Fort Augustus, though three platform roads were retained. As with the elaborate junction at

Spean Bridge, this layout far exceeded the needs of a branch line; but future hopes still ruled. It was outlay against the day (ever more distant?) when the Invergarry & Fort Augustus might be extended to Inverness.[15]

By October 1900 the permanent way was ready, save for the final section to Loch Ness. With share capital all paid up, the project remained broadly within budget. Signalling had yet to be installed, while station buildings and loading banks were unfinished. With a goods shed at Fort Augustus and engine sheds at either end of the new railway, the expenditure still outstanding might amount to £40-50,000; but debenture stock of £80,000 had been created (to which a further £10,000 would be added), on which basis bank loans could be obtained. Inspection by the Board of Trade during 1901 was thus an attainable target, before the five years prescribed by the Invergarry & Fort Augustus Act ran out.[16] That the company might acquire their own maintenance equipment, rolling stock and locomotives, not to mention fixed plant and operating staff, had been hitherto something of a bargaining counter. As a serious proposition it was sobering – which impelled the board, reluctant though they were, to resume contact with the North British before the year ended.

This time Reid dealt with general manager Jackson, who insisted that his hands were tied. Following a first meeting, the secretary reported to Burton:

Mr Jackson did not think there was the least chance of [their] doing without the Minimum. [They] could not see how it could be done for less than about £6,000, without loss to them. His Directors are under pledge to their Shareholders… not to incur further capital expenditure or loss of revenue in working other lines.

Reid had emphasised how the Invergarry & Fort Augustus Company remained confident of finding their entire capital. On the dubious evidence of the failed Lochend promotion, he had argued that Great Glen landowners were becoming more disposed to a through line along Loch Ness – which ought to influence North British calculations. But all to no effect:

[Mr Jackson] said that [his] Shareholders would not look with favour on any…expenditure in this district for some years to come. He would not admit that his Company would derive much benefit from being at Inverness.

Jackson, while protesting that he did not wish to appear "unfriendly or exacting", suggested only one concession – the minimum might be slightly reduced, in recognition that the West Highland stood to gain at least a little additional goods and passenger business.[17]

To work the railway independently – which in any case might well prove impossible – must entail delays and unpredictable costs. Arbitration under Board of Trade auspices was almost certain to confirm the junction arrangements at Spean Bridge which the North British had settled in principle; nevertheless, the Invergarry & Fort Augustus might be compelled to provide their own stationmaster and station offices. And the North British might attempt to bar second-hand locomotives and rolling stock – the Invergarry & Fort Augustus budget would permit nothing better – from West Highland metals. To keep the railway in good condition, should it lie unused for any length of time, meant a maintenance contract. (Would Young or another

Spean Bridge Hotel.

Spean Bridge Junction Station -- West Highland Railway.

The above First-class Hotel has recently been altered and re-furnished.

Being near Ben Nevis a good view of the Observatory can be obtained from the Hotel.

It is surrounded by beautiful and varied Scenery, and recommended by Mountaineers as very central, also within walking and driving distances of the Prince Charlie Cave, and Parallel Roads.

Spean Bridge is the junction for the new and beautiful Railway Route to Fort Augustus.

EXCELLENT CUISINE.

FISHING.   GOLF.   POSTING.

MODERATE TERMS.

J. ANDERSON, Proprietor.

By c.1907 the Abinger Arms, under new ownership, was transformed into the "modernised" Spean Bridge Hotel. Lochaber's meteorological observatories, on the summit of Ben Nevis and in Fort William, linked by telegraph, had operated from 1883 and were something of a tourist attraction.   (Scottish Railway Preservation Society archive)

bidder undertake "caretaker" duties?) At the turn of 1900-01, amid winter frosts, the immediate challenge was to protect the new plaster in empty station buildings and company houses. (Would Young engage to lay fires when required?)[18]

During the triangular contest of 1896-7, with the Highland Company, the Great North of Scotland and (less certainly) the Caledonian all in the field, the North British had behaved circumspectly, positing an eventual takeover of the Invergarry & Fort Augustus on reasonable terms. (See Chapter 6) If these others could be persuaded to reassert their respective interests in the Great Glen, George Wieland might be brought to a more moderate stance; and in the last weeks of 1900 George Malcolm despatched exploratory letters to the Caledonian and to the Great North – though what he wrote is unrecorded. That the Highland might operate the Spean Bridge–Fort Augustus line, despite the inevitable opposition of the North British, may have become for the first time a definite proposition, with Lord

Lovat a potential intermediary. The railway, though he had not wanted it, must do some good, and to do any good it must open for traffic. Caught up in the Boer War in South Africa as a serving soldier, Lovat could not readily influence the Highland board; and it seems that Captain Edward Ellice, likewise on active service, persuaded the Glengarry Trustees to enter their own appeal, stressing local need. In January 1901 Lord Burton made a definite proposal, dealing chairman-to-chairman with Sir George MacPherson-Grant. Would the Highland lease the Invergarry & Fort Augustus for a limited period? (This formula, excluding the North British, must have reassured the Caledonian.) There remained the possibility that Wieland could be softened and Reid, other moves notwithstanding, was to attempt a second meeting with Jackson.[19]

These hard-to-disentangle exchanges were interrupted by the news of Charles Forman's death on 8th February 1901, at the early age of 48, in Switzerland, where he had gone "to recover his health".[20] J. E. Harrison, already a partner in Formans & McCall, assumed responsibility for the Invergarry & Fort Augustus, while Sir John Wolfe-Barry offered an informal association to see the Callander & Oban Ballachulish branch completed. (James Forman, father of Charles, had died the previous year and David McCall was by this date an elderly man.) And it might well be said that Forman's unquenchable belief in an Oban–Fort William–Inverness railway now devolved on David Reid. The secretary, fearing that Burton risked appearing a helpless suppliant, thought it a better strategy to join with the Caledonian in resisting the North British portmanteau bill of 1900-01. This included a formal application (the second of its kind) for more time to build the West Highland Ballachulish Extension. On Reid's advice, the Invergarry & Fort Augustus directors sought a locus to oppose, citing their expectations of an eventual through line between Oban and Inverness and their misgivings that the Fort William–North Ballachulish line, authorised in 1896 and the subject of repeated North British assurances, had not even been begun. Moreover, Reid set out to rouse Lochaber, with the assistance of Fort William solicitors Allison & McNiven, Lord Abinger's agents. Thomas Allison should enlist "influential persons" and engage as many proprietors as he could, all ready to denounce North British procrastination and deceit, in the hope that the Callander & Oban, with the Caledonian's blessing, could be persuaded to attempt a new push across the Loch Leven frontier to Fort William and Spean Bridge.[21]

* * *

It was Reid's second experiment in applying what he termed the "Ballachulish lever". In parliamentary session 1898-9, the North British had sought three additional years (continuing the West Highland's powers beyond 1901); and the Invergarry & Fort Augustus Company, despite Burton's then tentative engagement with the North British, had resisted the application – by way of reminder that they retained some nuisance power. Two years had been granted, and John Conacher had suppressed his irritation at their intervention.[22] The North British now applied for three years more but were refused. Approval had been by no means certain – it would have carried matters to 1906, a full decade after the West Highland

Ballachulish Extension Act – but Wieland was to lay the blame at Lord Burton's door.[23]

The Caledonian gave Reid no encouragement and meanwhile the Highland Company had responded warily to all enquiries – leaving the Invergarry & Fort Augustus directors to ponder their narrowing choices. Given a successful appeal for the extension of their own parliamentary powers beyond August of 1901, they might postpone the statutory final inspection of the railway so that both the outstanding work and their hoped-for negotiations with the Highland could proceed unhurriedly. On the other hand, the North British, smarting at Reid's machinations, were likely to raise every possible objection, tit for tat. It was clearly desirable that the Highland be presented with a line ready for traffic – after a full Board of Trade inspection and a favourable verdict. And might the North British relent, matching or bettering any Highland offer, once assured that the Invergarry & Fort Augustus was in good order? The drastic answer was to declare insolvency, calculating that Highland and North British would squabble to acquire the bankrupt company and offer competing versions of a better-than-nothing take-over.[24]

What "lease" (above) meant does not appear. Burton may have envisaged the loan of engines, coaches and wagons to maintain a minimal train service, under cover of a nominal leasing arrangement. Reid's hope was *"[working at] 40% and no minimum"*.[25] Aware how the Invergarry & Fort Augustus were seeking here and there for a way out, the Highland directors remained properly suspicious. They took heed, too, when Wieland affected surprise and anger. Denying that the Invergarry & Fort Augustus and the North British were deadloked, he warned against any interference.[26] William Whitelaw, elected to the Highland board in 1898, exemplified the professionalism long demanded by the company's critics. He judged it not impractical, braving North British bluster, to undertake "isolated" operation out of West Highland Spean Bridge – and by this means his company might escape from the cycle of Great Glen confrontations. But Whitelaw was not yet chairman – that would come in 1902 – and he could not carry his colleagues with him. In April, Highland and Invergarry & Fort Augustus representatives met in London (at Burton's Chesterfield House), to examine several drafts of a seven-year agreement. It was rejected by a majority of the Highland board, unready as yet to undertake the working and maintenance of a line detached from their own system.[27]

When Burton felt compelled to fall back on the unyielding North British, a formal conference took place in that company's London offices on 15th May 1901. He was accompanied by Cunninghame, Lambrick and Reid. On the other side were Wieland and Jackson, with Watson in attendance. Though preliminary discussions between Malcolm and Watson had established no common ground, the Invergarry & Fort Augustus delegation persevered. They would accept responsibility for "extraordinary maintenance" for one year beyond the expiry of the contractor's liability – and the North British might satisfy themselves that the line was sound and stable by making their own examination, before the Board of Trade inspection or afterwards.[28] Burton was shocked to find that Wieland's central condition had hardened – all the Invergarry & Fort

---

CORRESPONDENCE BEFORE THE BOARD OF TRADE INSPECTION

Reid to Burton, 5th August 1901

Major Pringle R.E. proposes leaving Glasgow by the 5.50 a.m. …on Friday 16th and requests me to inform all interested. The inspection will begin on his arrival at Spean Bridge and go on all day. [Formans & McCall] are arranging the necessary engines and carriages with the North British at a fixed charge for each day…

The 5.50 train took the previous evening's West Highland coaches from London Kings Cross.

Reid to Wilkinson, Spean Bridge Hotel, 8th August

I shall…require a lunch basket to go with the saloon carriage on Friday morning. Please make this up as nicely as you can for…a dozen or so, and…include…a couple of bottles of champagne, two bottles of whisky and plenty of mineral waters.

That the inspection became in some measure a pleasure trip speaks to Reid's confidence in a favourable outcome?

Reid to Malcolm (telegram), 14th August

Please arrange to meet the Board of Trade Inspector and me at Spean Bridge on Friday…

Malcolm drove from Invergarry.

Reid to Wilkinson (telegram), 14th August

See me at station 5.20 p.m. tomorrow [to review arrangements].

Reid would travel by the afternoon West Highland train from Glasgow, staying overnight in Fort William and returning to Spean Bridge the next morning.

Reid to Pringle (telegram), 14th August

Will arrange to have breakfast basket at Crianlarich, Friday morning.

Reid to Refreshment Room, Crianlarich, West Highland Railway (telegram), 14th August

Basket for Pringle, 7.37 a.m. arrival Friday.

Until restaurant cars were introduced in the 1920s, Crianlarich's food baskets were a West Highland institution. The platform "dining room" there survives today in café guise.

NRS/BR/IFA/4/5

Augustus directors must bind themselves personally to the £6,000 minimum. At the conclusion of the morning session, Reid penned a downcast but still defiant summary:

We very reluctantly agree to the minimum of £6,000…but… cannot agree to make good any annual deficiency, still less to give a joint and several guarantee…We…believe that [the] risk is almost nil but…object in toto to the principle [which] gives a direct inducement so to work the line as to create a loss…[The Agreement will] remain a very favourable one for you – a very onerous one for us.[29]

Returning to the fray that afternoon, Burton argued that general traffic would be won from the Caledonian Canal, while the option of transfer at Fort Augustus, rail to steamer and vice versa, must stimulate summer tourist business, all to the advantage of the West Highland. To fix on £6,000 per year as the probable working cost was demonstrably excessive – translating into 3/- per train mile, against c. 2/- on the Callander & Oban and c. 2/6 on the West Highland. Unmoved, Wieland replied that little more exchange traffic could be expected than the Banavie branch already commanded, in summer or in other seasons.* The North British, he warned, would guard against loss as they saw fit, and he offered only one concession – "extraordinary maintenance" might become the working company's responsibility after three years.[30] In any case the conference was doomed to fail, as Reid explained, when he returned to Glasgow, in an urgent letter to Malcolm:

Lord B. and Mr Cunninghame would not hear of [a personal

guarantee] for a moment… Nothing has been gained by our efforts [and] these must cease…We must [somehow] arrange to open and work the Line ourselves.[31]

* * *

The Invergarry & Fort Augustus board settled on inspection as their next step, together with an application to continue their powers of 1896 until 1903.[32] While they could not tell how the Highland or the North British would react if the line was approved or what alterations the government inspector might demand, the two-year extension would pass unopposed – both Highland and North British held back. An awkward moment arose, however, when "a busybody about Spean Bridge" informed the Board of Trade that an illegal passenger service had begun. Reid's emphatic denial was the strict truth, but the record shows how George Malcolm, in his factor's capacity, had arranged that several of the Ellices' summer guests and shooting tenants would be fetched to Invergarry or Aberchalder by the contractor's "pug" engine and coach.[33] In due course Major John Pringle R.E. (who had carried out the final inspection of the Mallaig Extension) gave notice that he would assess the Invergarry & Fort Augustus over one or two days (16th and 17th August 1901). He requested two heavy locomotives and a saloon, which the Invergarry & Fort Augustus, of necessity, hired from the North British.[34]

In a round of letters and telegrams (see panel above), Reid alerted both J. E. Harrison of Formans & McCall and contractor James Young. The inspection party included others not professionally involved – Mrs Reid would accompany her

---

* When the Mallaig Extension opened that April, with its own Banavie station, the branch terminus had become "Banavie Pier".

George Wieland's reply to Lord Burton's memorandum, autumn 1901 (edited)

[I have demonstrated] the...obstructiveness of the Invergarry Company and their unfriendliness to [us]. The sanctioned Invergarry Line was made, and on several occasions during its construction Mr Forman saw...me with reference to the North British Company's working it; but [his] ideas required such sacrifices from [us] that nothing came of our many conversations. When the line was nearing completion, Mr Conacher, [our] late Manager...was invited by Lord Burton to a conference on the old subject of working the railway, and it speaks well of Lord Burton's powers of persuasion that Mr Conacher came back with a recommendation to the North British Board that we should work it at 50%, [when] it could not have been unknown to him that the West Highland Railway...was costing [us] more than 100% ...I naturally opposed [though] I only succeeded in getting the rate...increased to 60%* [but], wonderful to relate and much to my delight, Lord Burton declined the terms.

[I subsequently met] Lord Burton and...told him that, apart from the folly of promoting and interesting himself in the railway, he had never done a more foolish thing...I stated that [we] would... work the line at cost, or at 60% with an assured minimum. Neither of these suggestions was to Lord Burton's taste and [he] finally informed me that he would work the line himself.

At a subsequent meeting, I think with Mr Forman, we stated that we would work the line at 60% with a minimum of £6,000 per annum [and] an effective guarantee...This...led up to the meeting in London where...we reduced our requirements in respect of the maintenance of the line.

Whatever Mr Forman may have stated to Lord Burton, [he] put the traffic not at £7,000 or £8,000 per annum but at £15 per mile per week, which is equivalent to about £18,500 a year; but, taking Mr Forman's figures of £7,000 or £8,000, if they are reliable, Lord Burton runs no risk whatever in guaranteeing £6,000...

We are quite content that the Invergarry Company work the line themselves, as that will satisfy them of the reasonableness of our conditions. [If] there is a deficiency...between our receipts and our working costs, in what way does Lord Burton think that loss can be made up to us? [He] appears to think that...we should come to his assistance; but our undertaking exists for the purpose of earning a dividend for its shareholders and we have no funds [for] philanthropic purposes, even had we been indebted to the Invergarry Company instead of quite the contrary being the case.

NRS/BR/PYB/(S)1/410, Provisional Order (1902) to authorise working of Invergarry & Fort Augustus Railway by Highland Railway (with additional material): Wieland's account of Invergarry & Fort Augustus-North British negotiations, 1896-1901.

---

*   Conacher's starting figure was 60%. It is more than likely that Wieland misrepresented him as over-eager to compromise.

---

husband and other ladies came too. Spean Bridge Hotel was small, which compelled Reid to find additional accommodation in Fort William. He primed Malcolm to join him in greeting Pringle (coming overnight from London) and, as his final task, ordered the inspector's "on train" breakfast. Friday 16th August saw the new railway examined comprehensively from Spean Bridge junction to Fort Augustus. All spent that night there and on the following day, Pringle went over the short Loch Ness "extension", while the Invergarry & Fort Augustus directors met in their own Lovat Arms Hotel. Cunninghame was out of reach at Ben Alder shooting lodge. Lord Burton and Lambrick arrived by the Inverness mail steamer – the one from his son-in-law's Dochfour, the other from Burton on Trent via Perth; and Captain Ellice, newly returned from South Africa, was by chance another passenger aboard the vessel. Reid could report that the North British engine drivers had praised the condition of the track, while the inspector "seemed highly pleased".[35]

Pringle's verdict indeed proved positive. After the full Board of Trade Report had been received, Burton, Ellice and Malcolm went over the line for themselves, investigating the few faults identified and weighing up the improvements recommended. The board quickly decided to carry out all the work at once, so that re-inspection prior to opening would become a near formality; and their confidence was so far restored that they planned to confront the North British. Ellice, with Malcolm's assistance, would refresh the Invergarry & Fort Augustus case, then remonstrate with Jackson and Wieland.[36] Burton would prepare a supporting memorandum, detailing

the unreasonably severe conditions which had made the May conference a failure. ("*I half-incline to send [this] to each N.B. director.*")[37] Some five months had passed since the opening of the Mallaig Extension, and if (as rumour had it) the West Highland Company were soon to be fully absorbed into the North British, it might put negotiations on a different footing. Besides, Wieland was now installed as North British chairman, following the death of Sir William Laird. (See Chapter 7) Had his inflexibility hitherto been dictated by internal company politics? Might he now be ready to give and take? The North British, as beneficiaries of state aid, ought to look kindly on another socially desirable railway; and Parliament might be persuaded to make the extinction of West Highland independence conditional on North British concessions to the Invergarry & Fort Augustus.[38]

But Reid, as a rule the advocate of bold action, thought it pointless to target the North British board:

Even assuming that Mr Wieland's co-directors thought his terms onerous, it is very doubtful if they...would seriously differ from their chairman.[39]

And, contrary to Reid's half-expectations, the West Highland remained legally a separate entity until 1908, when amalgamation would finally be judged safe – after rating relief for the Mallaig line had been tested in the Scottish courts and payment of the Treasury Guarantee (applied annually from 1901) had become matter of fact.[40] Invergarry & Fort Augustus hopes were dashed when Wieland proved no more tractable. Having brushed aside Ellice's initiative, he savaged Lord

Burton's memorandum in a lengthy, unsparing rejoinder, which included a renewed attack on departed John Conacher. In 1896 Burton and his allies, said Wieland, had refused the reasonable request that they hold off until the North British gained experience of traffic between Glasgow and Fort William. Disregarding the territorial claims of the West Highland Company, they had promoted their line against North British wishes. Thereafter they had persisted in their Fort Augustus–Inverness scheme of 1896-7, precipitating a three-sided contest which in the end solved nothing, when they might have closed with the North British to achieve a line all through the Great Glen. And, by objecting to the award of additional time, they had jeopardised the West Highland Ballachulish Extension. In sum, for the Invergarry & Fort Augustus now to expect generous terms was shameless affrontery, and the North British Company were not a charitable body. (See panel on opposite page) This, as Reid put it, was "very strong", and he advised Burton to desist:

> [Mr Wieland] must be left severely alone. I suppose Captain Ellice and Mr Malcolm will now be satisfied.[41]

* * *

Could the Invergarry & Fort Augustus Company count on access to Spean Bridge station if they remained at odds with the North British? A time-consuming appeal to the Railway Commissioners might be unavoidable. Operating their line on their own account had come to seem less and less realistic. Following Harrison's more thorough costings, Reid noted Burton's deep dismay. (*"It almost seems a pity you showed them."*) The secretary believed that one "good strong tank engine" might suffice, though he had little idea of the likely price. On condition of the earliest possible reimbursement (by what means went unstated), Lord Burton and John Cunninghame pledged to find the purchase price of second-hand rolling stock from their personal resources. The sympathetic South Eastern & Chatham offered two elderly and doubtfully suitable tender locomotives, together with a selection of aged coaches and wagons, for approximately £7,000. Every calculation, however, led to the same sticking point: make-shifts might be contrived for the stabling and upkeep of rolling stock, but locomotive servicing and repair could not be skimped while North British good will remained in question and even the most basic provision was unaffordable.[42]

The North British were prepared, after the Board of Trade's favourable report, to send coaches, carriage trucks and horse boxes to Invergarry, for the convenience of Lord Burton and Mrs Ellice on their journeys south at the end of the 1901 season,[43] but there was no other sign that Wieland would relent. Having puzzled for several weeks, Burton, Ellice and Malcolm decided to request that the North British reassess the railway on the basis of direct running between Fort William and Fort Augustus, by the addition of a "fork line" (sketched by Harrison) at Highbridge.* Through workings, without reversal or change of train, would encourage those summer visitors who wanted to sample the classic Great Glen experience by day-excursion. It was time, they argued, to recognise the growing market for

round trips by train and steamer, as against the traditional extended tours patronised by the well-found middle class.[44] (See also panel above) This savoured of a desperate last throw. Tourist traffic alone could not justify the proposed Highbridge spur, which would have required a bridge over the main road, not inconsiderable earthworks and relatively complex points and signals. The real purpose was to re-engage with the North British and extract an admission (contradicting Wieland) that the Invergarry & Fort Augustus would attract an expanding summer traffic. In November Reid re-submitted the "fork" scheme as a definite proposal – and received general manager Jackson's "entirely discouraging" reply.[45]

The Invergarry & Fort Augustus board had already weighed capitulation to the North British against a second appeal to the hesitant Highland Company and they now decided on the latter.[46] Trusting to the good offices of William Whitelaw, they denounced Wieland's claim that they were already all but bound to his company. Nevertheless, directors and secretary were alike unwilling to admit how little leverage they would exercise in the ensuing discussions. For Reid, surrender in any guise remained unpalatable, and in his wishful thinking he still echoed the deceased Charles Forman – a through Oban–Fort William–Inverness railway must emerge in time and the Caledonian, choosing their moment, were sure to take a hand. His end-of-year letter was calculated to buoy up Burton:

> I have great hopes that by holding on…matters will develop in such a way as to get us out of our difficulties…better than we can at present. [When] the [Callander & Oban] Ballachulish Line is completed the Caledonian Company will be only too anxious to develop their property (sic) in conjunction with ours.[47]

* * *

The Highland board this time followed Whitelaw and declared themselves cautiously amenable. In January 1902 director Donald Grant first met with Reid, and thereafter Whitelaw and Cunninghame addressed the substance of a working and maintenance treaty. (Any leasing arrangement had been ruled out.) Ready in draft by late February, the Agreement was signed on 5th and 6th March – for the Highland in Inverness, by Grant, Whitelaw and company secretary Robert Park; for the Invergarry & Fort Augustus in London, by Burton, Cunninghame and Reid.[48]

The Highland pledged to work the Invergarry & Fort Augustus for ten years as a "single engine railway" (with

---

* Also described (confusingly) as the "loop line west of Spean Bridge" or the "new Spean Bridge curve".

Gairlochy station, above the River Spean, in 1914 looking east to the Highbridge gorge and Spean Bridge. The more than ample goods yard has a (solitary?) coal wagon, but there is no employment for a clearly marked platform barrow. The roof repairs in progress recall the Highland Company's allegation that inferior timber had compromised the station building.
(J L Stevenson collection, courtesy Hamish Stevenson)

another locomotive in reserve) and to develop the traffic by all feasible means. They would run four passenger or mixed trains daily in each direction during July, August and September, and two trains daily from October to June, giving West Highland and Loch Ness connections. They would pay the North British and West Highland charges at Spean Bridge. The owning company were to fix the timetables in detail and could vary fares when experience had been gained. They might require additional out-of-season trains, for which the working company would exact a surcharge. The Highland, like the North British, jibbed at unlimited "extraordinary maintenance"; they would undertake "ordinary maintenance", while for six years the Invergarry & Fort Augustus would be obliged to remedy any construction faults which came to light, bearing the whole cost of flood damage and similar. With accounts rendered monthly, the Highland were to receive £2,000 per half-year out of gross revenue. They might terminate the Agreement at six months notice, recovering any arrears if £4,000 per annum proved insufficient.[49]

Such gratitude as the little company showed was laced with suspicion and unstated reservations. Cunninghame warned his fellow directors not to communicate individually with their Highland counterparts until Whitelaw had won them over – they might harden the terms on offer if fully informed of North British demands. Thomas Wilson, the Highland general manager, was "put off" – he wanted to discuss (and might have opposed?) the concessions which Cunninghame had secured. That Grant might become his company's representative on the Invergarry & Fort Augustus board was grudgingly accepted.[50] And Reid not only counted on the Caledonian to temper the Highland's behaviour during the ensuing decade; he was ready to turn back to the North British, should Wieland, brought up short by the Highland's intervention, choose to offer better terms. It was a further complication that the North British contemplated another application (in parliamentary session 1901-2) to extend the West Highland's Ballachulish powers

– Reid calculated that the Invergarry & Fort Augustus could establish a new bargaining position by once more entering their objections.[51]

Wieland reacted with predictable rage when formally advised that the Highland meant to operate Invergarry & Fort Augustus trains in and out of West Highland Spean Bridge as soon as a Provisional Order could be obtained. In a personal letter to Lord Burton, he predicted that the Highland Company would prove a false friend but did not retract his scathing retort to Burton's reproachful memorandum of the previous year.[52] After he and Reid had crossed paths, and swords, at Westminster (both were on other business), Reid recounted their altercation to Grant. ("*I told him he should not act dog-in-the-manger. He had got his chance…*")[53] The North British would oppose the Provisional Order on several grounds, alleging that Whitelaw was determined to frustrate an all but completed agreement between the Invergarry & Fort Augustus and the North British. £4,000 was a quite unrealistic figure, which showed that the Highland were ready to sustain for a decade a loss unlikely to be retrieved from the owning company, whose finances must remain parlous – all to "block" the Great Glen. Though in 1897 the Highland claim for running powers between Fort Augustus and Spean Bridge had been logical, complementing their proposed line between Inverness and Fort Augustus, no like bill was before Parliament in 1901-2 and neither the West Highland Company nor the Invergarry & Fort Augustus contemplated a new scheme reaching to Inverness – so that the Highland's committing to work the Invergarry & Fort Augustus, separate from their own system, was utterly anomalous.[54]

With the 1902 summer season very much in mind, Whitelaw might have entertained a Whitsun opening, relying on the retrospective authority which the Provisional Order would confer. But at Spean Bridge the Invergarry & Fort Augustus possessed no powers east of the new junction, and to proceed in the face of implacable North British hostility and the possibility

The Calder Burn viaduct, near Aberchalder, was left to decay. It has been refurbished and given a new wooden deck, to carry the Great Glen Way.

(J L Stevenson, courtesy Hamish Stevenson)

of an interim interdict was demonstrably unwise.[55] Instead, the Highland concentrated on bringing the North British to confirm that they would honour the terms of access negotiated by Forman and settled with the Invergarry & Fort Augustus two years earlier – a 50/50 division of station costs (including general upkeep), wages, uniforms, stores and stationery; and a rental payment to the West Highland Company in proportion to traffic. Though Cunninghame proposed to challenge these heavy conditions, Reid warned that the North British might seize any excuse to "break off". It was safer to acquiesce, and even to submit to more demands. (*"[This will] show how reasonable we have been and how unreasonable they are."*)[56] He advised against arbitration:

> *I do not think that the Railway Commissioners would force them, simply to save us providing accommodation of our own.*[57]

Wieland at first insisted that any arrangement at Spean Bridge depended absolutely on his company's working the Invergarry & Fort Augustus. Faced with retaliatory opposition to that session's North British measures, in June 1902 he retreated – at which a gleeful Reid urged that *"we ask everything we possibly can"*.[58] But it next appeared that scrutiny of the Provisional Order would be devolved to the Scottish Office, in which case a decision in favour of the North British might not be subject to appeal (so Burton discovered, to his alarm).* The Highland Company, where Whitelaw's influence now thoroughly prevailed, resolved to push matters to a conclusion by different means. They would lodge a bill for powers to work and maintain the Invergarry & Fort Augustus in the next session of Parliament. This had two disadvantages – it gave the North British ample time *"to devise some new scheme of opposition"*,[59] and the line would lie unopened through another winter. Wieland's ingenuity indeed was not exhausted. He next suggested that a Highbridge connection might be reconsidered – prompting conjecture in the railway press that, after all, the North British would attempt for a third time to capture the Great Glen, by a third version of Forman's 1894 West Highland Inverness Extension.[60] Local traffic between Lochaber and the North would be encouraged and through running between Oban and Inverness brought one step closer, strengthening the West Highland case, if the Highbridge spur were included.

Though Wieland may have sanctioned the preliminaries

of a fresh North British-cum-West Highland bill (no Roy Bridge–Invergloy cut-off, but running powers between Spean Bridge and Fort Augustus and new construction onwards to Inverness?), he certainly did not intend that it should go forward. Rumour alone might suffice to deter the more nervous Highland directors and shareholders, whom he had loudly threatened with retribution unless they gave up their unnatural alliance with the Invergarry & Fort Augustus. David Reid was disposed to take these Great Glen whispers seriously. Financial constraints notwithstanding, his directors should make ready to do battle again for their own Inverness extension.[61] He requested that Thomas Allison (above) be alert for any North British activity "on the ground" at Highbridge (where Lord Abinger owned the left bank of the River Spean) – and Allison might report too whether Fort William and Lochaber could be mobilised behind an Invergarry & Fort Augustus scheme.[62] Where Reid deceived himself, Whitelaw stood his ground, discounting Wieland's sound and fury. The year closed with the Highland's enabling Bill in preparation, and no conflicting North British or West Highland bills had been deposited.

References

Keyden, Strang & Girvan abbreviated to KSG.

NRS/BR/LNE/8/764 – because the Treasury's Mallaig Guarantee ran till 1931, the North British general manager's files relating to the West Highland Extension were reclassified "LNE" from 1923.

1. NRS/BR/PYB(S)1/511/1, Invergarry & Fort Augustus Railway, brief for Parliament (1903) – including correspondence with North British Railway, 1898-1901.

2. Ibid. (See also NRS/BR/NBR/8/1401, North British Railway, files relating to Invergarry & Fort Augustus Railway, 1898-1903.)

3. Ibid. George Malcolm to John Conacher, 22 October 1898 and David Reid to Conacher, 20 December 1898.

4. Ibid. Conacher to Reid, 13 January 1899. NRS/BR/IFA/1/2, Invergarry & Fort Augustus Railway minutes, 27 January 1899.

5. NRS/BR/LNE/8/764/Box 2, general manager's files relating to West Highland (Mallaig Extension) Railway, Alexander Wilson to Conacher, 7 March 1899, enclosing plan of proposed Banavie

---

* In the event, this procedural reform was postponed.

station on western bank of Caledonian Canal. (The station as built was sited on the eastern side.) See also ibid, Simpson & Wilson to William Jackson, 13 December 1899.

6. NRS/BR/IFA/1/2, Invergarry & Fort Augustus Railway minutes, 15 June 1899, 17 August 1899 and 15 January 1900

7. NRS/BR/PYB/(S)1/410, Provisional Order (1902) to authorise working of Invergarry & Fort Augustus Railway by Highland Railway (with additional material): Wieland's account of Invergarry & Fort Augustus-North British negotiations, 1896-1901. NRS/BR/IFA/1/2, Invergarry & Fort Augustus Railway minutes, 7 October 1899 and 15 December 1900.

8. NRS/BR/PYB/(S)1/511/1, Forman to Watson, 12 February 1900, Watson to Forman, 14 February 1900, and ensuing correspondence between Reid and Watson, 15 February- 4 June 1900.

9. NRS/BR/IFA/1/2, Invergarry & Fort Augustus Railway minutes, 15 January 1900. NRS/BR/PYB/(S)1/511/1, Invergarry & Fort Augustus Railway, brief for Parliament (1903), Reid to Watson, 24 February 1900.

10. NRS/BR/PYB/(S)1/511/1, Watson to Reid, 19 and 22 February, 1 March and 31 May 1900; and Reid to Watson, 24 February, 9 March and 30 May 1900.

11. NRS/BR/PYB/(S)1/410, Wieland's account of Invergarry & Fort Augustus-North British negotiations, 1896-1901.

12. NRS/BR/LNE/8/764/Box 2, Simpson & Wilson to George Wieland, 22 May 1900, Wieland to Jackson, 23 May 1900, Jackson to Simpson & Wilson, 28 May 1900 and Simpson & Wilson to Jackson. 2 June 1900.

13. NRS/BR/PYB/(S)1/511/1, Reid to Watson, 4 June 1900.

14. NRS/BR/IFA/1/2, Invergarry & Fort Augustus Railway minutes, 15 January, 21 March, 19 July, 4 October and 6 December 1900, and 10 January 1901.

15. Ibid.

16. NRS/BR/IFA/1/2, Invergarry & Fort Augustus Railway minutes, 4 October and 6 December 1900 and 10 January 1901.

17. NRS/BR/IFA/4/5, KSG to Malcolm, 15 December 1900 and Reid to Burton, 17 December 1900. NRS/BR/IFA/1/2, Invergarry & Fort Augustus Railway minutes, 10 January 1901.

18. NRS/BR/IFA/1/2, Invergarry & Fort Augustus Railway minutes., 6 December 1900

19. NRS/BR/IFA/1/2, Invergarry & Fort Augustus Railway minutes, 6 December 1900 and 10 January 1901. NRS/BR/IFA/4/5, Reid to Burton, 17 and 18 January 1901.

20. NRS/BR/IFA/1/2, Invergarry & Fort Augustus Railway minutes, 21 February 1901.

21. NRS/BR/IFA/4/5, Reid to Allison & MacNiven, 20 December 1900; to Thomas Allison, 20 and 29 December 1900 and 3 January, 13 March, 9, 15 and 30 May 1901; to H.B. Neave, 31 January 1901; and to Malcolm, 4 April 1901; also, memorandum for Invergarry & Fort Augustus Railway board, 7 March 1901. NRS/BR/IFA/1/2, Invergarry & Fort Augustus Railway minutes, 16 April and 17 August 1901.

22. NRS/BR/IFA/1/2, Invergarry & Fort Augustus Railway minutes, 20 April 1899.

23. NRS/BR/PYB/(S)1/410, Wieland's account of Invergarry & Fort Augustus-North British negotiations, 1896-1901.

24. NRS/BR/IFA/1/2 Invergarry & Fort Augustus Railway Minutes, 21 February 1901. NRS/BR/IFA/4/5, Reid to Burton, 15 March 1901.

25. NRS/BR/IFA/4/5, Reid to Burton, 27 March 1901.

26. NRS/BR/IFA/4/5, Reid to Burton, 25 March 1901. NRS/BR/IFA/1/2, Invergarry & Fort Augustus Railway minutes, 6 June 1901.

27. NRS/BR/IFA/1/2, Invergarry & Fort Augustus Railway minutes, 6 June 1901, noting the Highland Railway's decision not to proceed to an agreement (letter dated 23 April).

28. NRS/BR/PYB(S)1/511/1, Invergarry & Fort Augustus Railway, brief for Parliament (1903).

29. Ibid.

30. Ibid. NRS/BR/PYB/(S)1/410, Wieland's account of Invergarry & Fort Augustus-North British negotiations, 1896-1901.

31. NRS/BR/IFA/4/5, Reid to Malcolm, 17 May 1901.

32. NRS/BR/IFA/1/2 Invergarry & Fort Augustus Railway minutes, 6 June 1901

33. NRS/BR/IFA/4/5, Reid to Burton and to Railway Department, Board of Trade, 5 August 1901. Article by A Buswell, *Highland Railway Journal*, 90, 2009. (See also Glenquoich letter books, Lochiel Papers, Lochaber Archive, June-July 1901.)

34. NRS/BR/IFA/4/5, Reid to Burton, 5 August 1901

35. NRS/BR/IFA/4/5, Reid to Burton and to John Cunninghame, 21 August 1901.

36. NRS/BR/IFA/1/2, Invergarry & Fort Augustus Railway minutes, 17 August and 10 October 1901. NRS/BR/IFA/4/5, Malcolm to Edward Ellice, 23 August 1901 and (?) September 1901.

37. NRS/BR/IFA/4/5, Burton to Reid, 30 September 1901, forwarded to Cunninghame, 1 October 1901.

38. KSG to Grahames, Curry & Spens, 14 February 1902.

39. NRS/BR/IFA/4/5, Reid to Burton, 4 October 1901.

40. NRS/BR/IFA/4/5, Reid to Burton, 19 March 1902. NRS/BR/WEH/1/2, West Highland Railway minutes, 9 April 1907.

41. NRS/BR/IFA/4/5, Reid to Burton, 15 November 1901.

42. NRS/BR/IFA/1/2, Invergarry & Fort Augustus Railway minutes, 10 October and 22 November 1901. NRS/BR/IFA/4/5, Reid to J.E. Harrison, 11 October and 14 and 22 November 1901, to J. Lambrick, 11 November 1901, and to Burton 14 November 1901.

43. Article by A Buswell, *Highland Railway Journal*, 90, 2009. (See also Glenquoich letter books, Lochiel Papers, Lochaber Archive, September-November 1901.)

44. NRS/BR/IFA/1/2, Invergarry & Fort Augustus Railway minutes, Reid's memorandum (following board meeting), 10 October 1901. NRS/BR/IFA/4/5, Reid to Burton 16 and 25 October 1901.

45. NRS/BR/IFA/4/5, Reid to Jackson, 6 November 1901, and to Cunninghame and Malcolm, 8 November 1901, reporting Jackson's reply.

46. NRS/BR/IFA/1/2. Invergarry & Fort Augustus Railway minutes, 22 November 1901

47. NRS/BR/IFA/4/5, Reid to Burton, 23 December 1901.

48. NRS/BR NRS/BR/PYB(S)1/511/1, Invergarry & Fort Augustus Railway – North British Railway correspondence, 1898-1901.

49. Ibid.

50. NRS/BR/I&FAR/4/5, Reid to Burton, 27 January, and 10 and 12 February 1902, and to Donald Grant, 1 March 1902

51. NRS/BR/IFA/4/5, Reid to Burton, 12 February and 19 March 1902

52. NRS/BR/IFA/4/5, Reid to Malcolm, 19 March 1902, and to Burton, 11 and 14 April 1902, touching on "a curious letter from Mr Wieland".

53. NRS/BR/IFA/4/5, Reid to Grant, 19 March 1902

54. NRS/BR/NBR/1/50, North British Railway Minutes, 13 March and 8 June 1902. (See also NRS/BR/NBR/8/1401, North British Railway, files relating to Invergarry & Fort Augustus Railway, 1898-1903.)

55. NRS/BR/IFA/4/5, Reid to Burton, 21 and 25 March 1902

56. NRS/BR/IFA/4/5, Reid to Whitelaw, 25 and 28 March 1902, and to Jackson, 2 April 1902.

57. NRS/BR/IFA/4/5, Reid to Burton, 2 April 1902

58. NRS/BR/IFA/4/5, Reid to Malcolm, 7 April and 6 June 1902, to Jackson, 9 April 1902, and to Burton, 5 May and 9 June 1902. KSG to Grahames, Curry & Spens, 6 June 1902. NRS/BR/NBR/1/50, North British Railway minutes, 3 July 1902.

59. NRS/BR/IFA/4/5, Reid to Burton and to Cunninghame, 10 June 1902.

60. For example, *Railway Times* (Inverness correspondent), 14 June 1902.

61. NRS/BR/IFA/4/5, Reid to Burton, 10 November 1902.

62. NRS/BR/IFA/4/5, Reid to Allison, 29 October 1902.

CHAPTER NINE

LAST BATTLE, 1902-03

The Meeting took into consideration the question of withdrawing the Company's Petition against the North British Company's Bill…and resolved that £125 [per annum] be offered…for the use of their Spean Bridge Station and Staff, and if this be accepted the Company's Petition is to be withdrawn.

A correspondence with Mr Neave, Solicitor, Caledonian Railway Company, and Mr Whitelaw was submitted, with reference to the facilities wanted by the Caledonian Company…in certain events…

[Letters] from and to Mr Park, Secretary, Highland Railway Company…were read, and a draft of a proposed Supplementary Agreement with the Highland Company was submitted. [The] Meeting resolved, after hearing Mr Whitelaw's view (he having attended for this purpose) that the opening of the Line be postponed till next year, owning to the impossibility of getting the Bill to authorise the Highland Company to work the Line through Parliament this Session…

[The] Meeting decided to delay the [Board of Trade] re-inspection till next year [and] instructed the Engineers to endeavour to arrange with Mr Young or others as to…the maintenance of the Line and buildings for another twelve months…

Invergarry & Fort Augustus Railway minutes, 25th June 1902

The Invergarry say they cannot; the North British say they will not, except on terms which the Invergarry will not accept; so…we are the only company…interested.

Thomas Wilson, general manager, Highland Railway, House of Commons, May 1903

* * *

As described in Chapters 5-7, the Invergarry & Fort Augustus Railway Act of 1896 had ushered in several months of inter-company manoeuvre, culminating in the triangular Great Glen contest of 1897, which left the vexed question of a westerly through route to Inverness unresolved. Four uncomfortable but comparatively peaceful years had followed, while the Spean Bridge–Fort Augustus line was completed (see Chapters 7 and 8) – an interlude which ended in March 1902, when the Highland Company, rather than see Lord Burton and his fellow-directors capitulate to the North British, had agreed to undertake working and maintenance.[1] To proceed by Provisional Order, against unrelenting North British opposition, was deemed hazardous, and by July they had turned to the surer course of parliamentary enactment

a year later. (See Chapter 8) In the interval, while the little railway stayed unopened, preparation and manoeuvre would grow feverish again.

The practicalities were not easily settled. Recognising that his company might be forced to provide their own booking office and waiting room at Spean Bridge station and perhaps a stationmaster too, David Reid reported that there was room enough for a small building "at the end of our platform" (i.e. the additional bay which Charles Forman had included in his junction layout). Lord Abinger, who offered a cottage for the prospective stationmaster, was ready to donate the parcel of land required for a separate entrance to the bay platform. Contractor James Young consented to continue watching over the railway into 1903 for the lump sum of £500, on condition that his quotation for the new entrance was accepted.[2] In the Highland's view, the Invergarry & Fort Augustus should be worked under one-engine-in-steam rules, as avowedly no more than a feeder to the West Highland – and on that basis the North British would have no reason to demand running powers. However, the line had been equipped for token (electric train staff) operation, and to dispense with it would signify lasting acceptance of branch line status and extinguish any lingering hope of advance to Inverness. Lord Burton and Reid had thought to purchase one all-purpose tank engine of sufficient power; but initially the Highland looked to deploy two tender locomotives (one of them the "spare") and stipulated that turntables be installed. In consequence, Spean Bridge would obtain Newtonmore's "redundant" table, dismantled and sent via Perth. (To Crianlarich, the Caledonian imposed no charge; the North British were predictably less obliging.) It had already been decided, before financial realities struck home, to have a two-road engine shed at Fort Augustus and a one-road shed at Spean Bridge. Among the Highland's other concerns was the water supply at Invergarry, as doubtfully adequate for both station and locomotive servicing.[3]

Reid and the Invergarry & Fort Augustus directors were to present their own case in Parliament (including, if they insisted, their expectations of one day recovering a real freedom of action). William Whitelaw and his officers would explain and defend the proposed working and maintenance treaty, without pretence that "blocking" had not entered the Highland's calculations. In rendering assistance to the Invergarry & Fort Augustus, he was also insuring against the "ruinous competition" which must ensue if the North British took possession of the southern half of the Great Glen and thereafter drove on to Inverness.[4] Such frankness might well be the best policy, but it indicated too how Whitelaw had taken the measure of George Wieland's bluster. The North British petition against the Provisional Order (which would become their petition against the Highland's 1902-3 Bill) he thought overblown and easily countered.[5] Burton, for his part, was eager to have the testimony of the two departed general managers, John Conacher and Charles Steel – the one would *"prove what he advised the NB Coy to agree to"* and the other would *"support the Highland Company's side"*.[6]

Reid was ready, as before, to contrast the Treasury's generosity to the West Highland (whereby, he implied, the North British had incurred moral obligations) with Wieland's harshness towards the Invergarry & Fort Augustus; and he intended to invoke North British "mistreatment" of the Clyde, Ardrishaig & Crinan Company a decade earlier.[7] He was left, with Whitelaw's approval, to reassure the Caledonian, where James Thompson (Sir James Thompson from 1897) had retired and joined the board (1900), becoming company chairman in 1901. During May 1902, Reid met with Thompson, Robert Millar (the new general manager) and company secretary H. P. Neave; and he saw Millar again two months later. It was settled that the Caledonian would receive balancing rights, should the North British obtain powers of any sort between Spean Bridge and Fort Augustus. Thompson warned that facilities over the West Highland should not be purchased by granting North British access to Fort Augustus – Lord Burton would be well advised to steer clear entirely of the Wieland regime. And, as if to demonstrate the once more febrile times, Neave voiced his apprehension that Highland and North British might reach a secret understanding, consigning all the West Highland's Great Glen traffic via Craigendoran and depriving the Callander & Oban of exchange at Crianlarich.[8] Though Wieland was forced to admit that he could not prevent the new Spean Bridge junction being brought into use, he was otherwise irreconcilable; and Reid remained on tenterhooks in the final months of 1902 to learn what the North British Bill for the new parliamentary session contained.[9] In the event there was no Great Glen element, while Wieland's threat to mobilise

dissent among Whitelaw's shareholders came to nothing – the Highland's Wharncliffe Meeting to endorse their 1902-3 Bill had passed off without incident.[10]

Reid nursed the suspicion that Whitelaw's sturdy confidence cloaked some undisclosed bargain with the North British, just as Neave had suggested. Burton must be vigilant:

> [There] is nothing to hinder [their] coming to some new Peace Agreement (sic) [We need] a binding agreement with the Highland Company that they are not to come to terms with the N.B. Co…[11]

With no more reason to trust the Invergarry & Fort Augustus, the Highland chairman had noted Reid's reluctance to engage wholeheartedly as long as there was any chance that Wieland would relent. Whitelaw insisted on seeing all the correspondence between Keyden, Strang & Girvan and the North British, back to 1896, and queried Reid's goal of a Callander & Oban alliance.[12] The secretary's stubborn belief that this could be achieved (which Whitelaw discounted), is partly explained by his regular dealings, as agent for the Lanarkshire & Ayrshire Railway, with certain Caledonian officers and directors – he made soundings, as opportunity offered, and glossed these as optimistically as he could. To Highland director Donald Grant, Reid responded that there had been no formal discussions as to "taking powers to make a line from Ballachulish to Fort William", but added ambiguously (perhaps to test the Highland's reaction?) that the Caledonian would be sure to welcome an independent promotion. In his reports to Burton he exaggerated every flicker of Caledonian goodwill. (*"I gather they are watching our movements carefully"*.)[13]

The Highland board reiterated their resolve to await the opening of the Invergarry & Fort Augustus under statutory authority. Though the "Law's delays" offered almost certain immunity, the risks attendant on an earlier, irregular beginning were not to be run. Like the Board of Trade's re-inspection, a comprehensive examination of the railway and its signalling equipment to the satisfaction of the working company was held over into 1903. In due course, the Highland engineer would

With North British notices much in evidence, a North British train pauses at Invergloy Halt, a little south from the summit of the line, in July 1914.

(J L Stevenson collection, courtesy Hamish Stevenson)

emphasise how well the line had withstood the winter floods. His evidence, like the testimony of other friendly witnesses, was calculated to show that maintenance need not be costly, so helping to justify the questionable estimate of £4,000 annually for working expenses, where the North British had demanded £6,000.[14]

* * *

George Wieland protested that the Invergarry & Fort Augustus, considered as a West Highland appendage, already all but belonged to his company; and it is striking how, in attacking the Provisional Order for which the Highland first applied, he chose to revive all the old North British pretensions in the Great Glen – pretensions which had very much receded under his chairmanship:

[Although] the original West Highland line ended at Fort William, it...was designed for the purpose of ultimately being extended to Inverness [and] our intention...has all along been well-known...The North British Company, as well as the public, are deeply interested in preventing anything being done to impair [the creation of] an...efficient and short through route from Inverness to Glasgow and the South. The Highland Company are already possessed of the route by Aviemore and Perth, and, if...allowed to appropriate...any part of the Loch Ness route (sic), they will have a monopoly... [Their] sole aim...is...to obtain a strategical benefit at [our] expense.[15]

When in parliamentary session 1902-3 the Highland resorted instead to their enabling Bill, the hostile North British petition, emphasising West Highland rights, was just as strongly worded and deplored Whitelaw's "blocking" intentions:

[The Highland Company] will lose money, but they know... and admit that this Agreement [with the Invergarry & Fort Augustus] will help to prevent [us] from completing the alternative route...[16]

The North British discovered new arguments, or at least new variations on the old. With the Aviemore cut-off in use since 1898, the Highland could face the challenge of a completed railway through the Great Glen on better than equal terms – why then, save for self-interest, should they resist? Why should Parliament any longer heed their traditional plea of disadvantage and imminent ruin? Moreover, the revenues of the West Highland Mallaig Extension, opened in 1901, had fallen short of expectations, while working expenses had exceeded all projections. Having committed £2½ million to the West Highland route, the North British had more than fulfilled their public duty; and only by securing a larger share of the traffic between the Central Belt and Inverness (i.e. larger than they commanded at Perth) could they hope to recoup some fraction of this heavy outlay. An amicable settlement with the Invergarry & Fort Augustus was self-evidently the first step, and the Highland were unscrupulous interlopers, bent on preventing it.[17]

But earlier Wieland had declared his opposition for the foreseeable future to any further expenditure in the western Highlands; and general manager William Jackson had warned Reid only a year before that the North British directors had come to doubt the value of access to Inverness. On-the-record,

in any case, was the North British pledge of 1889 that a west-coast railhead would remain their primary goal, after the West Highland had been completed to Fort William. Incontrovertible likewise were their several statements in 1894, specifying the Mallaig Extension as an urgent commitment, with connections to Ballachulish and into Strathspey next for consideration, after the newly opened West Highland had proved its worth. Despite the North British claim to have "reserved" the Great Glen, a West Highland move on Inverness had been treated as something for the vague long-term. In 1895, following the collapse of their ten-year Agreement with the Highland Company shutting up the Glen, they had willingly seen it rewritten; and in 1895-6 they had opposed the Invergarry & Fort Augustus as a premature scheme. They had complained that the two West Highland Inverness Extension Bills (the one withdrawn in 1895 and the other defeated in 1897) were forced on them by circumstances.

It strained credulity for the North British to assert that entry to Inverness was not only their due but had always been their purpose. Their plea that the Mallaig Extension had turned out badly invited the old retort – they had been misguided to back the West Highland in the first place and must pay the price. Their whole stance defied the known facts; and it rested on a forced reading of the defunct 1889 Agreement – that the Highland had conceded a West Highland title to the Great Glen which the North British might assert whenever they chose. Wieland, with no real intention of furthering a third West Highland Inverness Extension, may have counted on convincing the Highland directors that, unless they withdrew, they faced a renewed fight of 1897 proportions; and his reported second thoughts on a Highbridge connection (see Chapter 8) point to some such strategy. But Whitelaw was not deterred, and the North British could only persist in the thin pretence of violated rights, coupled with the fiction that the Highland's wanton intervention had frustrated an amicable, next-to-finalised settlement with the Invergarry & Fort Augustus. It became, perforce, the North British argument that Wieland had merely been cautious (and unintentionally irascible?) in stating his terms. ("By...1901 we had very considerable experience of what the receipts of lines in the western Highlands ... are...") Misunderstandings had unfortunately arisen, and the minimum, which Lord Burton found so oppressive, might now be submitted to an arbiter nominated by the Board of Trade, together with any other clause to which the Invergarry & Fort Augustus objected.[18] This picture was altogether unconvincing.

* * *

In Parliament in 1903 the Highland stood on surer ground: some means must be found to bring the Spean Bridge–Fort Augustus line into use, and North British interests, for what these might be worth, need not be injured.[19] Whitelaw instructed his general manager and departmental officers that their testimony should be low-key. Here was an unexceptional working and maintenance pact, and administration of the Invergarry & Fort Augustus, detached from the Highland system, need not be problematic. On this, the two companies must speak as one in Parliament. David Reid could not dissent, but he pressed his directors to make sure that they were not nudged into a subordinate role.[20] Because Lord Burton planned to spend the spring in Spain, George Malcolm and John Cunninghame were designated as principal witnesses.[21] However, Burton returned to give his evidence and Cunninghame's testimony was not required. In the end John Conacher and Charles Steel were not invited to appear – either of them might have said too much.

It became Malcolm's task to explain why the Invergarry & Fort Augustus had turned to the Highland Company, as their last hope of friendly assistance. Drawing on his experience as factor at Corrour, he enlarged on a favourite theme – the North British, for all their talk of loss and sacrifice, had not done their best for the West Highland. Control of territory, not patient development of traffic, was their watchword; and they had brought the same attitude to their negotiations with the Invergarry & Fort Augustus, during which he had tried in vain to coax Wieland towards a larger view. Though determined to treat the line as a West Highland branch, the North British had refused an equivalent guarantee. Their unexpected offer to work at cost had been of no advantage, and afterwards Wieland had insisted on the impossible minimum, adding the insulting demand that the Invergarry & Fort Augustus directors bind themselves personally.[22] Malcolm pointed out, as did Whitelaw and other witnesses, how in 1897 the North British had indicated (between Houses, after the Highland's Inverness–Fort Augustus Bill had prevailed in the Commons) that they were prepared to share the Great Glen. (See Chapter 6) Why should they now object to the Highland's stepping in, on terms in no way sinister and probably for a finite period, to succour the Invergarry & Fort Augustus? Whitelaw did not deny that his company looked to protect themselves – this being so, Wieland's prediction that the Highland would tear up their bargain made no sense. And if good faith were the question, what of the North British record? Ten years earlier, they had deserted the Clyde, Ardrishaig & Crinan Company, in favour of the West Highland. The promised Loch Fyne Light Railway had not been built. That the West Highland Ballachulish Extension was a sham could no longer be doubted.[23]

All in all, though the Highland found ample scope to put the North British on the defensive, it mattered more that Whitelaw's instincts proved sound. Public and press demanded a resolution, and John Dewar MP, who had recaptured Inverness-shire for the Liberal Party in the general election of 1900,* spoke out in support of his constituents – Parliament must make sure in session 1902-3 that trains would begin to run between Spean Bridge and Fort Augustus.[24] The House of Commons Committee, not uninfluenced, heard the evidence

Thomas Wilson, ex-North Eastern Railway, the Highland Company's general manager from 1899 to 1910. He "missed the excitement" of the Great Glen parliamentary set-piece in 1897 but played his part in the final contest of 1903. (Railway Magazine)

for and against the Highland Bill over three days (19th-21st May 1903) and the outcome was in little doubt.

* * *

Lord Burton and George Malcolm were not pressed to recount the whole story of the Invergarry & Fort Augustus, and neither volunteered it. The North British Company, they both agreed, ought to be able to work the line more cheaply than the Highland ever could; but Wieland had refused, save on the harshest of conditions. Even a renewed and genuine offer to work at cost would not better the Highland's terms. The North British professed good will, but their requirements had grown more and more stringent. Independent operation could no longer be thought of (though it remained a long-term hope), and the little company were ready "to accept almost anything", which meant bowing to Wieland if Parliament did not approve the proposed Highland–Invergarry & Fort Augustus Agreement. "Lease" was a debatable word, but the arrangement was certainly terminable and could not extinguish the West Highland's so-called right to reach Inverness. The Highland directors were not "Greeks bearing gifts", and Whitelaw's formula allowed the owning company some discretion in respect of timetable, fares and other charges.[25]

Burton confirmed that the Invergarry & Fort Augustus board were collectively more-or-less their railway's owners – though John Neilson, no longer a director, held £50,000 in shares and the Forman Trustees £35,000. His personal stake, much to his anxiety, had increased to £150,000. £331,000 had been expended (only some £10,000 more than the company's original Act had authorised), though this did not include outlay on the latest parliamentary contest. The adverse balance was covered by Lloyds' Bonds, which he and the other directors now held. On the positive side, every Board of Trade requirement had been met, and the line, which had suffered little over two winters, might open almost at once. Better local transport along the Great Glen was the urgent need and local traffic would just suffice to make the railway viable, if summer tourist earnings were maximised.[26] The proposed Highbridge spur, for direct connection with Fort William, was therefore very desirable, but it could not be installed without North British cooperation. Malcolm struck a similar note. (*"My only object, as a public man in the district, is to get railway facilities."*) The off-season service on the Caledonian Canal had deteriorated (he did not say why) and it was more important than ever to improve communication between Fort William and Inverness. In conjunction with a fast Loch Ness steamer, the Invergarry & Fort Augustus would facilitate same-day return travel, something hitherto impossible – and there had been much complaint, after the Highland Company's intervention became known, that the line was not brought into use during 1902.[27]

Lord Lovat confirmed that there had been general dismay. Speaking as a county councillor, Lachlan MacKintosh concurred – he divided the former Letterfinlay estate with Miller of Corriegour and others, and they would all use the railway halt at Major Bailey's Invergloy, instead of driving to Spean Bridge or joining MacBrayne's steamer at Laggan Locks. The Duke of Portland, testifying on behalf of the fishing and shooting lessees along the Great Glen, thought it "immaterial" whether Highland or North British became the working company.[28] Abbot Linse acknowledged how the people of Fort Augustus had distrusted the Highland Company, but now, he felt sure, they all wished *that [the Highland] should come*", and the Abbey tenants were certainly of this opinion. With a train service established, he hoped to reopen the Abbey School, which had been handicapped by unreliable transport since its first establishment. In 1897 the Highland had admitted that, at heart, they wanted no railway at all, while the Invergarry & Fort Augustus had just begun to build. The situation in 1903 was not at all comparable. (Linse, like Malcolm, also harped on the undependable canal service.)[29]

Both Lovat and MacKintosh stressed that they had engaged to give evidence in the public interest, while admitting "a partiality" for the Highland Railway. (The latter's family roots were in Highland territory.) Lovat told how in 1896-7 he had made known his distaste for a line along Loch Ness, whether Highland, Invergarry & Fort Augustus or West Highland-cum-North British. Steamers serving both shores were sufficient, and all the proprietors would prefer that a through railway, whether conventional or of light construction, was not again attempted – though some thought that a light line to Lochend, if revived, might be a useful improvement. He agreed that traffic from Invermoriston and points south would tend to the West Highland, no matter who worked the Invergarry & Fort Augustus, and that there was, in addition, a "draw" to Glasgow *for work in the winter season*". Though the large, well-established Inverness markets for livestock and wool would exert their own draw and water transport would remain competitive for coal and other heavy goods, Lovat believed that the Spean Bridge–Fort Augustus line could narrowly pay its way once tourist business had been developed to the utmost.[30]

William Whitelaw stated bluntly that the Highland Company ("*as long as I have anything to do with them*") would resist a North British advance to Inverness, but he submitted that this was not the matter before Parliament. In assisting the Invergarry & Fort Augustus, the Highland were doing only what the North British should have done; and the West Highland claim to the Great Glen – which, in any case, he denied – could not be impaired by any clause in the proposed working and maintenance treaty. The North British must have realised long since that the Highland's territory afforded a living for only one trunk railway, and their latest remonstrations could be dismissed. The truth was that they had expected the Invergarry & Fort Augustus directors to capitulate. Whitelaw did not count on operating the little line at a profit, but neither should there be a serious loss, and his shareholders were

content to make the experiment. The North British might make difficulties over exchange at Spean Bridge but the Caledonian were most unlikely to hinder any Great Glen traffic handled by the Callander & Oban and transferred at Crianlarich – and, in either event, the Railway Commissioners could be counted on to provide a remedy. Small consignments of sundry needs would be sent to Fort Augustus by steamer, and office staff could travel to and fro by the same means, ensuring administrative overview. For goods traffic on their own system, the Highland Company made much use of "foreign" vans and wagons which had been worked north through Perth, and he anticipated a similar pattern on the Invergarry & Fort Augustus. There would be little occasion to send more vehicles from Inverness.[31]

There were few plausible Scottish precedents for working the Spean Bridge–Fort Augustus line at long range; south-of-the-Border examples in districts quite unlike the Great Glen scarcely applied. Here, under cross-examination, Whitelaw floundered. (North British experience, with their system divided for many years by the water breaks of Forth and Tay, was no true parallel.) Pressed to justify the long roundabout trundle of Highland engines and rolling stock from Inverness to Spean Bridge via Perth, Dunblane and Crianlarich, he replied (clutching at straws?) that the journey would be a little shortened by the impending new link from Comrie along Loch Earn to Callander & Oban Balquhidder.* General manager Thomas Wilson, coming to his chairman's aid, played down how unusual it all was. The Railway Clearing House would determine a reasonable charge for the passage of the Highland convoy over Caledonian and North British metals, and he expected the Caledonian to remit their share. He had satisfied himself that "one locomotive plus a reserve" would prove adequate. Two engines could readily be spared – over nine months of any year, outwith hectic August-to-October, the Highland were, if anything, over-provided. Keeping in touch with Fort Augustus by steamer should be a simple matter, Wilson added, in contrast to the difficulties which he experienced daily in communicating with Wick and Thurso, at his own company's northern extremity.[32] William Roberts, the Highland engineer, gave similarly emollient evidence. He had found the Invergarry & Fort Augustus in good condition. Given the proposed timetable, routine upkeep would not be troublesome. "Extraordinary maintenance" was to remain the owning company's responsibility for six years, time enough for any flaws in construction to be revealed – which had gone far, he believed, to reassure the Highland directors and shareholders. And fellow-engineer John Ferguson, of Formans & McCall, asserted that the Invergarry & Fort Augustus must prove cheaper to maintain than the West Highland – the Great Glen did not compare with bleak and exposed Rannoch Moor.[33]

Wilson, who had "*missed the pleasure*" (so counsel for the Highland Railway put it) of previous parliamentary bouts, copied Whitelaw's disarming style – the proposed arrangements were quite unexceptional and parliamentary proceedings almost a formality – so that the necessary powers (not specified in any of the company's acts) might be rendered explicit. It was fatuous to suggest that the Highland could

_____

* The Lochearnhead, St Fillans & Comrie Railway, a Caledonian subsidiary, was not completed until 1905.

Gairlochy station, looking west, with Glen Spean debouching into the Great Glen. As at Invergarry, the signal box seemed in appearance something between the little cabins on the West Highland proper and the roomier boxes on the Mallaig Extension. In fact, all the Railway Signal Company boxes on the Mallaig line and on the Invergarry & Fort Augustus were of very similar design and construction. (D Yuill collection)

impose an effective "block" or coerce their customers to send via Inverness and Perth. The farmers of the Great Glen knew their own minds and would consign by the West Highland whenever they chose. Some of the existing traffic which reached the Highland by the vessels plying the Caledonian Canal would go instead to Spean Bridge, but he held to the precept that a new railway invariably generated new business, not all of which, in this instance, need be captured by the North British. A small proportion at least, from the southern end of the Great Glen, would pass to Inverness by Loch Ness. The Highland's 1903 tourist programme had been amended, demonstrating their confidence that the multiplication of rail-and-steamer excursions must benefit his company besides the Invergarry & Fort Augustus. Examination and cross-examination brought Wilson to a single damaging admission: he expected a Spean Bridge–Fort Augustus service to pay its way, but only if the line could be worked and kept in order at a lower figure than the Highland Company's own average costs.[34]

Lord Burton sought reinforcement from two other general managers, Vincent Hill of the South Eastern & Chatham Railway* and Sir Joseph Wilkinson of the Great Western, who both declared that the Invergarry & Fort Augustus directors were entitled to seek the best terms available, treating Highland and North British as "rival contractors". Hill, who had advised Burton to reject Wieland's conditions, condemned the demand for personal guarantees as outrageous. Refuting the North British claim that Whitelaw wanted only to "block" and would bear a loss to do so, he estimated that the Invergarry & Fort Augustus might show a profit if working costs were contained at c. 2/- per train mile, equivalent to the Highland Company's experience on their Black Isle branch (in operation since 1894). Wilkinson agreed, adding that the summer season was key. With through rail travel from Edinburgh and Glasgow to Fort Augustus (which of course assumed North British cooperation), circular tours centred on the Great Glen would become distinctly more attractive. The two concurred that the Caledonian Canal between Banavie and Fort Augustus was outmoded. Local needs justified a railway, linked to the Loch

Ness steamers, though the line would depend on sporting traffic and tourism to survive. And they saw no difficulty in one company's working another at a distance.[35]

Wilkinson's testimony was for the most part measured. He forecast profitable summers, loss-making winters, and lean intermediate seasons. All possible business should be thoroughly re-investigated. What, for example, of the North British Aluminium Company, whose traffic went by water between Foyers and Inverness? Though they had severed their association with the Invergarry & Fort Augustus after 1896 (see Chapter 5), they might be cultivated anew. Though no second trunk line, in competition with the Perth–Inverness route, would ever be needed, he judged that, in the very long run, a railway along Loch Ness might prove viable. The through West Highland-cum-Great Glen route so completed would have secondary value, but only if Parliament took steps to restrain Highland–North British strife. Veering into distinct over-optimism, Wilkinson suggested that the Invergarry & Fort Augustus directors might gradually accumulate the resources to acquire their own equipment and reclaim full independence. He insisted that their immediate prospects, under Highland patronage, were promising:

> I have looked at similar lines in England serving a similar district** [and] the bargain is a very fair one... I should not hesitate to open [the railway] for goods traffic at once, and it could be made ready...for passenger traffic in a fortnight.

But his quite unrealistic description of the new railway as "*a... practically level line running alongside...loch and river [and] as inexpensive to work as you can imagine*" called in question whether he had indeed made the careful end-to-end examination that he claimed.[36]

* * *

For the North British Company, general manager Jackson understandably echoed his chairman. Though the Invergarry & Fort Augustus had expected assistance, almost as of right, they were owed nothing. They had been "unfriendly all along"; and their meddling had prevented a further continuation of parliamentary powers for the West Highland

---

*   Successor to Alfred Willis, so unceremoniously dismissed by George Wieland. (See Chapter 8.)

**   The Great Western general manager did not say where.

Ballachulish Extension – now a new promotion would be needed. In these circumstances, the North British deserved praise for their forbearance and generosity, not condemnation. He harked back to the original Invergarry & Fort Augustus prospectus and the promoters' arguments in 1895-6, when they had presented their scheme as essentially "a landowners' line", wanted by proprietors and sporting tenants. It was therefore not unreasonable that the gentlemen who now effectively owned the company – and not least their chairman, Lord Burton, who was a large-scale sporting lessee – should give their guarantees in return for North British aid.[37]

Parliament might wish to deal tenderly with a small company, whose line certainly promised local benefits, but that, Jackson argued, would be to miss the point. The Invergarry & Fort Augustus were no longer in any position to aim for Inverness. A through railway was demonstrably in the public interest, as the natural extension of the West Highland – and this only the North British could achieve efficiently, at the same time serving all the communities along the Great Glen. Operating expenses on the Spean Bridge–Fort Augustus line were sure to exceed £4,000 per annum, and the Highland, whatever they might pretend, had decided to bear the loss in order to bar the way. ("*[There] must be something more...to induce anyone to work and maintain [the line] on that figure.*") Though the larger share of traffic might fall to the West Highland, for that very reason the Highland would have no incentive to be enterprising; and they would divert all that they could by Loch Ness and Inverness. In their hands, the railway would stagnate. To the accusation that the North British had frustrated the best efforts of the Invergarry & Fort Augustus board, Jackson replied that he had only recently costed the proposed Highbridge spur for a second time. The necessary outlay was excessive, merely to achieve direct working between Fort William and Fort Augustus. North British experience showed that tourists continued to favour the traditional all-day voyage between Banavie and Muirton. Passenger exchange at Spean Bridge station would be not in the least inconvenient, and Fort William trains could readily reverse, as had always been envisaged. Summer-season "specials", which Lord Burton and his friends thought so important, would suffer very little delay.[38]

Jackson made a powerful attack on the Highland Company's claim that they could ensure a reliable, within-budget service. What if a break-down squad or heavy crane were required, following a derailment? Would Whitelaw seek North British help? Although the line lay in relatively easy country, allowance must be made for treacherous weather. Built, like the West Highland, to Forman's "contour" technique, it was terraced above Loch Lochy and vulnerable to landslide and flood. That the timetable would be slender did not greatly matter. Wear-and-tear depended not so much on train-miles but on general conditions in the North of Scotland. The true measure was train-miles-per-mile-of-route. By that test, working and maintenance on the Black Isle branch amounted to fully £4,000 per annum – and yet the Highland proposed to work the Spean Bridge-Fort Augustus line, ten miles longer, for the same sum.[39] Appearing once again as a North British witness, Benjamin Hall-Blyth endorsed Jackson's arithmetic:

> *To base the calculation of...maintenance...upon [train-miles] is absolutely fallacious...You must take it by [route miles] and you must have in mind the nature of the route.*

On the descent from Letterfinlay summit, where the numerous streams brought down mountain scree, he thought the Invergarry & Fort Augustus "*worse than almost any part of the West Highland*"; loose rock, choked culverts and washouts would be a permanent risk.[40]

Together Jackson and Hall-Blyth contrived to present a picture purporting to explain all Wieland's stern reservations about working the Invergarry & Fort Augustus. The promoters had emerged victorious in 1896 only because Parliament assumed that an arrangement with the North British must follow; and the North British, tolerating the little company's provocative pose of independence, had made ready to obtain

Thanks to timber-clearance for a refurbished high-voltage power line (note pylons), the trackbed, seen here from a vessel on Loch Lochy in July 2021, is visible again, climbing south from Invergarry. Note the many seemingly innocuous mountain streams which so readily turned to spate, bringing down scree and other debris and threatening the railway formation.

(Keith Fenwick)

Aberchalder station looking north in 1914 – with simple siding accommodation although goods traffic was not normally handled. While the Ellice Trustees enjoyed special facilities at Invergarry station, Aberchalder was more convenient for several of their tenants and "sportsman" lessees.
(J L Stevenson collection, courtesy Hamish Stevenson)

the necessary powers when the line neared completion. All might easily have been resolved by 1901. Though Lord Burton had every right to search out the best bargain, keeping open the possibility that the Invergarry & Fort Augustus would one day find the means "to work themselves", he had no cause to expect any special indulgence and no right to impose more burdens on the West Highland Railway, which had never achieved its projected earnings. For the Highland "*to come 125 (?) miles out of its own district to help another company like this*" was without precedent. Their policy of obstruction dated from the defeat of the Glasgow & North Western Bill in 1883, and it spoke volumes that they had so eagerly accepted the long neutralisation of the Great Glen by the 1889 Agreement. Parliament, knowing their "blocking" intentions, had rejected their Inverness to Fort Augustus line in 1896-7. Now the Highland had seen the chance to "block" the Great Glen "for all time", by pretending to assist the Invergarry & Fort Augustus. As before, Hall-Blyth held that the North British, who made good the West Highland's losses, were entitled to advance to Inverness – if thereby they could compensate their shareholders. As before, he made no comment on the wisdom of this course. He did not agree, in so many words, that the West Highland's "right" to the Great Glen had been widely acknowledged; but he remembered what the whole railway industry expected after 1889:

> Everyone…had no doubt whatever that [the West Highland] would become an alternative route from Glasgow to Inverness.[41]

To counteract the testimony of Hill and Wilkinson, the North British relied on the evidence offered by two representatives of the company's East Coast English allies – Henry Tennant, former general manager of the North Eastern Railway, and Sir Henry Oakley, general manager of the Great Northern. They both declared Whitelaw's figures flawed and aired their suspicions of his purpose. The Highland's proposed agreement with the Invergarry & Fort Augustus was "not commercial", not justifiable "on its individual merits", and would "impede the development of the district". The expense of a separate establishment could not be negligible – an establishment too large for economic day-to-day operation yet insufficient for emergencies. By contrast the North British, with the resources already allocated to the West Highland, could offer flexible working from Fort William. Moreover, it was unbelievable that the Highland, once in possession, would feed goods and passengers to the West Highland at Spean Bridge with any enthusiasm; and they would not hazard their own existing traffic, gathered to Inverness from Loch Ness.[42]

Oakley and Tennant conceded that, with a fresh injection of capital, the Invergarry & Fort Augustus might recover some freedom of action – when, conceivably, they would turn again to the North British or perhaps purchase a steam railcar and operate the line themselves. (Hall-Blyth had made the same suggestion). But Whitelaw's conditions lacked "mutuality", and Burton and his fellow-directors could not easily break away. The Highland would hold the North British at Spean Bridge for up to a decade, to the further detriment of West Highland finances. Indeed, the Highland might play a longer game. What if, to consolidate their grip, they revived their lost line of 1896-7 between Inverness and Fort Augustus or, with railcar operation in mind, sponsored an equivalent light railway? In Oakley's opinion, Parliament, the Board of Trade and the Railway Commissioners must take note of these eventualities. If the Highland–Invergarry & Fort Augustus Agreement prevailed, the North British deserved running powers to Fort Augustus (and prospectively to Inverness), so that they could not be denied a locus to oppose any future Highland scheme.[43] Tennant was of the same opinion. The Highland must not be permitted a permanent "block". If they absorbed the Invergarry & Fort Augustus then built on along Loch Ness, they must share the through line thus created with the North British, on terms which ensured meaningful competition with the Perth-Inverness route.[44] Wary that the North British, with a foot in two Anglo-Scottish camps, might entice the Midland Company to participate in a westerly through route to Inverness, the North Eastern and the Great Northern had obtained protection clauses in every West Highland act; but they wanted no involvement in the Great Glen, beyond securing East Coast interests, and neither Oakley nor Tennant suggested otherwise. However, Tennant expected "other companies" (the Caledonian or the Great North of Scotland?) to demand their say; and, whatever happened, the Highland must not aspire to sole possession:

> The district should be left open for anyone who feels disposed to spend money…making a railway up to Inverness, and the Company that has the other line, from Inverness to Perth, should not gain a special advantage…[45]

The North British persisted in their assertion that, if not for the stubbornness of Lord Burton and the Highland's interference, they would have been in possession of the Invergarry & Fort Augustus already; and they implied that a third edition of the West Highland Inverness Extension would have followed before long. But it was much more believable that Wieland wanted only a return to impasse, by frustrating the bargain which the Invergarry & Fort Augustus had achieved. The truth, declared the Highland's counsel, was that the North British had over-reacted, "*vexed…that a poor little company, which they hoped to devour, is passing out of their hands*". And he utterly rejected any West Highland "right" to the Great Glen:

> [It is] the basis of the North British case…that the West Highland was laid out…as an instalment of the route to Inverness (sic), and that Parliament so treated it from the beginning, and has so treated it ever since. That I completely contradict…[46]

* * *

On 21st May 1903 the Commons Committee approved the Bill, as their demeanour throughout the hearing presaged. They had neither probed deeply into history nor considered whether any branch line elsewhere in the British Isles was comparable with the Invergarry & Fort Augustus. The chairman had prevented first Wilson and then Jackson from going more deeply into operational detail. He had intervened again to request that Oakley, as a North British witness, answer two straightforward questions. Could the line earn £4,000 a year –

from local traffic and from traffic exchanged at Spean Bridge? Would £4,000 a year cover costs? Oakley's response may well have been decisive. At bottom, he was of Wilson's opinion – it could be done, though "*a very near thing indeed*", given "*nothing exceptional in the way of maintenance*".[47] Experience would show how an utterly inadequate revenue, not cost of working, was the fatal flaw (see pages 105 and 107).

For the future, the Committee preferred a fence-sitting verdict:

> [We] find the preamble…proved, but in doing so, in allowing the lease (sic) to the Highland line for ten years, [we] do not wish in any way to be considered to express an opinion on the desirability or otherwise, in the public interest, of the West Highland line getting [eventually] into Inverness.[48]

This encouraged Wieland to persevere in the House of Lords, if only to pursue a more explicit protection clause for the North British in the finished Act. The Caledonian persisted too, seeking a clause to balance any advantages which the North British might obtain. Nevertheless, the first House had set the tone. That the Lords Committee would remember 1897 and again declare against the Highland's "blocking" proclivities was improbable, and they too chose to steer by public interest – rescuing the Invergarry & Fort Augustus Company was imperative and running powers to Fort Augustus for the North British, who had not been left helpless, were an unnecessary complication. Parliament, they held, could think again if the Highland exploited their interim possession of the Great Glen to the injury of the West Highland. Meantime, the North British should have the simplest of protection clauses – and with this the Caledonian were content. The proceedings went swiftly and by mid-June the Highland–Invergarry & Fort Augustus Agreement had cleared every hurdle.[49] The covering Act would receive the royal assent on 21st July.

Though dismayed that the Caledonian had not played a more active part, David Reid still saw in his mind's eye the Connel Ferry–Ballachulish line extended to Fort William and a Caledonian application for running powers between Fort William and Spean Bridge. Throughout the first six months of 1903 he had expected overtures from the Callander & Oban Company, whose new branch was all but complete. In April, at an inspection of the Lanarkshire & Ayrshire Railway,* he seized the chance to propose a visit by Caledonian officers to the Invergarry & Fort Augustus – and they were, Reid thought, receptive. He subsequently claimed to have received "private information" that Sir James Thompson was amenable. ("*This tends to the position I have long looked forward to.*")[50] But Whitelaw and Wilson paid little attention – certain that the Caledonian would be broadly supportive of their Bill unless the North British were to gain some unexpected benefit. If Reid was ultimately disillusioned, he was also alarmed. During the preparations for Parliament, though fully consulted, he had been several times reminded how Whitelaw was master. Worse, with the Bill "between Houses", the Highland chairman had responded positively to Jackson's suggestion of one-to-one discussions, though these in the event led nowhere.[51] Realistically, the Invergarry & Fort Augustus directors could

---

* The Lanarkshire & Ayrshire, built incrementally, would open throughout in 1904.

expect nothing better. Whitelaw was not bent on betrayal, but neither need he have deferred to them, had the North British proved amenable to compromise.

Reid had advised Burton more than once to conceal his financial anxieties as much as possible – or the Highland might take advantage. After the enabling Bill had cleared the Commons, the secretary wrote to Captain Ellice, who of all the Invergarry & Fort Augustus directors had been the least satisfied with Whitelaw's terms and wanted to modify the Agreement:

[We] have avoided complications and our arrangements with [the] Highland are only temporary; and my view is to keep ourselves free and independent and see what the future holds.[52]

The secretary and George Malcolm, in an encounter at Westminster, had clashed not only with George Wieland and North British solicitor James Watson but also with the Highland's representatives.[53] Reid reported how he had "spoken plainly", insisting on "the normal courtesies"; and the Invergarry & Fort Augustus board were sufficiently perturbed to agree that he should address a formal complaint to Wilson:

My directors think that no communication should pass directly between either your Company or my Company and the North British without each knowing what is being done.[54]

By his own account, Reid had confronted Watson defiantly – the battles for the Great Glen were not over and one day the Invergarry & Fort Augustus, "entirely unfettered", would deal on equal terms with all contenders and name their own price. It was a wildly unrealistic prediction.

References

Highland Railway–Invergarry & Fort Augustus Railway Joint Bill, 1902-3, House of Commons evidence, cited as HR-IFAR.

1. NRS/BR/PYB(S)/1/410, Provisional Order, promoted April 1902, to confirm Highland Railway – Invergarry & Fort Augustus Railway Agreement of March 1902
2. NRS/BR/IFA/4/6, David Reid to Lord Burton, 25 March and 5 April 1902, and to George Malcolm, 4 August 1902. (See also NRS/BR/IFA/1/2, Invergarry & Fort Augustus minutes, 17 January 1901.)
3. NRS/BR/IFA/4/6, Reid to Burton, 25 March, 2 April and 5 May 1902, to William Whitelaw, 25 March and to Donald Grant, 1 May 1902. (See also NRS/BR/IFA/1/2, Invergarry & Fort Augustus Railway minutes, 17 January 1901.)
4. NRS/BR/IFA/4/7, Reid to Burton, 24 January 1903 (enclosing letter from Whitelaw as to parliamentary counsel's opinion). NRS/BR/IFA/4/6 and 7, Reid to Malcolm, 30 May 1902 and 26 and 27 January 1903.
5. NRS/BR/IFA/4/6, Reid to Malcolm, 17 and 30 May 1902
6. NRS/BR/IFA/4/6, Reid to Burton, 14 May 1902, and to Malcolm, 15 May 1902
7. NRS/BR/IFA/4/7, Reid to Park, 16 April 1903, and to MacLachlan, Dewar & Henderson, 17 April 1903.
8. NRS/BR/IFA/4/6, Reid to Burton, 14 May and 4 July 1902.
9. NRS/BR/IFA/4/6, Reid to Burton and to John Cunninghame, 10 June 1902, and to Malcolm, 4 August 1902. NRS/BR/IFA/4/7, Reid to Burton, 10 November 1902, to Cunninghame, 14 November 1902, and to Thomas Allison, 29 October 1902.
10. NRS/BR/IFA/4/7, Reid to Whitelaw, 14 November 1902
11. NRS/BR/IFA/4/7, Reid to Burton, 10 November 1902.
12. NRS/BR/IFA/4/6, Reid to Whitelaw, 23 May 1902.
13. NRS/BR/IFA/4/6, Reid to Grant, 25 March 1902, and to Burton, 14 May and 4 July 1902.
14. NRS/BR/IFA/4/6, Reid to Burton, 11 June 1902. NRS/BR/IFA/4/7,

Reid to Malcolm, 18 February 1903, and to Robert Park 26 February and 2 March 1903. NRS/BR/IFA/1/2, Invergarry & Fort Augustus Railway minutes, 25 June 1902.
15. NRS/BR/NBR/1/50, North British Railway minutes, 13 March and 8 June 1902. NRS/BR/PYB(S)/1/410, Provisional Order to confirm Highland Railway–Invergarry & Fort Augustus Railway Agreement, North British Railway "petition against".
16. NRS/BR/PYB(S)/1/511, Highland Railway and Invergarry & Fort Augustus Joint Bill, 1902-3, North British Railway "petition against".
17. Ibid.
18. NRS/BR/PYB (S)/1/511, Highland Railway and Invergarry & Fort Augustus Railway Joint Bill, 1902-3, brief for North British Railway and West Highland Railway.
19. NRS/BR/PYB (S)/1/511, Whitelaw, HR-IFAR, 19 May 1903.
20. NRS/BR/IFA/4/7, Reid to Burton, 30 January 1903, and to Malcolm, 26 and 27 January and 18 February 1903. NRS/BR/PYB(S)/1/511, Thomas Wilson and William Roberts, HR-IFAR, 19 May 1903.
21. NRS/BR/IFA/4/7, Reid to Burton, 30 March 1903.
22. NRS/BR/PYB(S)/1/511, Malcolm, HR-IFAR, 19 May 1903.
23. NRS/BR/PYB(S)/1/511, Whitelaw, HR-IFAR, 19 May 1903.
24. NRR/BR/IFA/4/6, Reid to Burton, 31 July 1902. *The Scotsman*, 30 July 1902 and passim 1902-3.
25. NRS/BR/PYB(S)/1/511, Burton and Malcolm, HR-IFAR, 19 May 1903.
26. NRS/BR/PYB(S)/1/511, Burton, HR-IFAR, 19 May 1903.
27. NRS/BR/PYB(S)/1/511, Malcolm, HR-IFAR, 19 May 1903.
28. NRS/BR/PYB(S)/1/511, Lord Lovat, Lachlan Macintosh and Duke of Portland, HR-IFAR, 19 May 1903.
29. NRS/BR/PYB(S)/1/511, Abbot Leo Linse, HR-IFAR, 19 May 1903.
30. NRS/BR/PYB(S)/1/511, Lovat, HR-IFAR, 19 May 1903.
31. NRS/BR/PYB(S)/1/511, Whitelaw, HR-IFAR, 19 May 1903.
32. NRS/BR/PYB(S)/1/511, Wilson, HR-IFAR, 19 May 1903.
33. NRS/BR/PYB(S)/1/511, Roberts and John Ferguson, HR-IFAR, 19 May 1903.
34. NRS/BR/PYB(S)/1/511, Wilson, HR-IFAR, 19 May 1903.
35. NRS/BR/PYB(S)/1/511, Sir Joseph Wilkinson and Vincent Hill, HR-IFAR, 20 May 1903.
36. NRS/BR/PYB(S)/1/511, Wilkinson, HR-IFAR, 20 May 1903.
37. NRS/BR/PYB(S)/1/511, William Jackson, HR-IFAR, 20 May 1903.
38. Ibid.
39. Ibid.
40. NRS/BR/PYB(S)/1/511, Benjamin Hall-Blyth, consulting engineer for North British Railway, HR-IFAR, 20 May 1903
41. Ibid.
42. NRS/BR/PYB(S)/1/511, Henry Tennant and Sir Henry Oakley, HR-IFAR, 20 and 21 May 1903.
43. NRS/BR/PYB(S)/1/511, Oakley, HR-IFAR, 21 May 1903.
44. NRS/BR/PYB(S)/1/511, Tennant, HR-IFAR, 20 May 1903.
45. Ibid.
46. NRS/BR/PYB(S)/1/511, counsel for Highland Railway, closing speech, Highland Railway and Invergarry & Fort Augustus Railway Joint Bill, 1902-3, Commons, 21 May 1903.
47. NRS/BR/PYB(S)/1/511, Oakley, HR-IFAR, 21 May 1903.
48. NRS/BR/PYB(S)/1/511, Highland Railway and Invergarry & Fort Augustus Railway Joint Bill, 1902-3, Commons, 21 May 1903.
49. NRS/BR/NBR/1/52, North British Railway minutes, 18 June and 2 July, 1903. NRS/BR/PYB(S)/1/511, Highland Railway and Invergarry & Fort Augustus Railway Joint Bill, 1902-3, Lords. NRS/BR/IFA/1/3, Invergarry & Fort Augustus Railway minutes, 30 June 1903.
50. NRS/BR/IFA/4/7, Reid to Burton (in Spain), 24 and 25 April 1903.
51. NRS/BR/IFA/4/7, Reid to Burton, 26 May 1903.
52. NRS/BR/IFA/4/7, Reid to Edward Ellice, 12 June 1903.
53. NRS/BR/IFA/4/7, Reid to Burton, 26 May 1903.
54. NRS/BR/IFA/4/7, Reid to Wilson, 8 June 1903.

CHAPTER TEN

RECKONING, 1903-14

With the opening of the Invergarry & Fort Augustus in sight, on 30th June 1903 Lord Burton and David Reid together called at the Railway Department of the Board of Trade to request that Major Pringle ("conversant with the state of affairs") be assigned to carry out the necessary re-examination of their railway – and as soon as possible. Reid, back in Glasgow, wrote in similar terms three days later.[1] William Whitelaw was equally eager to move swiftly; on his instructions, a Highland locomotive and coach were sent via Perth for Pringle's use[2] – which implies that the other engine chosen for Great Glen duty (see Chapter 9) brought an assortment of rolling stock to Spean Bridge some time afterwards. The North British, it seems, made no more difficulties about passage over the West Highland from Crianlarich. To Reid's great dismay, Sunday 5th July ("very wet") saw a serious landslip – and at least 48 hours were needed to restore the track. Without fully admitting what had happened, he succeeded in putting off the re-inspection (scheduled for Thursday 9th) until the following Tuesday, when all went smoothly. This time Pringle gave particular attention to the signals protecting the junction at Spean Bridge and he queried the interlocking of the swing bridge at Fort Augustus; but the inspector was otherwise satisfied.[3] The official opening took place on Wednesday 22nd with three trains each way between Fort Augustus and Spean Bridge. The full timetable of four trains, including services to "Pier", the baldly designated terminus on Loch Ness, started the following day. Though half

the year had already gone, there remained at least a dozen weeks in which tourist and sporting traffic could be tested. (The West Highland had opened in August 1894 – officially on the 11th, in fact four days earlier, to undergo the same experiment.)

While the Invergarry & Fort Augustus directors would enjoy free passes over their own railway, a blanket North British concession for travel between the South and Spean Bridge was a different matter, and Reid warned Burton not to count on it. He also pressed Thomas Wilson, general manager of the Highland Company, to obtain confirmation that David MacBrayne's steamers would call routinely at the railway pier on Loch Ness. Wilson should make sure, too, that Robert Millar, general manager of the Caledonian, received an invitation to the opening ceremony, together with his wife.[4] Future relations with Callander & Oban and Caledonian were seldom absent from Reid's mind, and he thought it an advantage that the Invergarry & Fort Augustus line was to open a few weeks ahead of the Ballachulish branch (where traffic would begin on 20th August). He was soon to suggest, looking to the summer season of 1904, that the Caledonian sponsor a "motor carriage" between North Ballachulish and Spean Bridge, linking the Callander & Oban with the Invergarry & Fort Augustus, and by-passing North British Fort William.[5]

In his opening day speech Whitelaw spoke of a new beginning. Great Glen quarrels, he said, were at an end. It was self-evident that a Fort Augustus–Inverness extension would

A "period" scene of 1903 at Fort Augustus station, complete with bicycles and bicyclists, where a typical Highland train of three 6-wheeled coaches, behind Yankee Tank No. 52, has arrived from Spean Bridge. The Highland Company's first intention had been to employ two tender locomotives.
(Highland Railway Society collection)

never be needed:

> As between Spean Bridge and Fort Augustus no one could doubt the value of the [line]. But in a sparsely populated district, through which passed a splendid waterway (i.e. Loch Ness and the northernmost reach of the Caledonian Canal), the making of a railway would be utter nonsense.[6]

Parliament, however, had not pronounced decisively against an eventual West Highland advance to Inverness – for which the North British had argued strenuously only a few weeks earlier; and there remained a body of opinion that a secondary Glasgow–Inverness line might eventually be justified (see Chapter 9). The Highland chairman disagreed but repeated that he had no "blocking" intentions, no starvation agenda; though he would remain vigilant until the North British finally forswore all designs on his company's territory, the Highland, operating the Invergarry & Fort Augustus, would honour their commitment to feed the West Highland and connect with the Loch Ness steamers.

This echoed the *Railway Times* three months before. ("*It is ridiculous to suppose that…traffic requirements necessitate another through route…and the Highland shareholders are surely entitled to some protection…*")[7] Wilson spoke too, and in like manner. He looked to cooperation with the MacBrayne Company, the West Highland and the Callander & Oban. When Inverness, Fort William and Oban were linked by a combination of trains and steamers, all the intermediate communities would be more than adequately served.[8] Whitelaw had added that Caledonian and North British must decide for themselves whether the Ballachulish–Fort William gap should ever be filled – but he showed no enthusiasm for a Caledonian presence in the Great Glen.

* * *

From the autumn of 1903 the Invergarry & Fort Augustus board set out to clear their outstanding obligations. These included a reckoning with the North British for point work, signals and the new signal cabins at Spean Bridge, besides a final accounting with contractor James Young (who eventually settled for a further £1,800). While Formans & McCall obligingly reduced their account, the Railway Signal Company demanded payment in full. Materials left over from construction were sold to bridge-builders P. & W. McLellan.[9] It was a small bonus that the North British refrained from a strict exaction of "terminals" (handling charges)

for goods traffic exchanged at Spean Bridge; but friction soon arose over domestic coal for the Great Glen, brought to Crianlarich by the Caledonian via the Callander & Oban and taken forward by the North British.[10] Rates were determined by mileage from the Stirlingshire pits, disadvantaging the longer route over the West Highland via Craigendoran (cf. how from 1894 the Caledonian had been forced to reduce their rates for

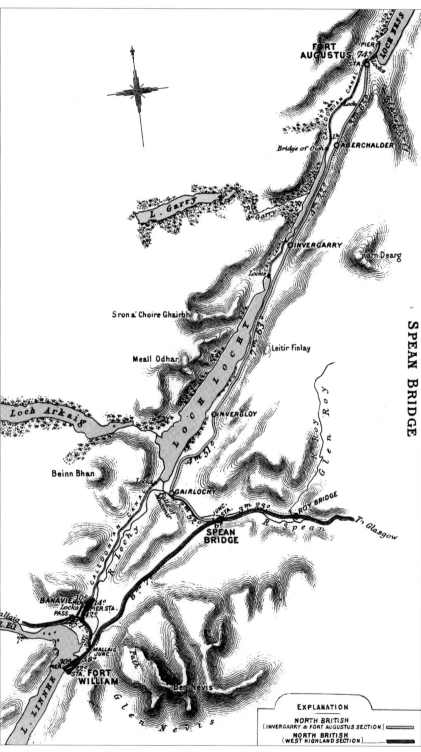

The Railway Clearing House Junction Diagram of 1915 showed the Invergarry & Fort Augustus Railway, finally purchased by the North British Company in 1913-4, as still a separate entity. "Leitir Finlay" appears among several Gaelic spellings. Letterfinlay summit, so designated, was closer to Invergloy – see page 54.

Lanarkshire coal by the Callander & Oban to Crianlarich and Tyndrum, because the distance by the new West Highland Railway was shorter). In any case, lighters had been delivering coal all along the Caledonian Canal for several decades and it was soon discovered that only by sizeable reductions in rail charges could modest mineral depots be maintained at Gairlochy, Invergarry and Fort Augustus.[11]

George Malcolm, who put his faith in estate traffic, wanted porters at Gairlochy, Invergarry and Aberchalder each summer and autumn, for the convenience of "sportsmen", and he later complained that the Highland Company had not provided them.[12] "Sporting" revenue, though in itself far from sufficient, was indeed worthwhile (and not without an out-of-season element, when proprietors undertook repairs and improvements). In pursuit of tourist traffic, a guide to the district had been distributed free of charge and advertisers at first escaped any charge. July-to-October 1903 could not be considered a fair test (above) and better things were expected in 1904, with interchangeability of rail and steamer tickets fully established. The *Railway News* issued a special supplement

CALEDONIAN RAILWAY.

CALLANDER AND OBAN LINE.

Opening Ceremony—Ballachulish Extension

On FRIDAY, 21st AUGUST, 1903.

SPECIAL TIME TABLE.

	a.m.		p.m.
GLASGOW (Buchanan Street), dep. 8.20		BALLACHULISH HOTEL by	
EDINBURGH (Princes Street)		Coach, - - - - dep. 3.40	
(Ordinary Train), - - „ 8.0		KENTALLEN by Coach, - - arr. 3.52	
STIRLING, - - - - „ 9.0		„ by Train, - dep. 3.55	
DUNBLANE, - - - - „ 9.10		CONNEL FERRY, - - - „ 5.8	
CALLANDER, - - - „ 9.35		DALMALLY, - - - - „ 5.44	
KILLIN JUNCTION, - - „ 10.18		KILLIN JUNCTION, - - - „ 6.41	
DALMALLY, - - - „ 11.10		CALLANDER, - - - - „ 7.23	
CONNEL FERRY, - - - „ 11.50		DUNBLANE, - - - - „ 7.45	
„ BRIDGE, - - „ 12.2p		STIRLING, - - - - „ 7.54	
CREAGAN BRIDGE, - - „ 12.37		EDINBURGH (Princes Street)	
BALLACHULISH, - - arr. 1.30		(Ordinary Train), - - arr. 9.27	
„ by Coach, - dep. 1.35		GLASGOW (Buchanan Street), - „ 8.40	
For drive up Glencoe and return			
by Coaches to Hotel, - - 2.45			

LUNCHEON
IN BALLACHULISH HOTEL.

Construction of the Callander & Oban Ballachulish branch (1897-1903) was unhurried. It became the fading hope of the Invergarry & Fort Augustus directors that somehow the Caledonian Company, once traffic to Ballachulish had begun, would take a hand in the Great Glen as a third player alongside the Highland and the North British.
(National Records of Scotland)

"puffing" the new opportunities for holiday travel in the Highlands; but a 20-mile line could never obtain a princely share of the pooled receipts from extended tours and the Lovat Arms Hotel at Fort Augustus would prove a dubious asset.[13] As for livestock, there was a warning already in what had turned out to be over-provision of pens and sidings at West Highland Spean Bridge – the two companies were pursuing much the same drove traffic from the districts north-west of the Great Glen. Nevertheless, the new railway had shortened several existing "walks" for cattle and sheep and Fort William auctioneer Donald Cameron (who had been an itinerant cattle dealer until the West Highland opened) saw possibilities in another mart at Fort Augustus. During 1904-6 Malcolm met Cameron more than once but with the result that a fenced drove stance was proposed instead.[14]

The final adjustment of the railway boundaries entailed the purchase of yet more land at Gairlochy. When the Highland demanded a clutch of small repairs and alterations, they were offered £200 all-in, on condition that their engineer attend to everything he thought essential. A further £200 went to extend and reinforce a retaining wall near Aberchalder, which gave more trouble only two years later. There was little economy to be found in simplifying the signalling at Fort Augustus swing bridge and the proposed alterations, estimated to cost at least £100, were not carried out. (By contrast, the West Highland Company were able to eliminate the west-side signal box at Banavie swing bridge, on the Mallaig Extension, after the Board of Trade had relaxed their original requirements.) On either side of Letterfinlay summit, the formation proved liable to floods and earth falls. In 1905 came a warning that the foundations of the Loch Ness pier were suspect and the verdict followed that £250 would be needed to make the structure safe. More hopeful was the opening of the promised halt, with siding and loading bank, at Invergloy (see Chapters 8 and 9); and in 1906 Lewis Miller was permitted to erect a private platform above Corriegour House, on condition that this would become in due course Invergarry & Fort Augustus property.[15]

It was an axiom across the railway industry that in country districts other traffic "followed the mails". Bags were charged by weight at first while the Highland Company negotiated with the Postmaster-General, and the outcome fell short of Lord Burton's hopes – Glen Garry, Glen Quoich and Loch Hourn would be served from Invergarry station, on a fixed contract which earned only £75 per annum.[16] Experience in 1904 and 1905 showed that the Invergarry & Fort Augustus could afford neither an elaborate July–September timetable nor payments to MacBrayne for the extension of tourist sailings into early autumn; and the directors, in discontinuing these outlays, reconciled themselves to a finite income from the summer season. They had expected Whitelaw to be generous in small matters, for instance the cost of empty mileage accumulated by any special summer workings; but the Highland held the owning company to almost every clause of the 1903 Agreement, including payment of all rates and taxes.[17]

To his own shareholders Whitelaw conceded that Great Glen earnings, especially tourist earnings, were dispiriting. Uncertainty over the long-postponed opening had deterred not only excursionists but also sportsmen-enquirers seeking

Edward VII twice visited Glenquoich, in 1904 and 1905. The shadows show that it is morning at Invergarry station and the flags are flying for a royal occasion, though the royal train is nowhere to be seen. Lord Burton can be identified tentatively in both photographs – as the right-hand figure of the two posed at the gable door, and as front-seat passenger in the motor car. Behind the Highland Railway Skye Bogie class 4-4-0 is an ordinary Highland First Class coach. Note the generous proportions of the station building, which included a private waiting room for the Ellice family. The projecting canopy was likewise distinctive.

(Highland Railway Society Roberts collection)

The Highland Railway's 4-4-0T No 54, another Yankee Tank, at Fort Augustus in August 1906. As in so many railway scenes, the photographer has captured a casual moment in time – on this occasion a seemingly earnest platform conversation. (LGRP)

summer lets. More publicity might produce better results, and to this end Highland and Invergarry & Fort Augustus would continue to share advertising expenses. In 1905 the Highland attempted to introduce their own vessel on Loch Ness. David MacBrayne's opposition had been expected (and, in the event, could not be overcome); but Whitelaw's patience was strained when the Invergarry & Fort Augustus board objected too (at the instigation of David Reid?), on the grounds that a better service must tell against any future railway extension to Inverness – this despite their old pledge that an efficient rail-and-steamer service would be achieved all along the Glen. The 1903 Agreement bound the Highland Company only from year to year (as the North British had emphasised in advising Lord Burton to beware), and Whitelaw now warned that he could not persevere indefinitely if Invergarry & Fort Augustus income consistently failed to meet outgoings. His shareholders, who had assented to the Agreement as insurance against renewed North British attack, might well decide that the insurance cost too much – or was no longer needed.[18]

From 1904-5 the county assessor for Inverness-shire would value the line at nil. Ominous also was Burton's increased preoccupation with every financial detail. £7 to fence the planned livestock compound at Fort Augustus (above) was eventually judged unaffordable. All came under apprehensive scrutiny – the annual gratuity for the North British stationmaster at Spean Bridge; a "small shelter", probably intended for Invergloy; the derisory income from station advertising; and

the minor charges levied for grazing rights on the railway embankments*. So too did such items as the token shooting rents paid by landowners, whereby they and their tenants secured a legal right to confront the occasional poacher who took advantage of the railway track.[19] The visits of Edward VII to Glenquoich Lodge in September 1904 and again the following year, travelling by the Invergarry & Fort Augustus, were the company's only triumphs. Lord and Lady Burton made shift to accommodate the royal entourage; the private papers of the Ellice family, who were closely involved, reveal all the hectic preparations.[20]

Lord Abinger had died in 1903, to be replaced on the Invergarry & Fort Augustus board by G. W. Robertson, representing the Forman Trustees. At a by-election (1903) Captain Ellice had become Liberal MP for St Andrews, a constituency previously associated with his family (see Chapter 2, page 19) and in 1905 he resigned his directorship.[21] Burton, who felt increasingly weighed down, mooted (but in vain) a one-of advance payment of £1,000 to the Highland Company, on condition that they saw out the full ten-year span of the 1903 Agreement, waiving all "extras" for which compensation was due. Working and routine maintenance at an annual £4,000 had proved just attainable, but with no margin whatever, while income felt hopelessly short. The real question was different – could the railway ever earn enough to meet all the Highland's

---

* Grazing had been allowed, even encouraged, during 1901-3, while the line lay completed but unused.

legitimate claims and, sooner or later, the cost of large repairs or renewals? With no alternative to be found, the directors resolved that from 1906 the increasing deficit would be made good in the proportions Lord Burton, 65%; Forman Trustees, 20%; and John Cunninghame, 15%.[22]

* * *

From the mid-1890s, Britain's railway industry would be subject to increasing financial pressures and to a mixture of government cajolery and compulsion. Legislation remained piecemeal, aimed principally at improving wages and working conditions for railwaymen. (Recognition of the railway trade unions came very slowly and would be consolidated only under the wartime conditions of 1914-18.) As quid pro quo, the companies sought both a relaxation of their common-carrier obligations and a greater freedom to conclude traffic-sharing agreements or outright mergers, but with little success because traditional opposition to "monopoly" died hard while their critics remained both vocal and influential.

In Scotland, the general trend to retrenchment was exemplified in the Clyde Coast traffic pool of 1905 (Caledonian, Glasgow & South Western and North British), and even more by the rapprochement of Highland and Great North of Scotland. From shared locomotive workings between Aberdeen and Inverness, these two old enemies moved towards amicable amalgamation in 1905-6. Though their joint bill was dropped (fear of injury to the local economy of Inverness again entered), it told an incontrovertible tale of changing times.[23] The North British, properly concerned both for their own traffic and for that of their English partners through Aberdeen, had petitioned against the merger of Highland and Great North, adding a weary, scarcely-to-be-taken-seriously, demand that West Highland "rights" in the Great Glen be recognised, whatever the outcome. Despite multiplying woes, the Invergarry & Fort Augustus had entered their own petition against – if the proposed union were approved, Parliament should ensure that a Fort Augustus–Inverness extension was not jeopardised.[24] When amalgamation with the Great North was frustrated, the Highland made it known that a general financial review would follow. It was their cue to announce, in October 1906, that they would cease to work the Invergarry & Fort Augustus six months later.

Whitelaw reiterated that his prime duty was to the Highland's shareholders. Whatever his own inclinations, they must soon have called a halt:

We have worked the line within the estimated cost...and [given] it every opportunity. It has not shown any...expansion of traffic, and we have been experiencing a loss of £2,000 a year...which [we] cannot continue to face. We foresaw [this] possibility and...we will now recover the difference between

The Loch Ness railway pier (middle, right), designated simply "Pier" and out of use from 1907, has been left to decay for more than a century. Though folly it must now seem, in extending their line beyond Fort Augustus village, the Invergarry & Fort Augustus promoters had two goals – their pledge of an improved steamer service would ring true, while a later extension to Inverness by the loch's north-western side would become all the easier, with the Caledonian Canal and the River Oich already bridged. This photograph was taken in 1993; since then the trackbed had become a private road.

(Keith Fenwick)

Highland Railway–North British Railway, provisional agreement, 2 April 1907

1. The Highland Company's two locomotives and twenty-four vehicles to be withdrawn via Crianlarich, with North British conductors, on or before 30 April.
2. The Highland to take wagon sheets and ropes, the North British to retain weighing machines, hurleys, hand lamps, office furniture, tickets, ticket cases and ticket machines.
3. To be further considered – rate books and similar, permanent way materials.
4. Invergarry to be only postal station, with North British parcel rates applied pro. tem.; no provision for postal deliveries; no advertised mail coach connections.
5. Mixed trains to be run and the Railway Clearing House notified accordingly; Invergloy up traffic to be invoiced Gairlochy, down traffic to be invoiced Invergarry; existing arrangements at Aberchalder (sometimes worked from Fort Augustus) and Corriegour (Mr Miller's platform) to continue.
6. Landowners' shooting rights (Invergloy and Culachy) already revoked.
7. Board of Trade report on Invergloy siding mislaid. (Noted that *"a woman is in charge who received £5 a year from Highland Company in addition to what she is paid by Major Bailey".*)
8. Fort Augustus signalman and porter to be taken into North British employment; North British employees to take over other stations from 29 April; Highland Company's driver to be redeployed as soon as possible, making house at Fort Augustus available for North British driver.

List scheduled to Invergarry & Fort Augustus Railway–North British Railway Agreement, May 1907

Gairlochy Station – stationmaster's house, three rooms and kitchen (at 2 miles 60 chains) Gairlochy Station – double house for surfacemen (3 miles)

Letterfinlay passing place – two-room and kitchen house intended for signalman (8 miles)

Altrua – double house for surfacemen (9 miles)

Laggan – double house for surfacemen (14 miles)

Invergarry Station – stationmaster's house, three rooms and kitchen (15 miles)

Aberchalder Station – double house for surfacmen (19 miles 40 chains)

Pier Station – two-room and kitchen house (24 miles).

NRS/BR/NBR/8/1198

£4,000 and the total of last year's receipts.[25]

Lord Burton could only turn helplessly to the North British and their new chairman, the Earl of Dalkeith (subsequently seventh Duke of Buccleuch), who had succeeded George Wieland on the latter's death in 1905. On 30th November 1906 he wrote to Dalkeith in his own hand, chairman to chairman and peer to peer, begging an early meeting in Edinburgh or London:

> *The Highland Coy have given…notice to terminate their working arrangement next April. I would be grateful if you could grant me a private interview…to discuss the position, and the possibility of some arrangement with your Company.*[26]

On 9th December (a Sunday, with no scheduled trains) the North British engineer James Bell and other officers examined the Invergarry & Fort Augustus from end to end.[27] Their Highland Railway counterparts cooperated fully, under orders from Whitelaw who was confident that matters had come at last to the operation of a chronically unremunerative branch which would never reach beyond its existing terminus.

The Highland chairman's personal letter* to Dalkeith, on New Year's Day 1907, was so altogether forthcoming as to suggest that the two had anticipated the situation (and had already discussed it?):

> *The cost of working…is about £3,800 a year and the income is barely £2,000; I believe you could work…for about £1,000 less…and by running the trains through from Fort William you might very considerably increase the passenger traffic… If you want to [make a further inspection], we can give you [an] engine and carriage any day [without] charge…If you like we will send our Engineer…to meet yours, and…your Accountant …can see all the accounts since the line opened.*

Bell's relatively favourable report had surprised the Highland chairman, who warned of looming difficulties and dangers. Concrete work, he alleged, had been found generally "very shoddy", while Gairlochy station had been built with green timber. The contractor *"had taken much wear out of the track"* during construction. Loose rock remained near Aberchalder, where the Highland had introduced precautionary patrols. The North British would need luck and must keep control of the timetable. They should accept no liability for "extraordinary maintenance", or for repairs consequent upon landslip or flood. The "extension" to Loch Ness could be abandoned:

> *[You] should…not send any trains across the Canal; it would be cheaper to drive luggage and parcels from the steamer… than to maintain the pier and line…The transfer can be made at the top lock, close to the station, in the case of through boats.*

And with a little judicious spending, Whitelaw concluded, the railway might be reduced to an unstaffed tramway.[28]

Simpson & Wilson, the engineers of the West Highland Mallaig Extension, made a further inspection and endorsed

---

* Whitelaw's letter began with commiserations on the Elliot Junction accident (28th December 1906), which had revealed embarrassingly slack management on the Dundee & Arbroath Railway, jointly owned by Caledonian and North British.

NORTH · BRITISH · RAILWAY.

GENERAL MANAGER'S OFFICE,
EDINBURGH, *April* 1907.

CIRCULAR G.M.

Invergarry and Fort Augustus Railway.

The Staff are hereby informed that this Company will take over the working of the above Railway on WEDNESDAY, 1ST PROXIMO.

The names of the Stations on the Line are as follows, viz. :—

Gairlochy,

Invergarry,

Aberchalder,

Fort Augustus.

Goods and Passenger Traffic can be dealt with at each of the Stations named, with the exception of Aberchalder, which is a purely "Passenger" Station ; no Goods, Parcels, or Miscellaneous Traffic being dealt with.

W. F. JACKSON,
General Manager.

The North British takeover becomes official. (NRS/BR/NBR/8/1198)

Bell's findings.[29] Negotiations for the North British takeover proceeded with little or no reference to the Invergarry & Fort Augustus directors, save to confirm factual detail. At departmental level, there was a little friction. (How much locomotive coal would the Highland leave behind? Who was to account for missing carriage end-boards and ticket clippers?) James Watson, the North British solicitor, warned that Inverness-shire County Council might impose a rating revaluation "prejudicial to us", while Bell feared that the Highland would "let maintenance go down" in the interval before he assumed responsibility. Coal, permanent way materials, stores and sundries, taken over by the new operators, were valued in the end at some £550, a proportion of which was paid to the Invergarry & Fort Augustus.[30] Other concessions to the owning company included the creation of a joint committee of directors to overview timetables, rates and fares, with provision for arbitration by the Board of Trade in the event of disagreement. Charges for facilities at West Highland Spean Bridge might be adjusted. Traffic returns would be made available quarterly,

Drafted during March, the formal North British–Invergarry & Fort Augustus Agreement was finalised in April and took effect from 1st May 1907.[31] Little less daunting than Wieland's uncompromising prescription, Dalkeith's terms reflected Whitelaw's recommendations. The Agreement might be ended after three years, subject to six months prior notice by either party. If Parliament were to impose unacceptable alterations, either party might resile. Four services ("passenger" or "mixed") would be run each way during July, August and September, giving transfer in and out of West Highland trains and connection with the steamers between Fort Augustus and Inverness; and there would be through coaches once daily in each direction between Glasgow and Fort Augustus. (See

panel on page 109) From October to June two "mixed" workings in both directions, with West Highland connections, were deemed sufficient. The North British took responsibility for fire damage to stations, and for accidents and any ensuing liability under the Workmen's Compensation Acts. Measured against experience since 1903, the obligations of the Invergarry & Fort Augustus Company remained onerous – and all but certain to prove finally crushing unless income increased. The board undertook to pay for "directorial and financial management"; for any initial outlay putting the line in order ("to the reasonable satisfaction of the North British engineer"); and for all instances of "extraordinary maintenance" exceeding £100 – this to include remedying any further defects in construction which came to light, when the North British would decide what expenditure was required. To meet the notional working and maintenance figure of £2,000 per half-year, the North British would claim 60% of gross revenues – making up any shortfall from the other 40%. In the still worse case that income did not reach £4,000 per annum, the owning company were to find half the difference.

Invergarry & Fort Augustus board meetings during 1907-10 took place variously in Glasgow and London and were dominated by financial worries. The North British asked some £550 for "putting in order", later reduced to £400. Their request that a house be rented, purchased or built for their stationmaster at Fort Augustus could not be met. (The Highland's earlier provision is unclear.) Prospective buyers of the Lovat Arms Hotel showed only tepid interest. Towards settling with the Highland Company (who claimed more than £2,000), Lord Burton gave £1,100, to which the Forman Trustees added £250 and Cunninghame £150. With smaller sums from the other directors (Malcolm contributed £15), the total inched upwards but still fell short. Experience by the end of 1908 suggested that the figure to be made good annually would rest at something less than the Highland's recurring claims during 1903-6, though storm damage had threatened to reverse this very modest improvement. Breaking even was a remote prospect, and quite out of reach as matters stood.[32] Lord Burton's death in February 1909 spelt crisis. In April the board elected Cunninghame

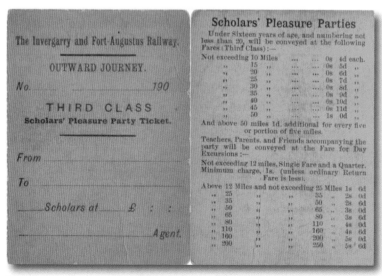

How many such excursion tickets were ever issued? The Invergarry & Fort Augustus Company's supply of regular tickets outlived the North British, to be over-printed "LNER" in the 1920s.   (Keith Fenwick collection)

FROM SUMMER PROGRAMME 1907, WITH THE NORTH BRITISH NEWLY IN CHARGE

Inverness
Improved Facilities via West Highland and Fort Augustus Railways
One Change only between Glasgow and Inverness.
Through carriages between Glasgow and Fort Augustus
Shortest and Best Tourist Route between Glasgow (Queen Street) and Inverness
Glasgow d. 7 13 am, Fort Augustus a. 12 55 pm, Inverness (Muirtown Wharf) a. 5 15 pm
Inverness (Muirtown Wharf) d. 7 00 am, Fort Augustus a. 10 35 am, Glasgow a. 5.20 pm

Circular Tour Tickets are also issued, going via Fort Augustus and returning via Dunkeld or Aberdeen, or vice versa.

1st Class and Cabin	Single 25/7d	Return 41/5
3rd Class and Steerage	Single 13/5½d	Return 22/5d

Local Tours from Fort William
Caledonian Canal, Fort Augustus and Invergarry
Going via Banavie and Fort Augustus, returning via Invergarry and Spean Bridge or vice versa.

1st Class and Cabin	13/6
3rd Class and Steerage	6/3 #

Holders can travel in Cabin of the Steamers of David MacBrayne Limited, on payment of 4/6 extra to purser on board.

Scottish Railway Preservation Society Archive

---

as chairman. Though other questions called for attention, including the future of Corriegour platform following the decease of Lewis Miller, it had become all-important to halt the slide into indebtedness – and David Reid, who could discover not the faintest hope of Caledonian intervention, finally fell silent. Burton's executors, like the Forman Trustees, were bound by legal restraints on any payments into Invergarry & Fort Augustus funds, while Cunninghame could not bear the burden alone. That autumn the directors resolved to abide by the 1907 Agreement throughout 1910; but abandonment of their railway was the inevitable prospect thereafter.[33]

Dalkeith remained cautiously amenable to any viable solution consistent with his general strategy of putting the North British house in order after half a dozen years of marking time under Wieland. Formal amalgamation in 1908 had ended the long pretence of West Highland independence; the retiring district superintendent at Fort William was not replaced and thereafter management would be based entirely in Glasgow. New investment at Mallaig was ruled out, unless matched by further Treasury assistance. However, under pressure from fishermen, wholesale merchants and curers, the North British directors would eventually contemplate an arrangement approximating to a traffic pool, with landings at Mallaig, at Caledonian Oban and at Highland Kyle of Lochalsh all coordinated. The sticking point was Treasury approval – might the Mallaig Extension Guarantee be endangered if "pooling" were adopted? In this broad picture of catching up and rationalisation, the precarious existence of the Invergarry & Fort Augustus Company had become an inconvenience.

Britain's stormy politics in the years immediately preceding

The MacBrayne Company's first venture into scheduled bus services began with this vehicle, operating between Fort William and North Ballachulish. There would be no West Highland Ballachulish Extension.
(Author's collection)

The station buildings at Gairlochy, Invergarry and Aberchalder, and especially the long range at Fort Augustus, backing the generous platforms, were similar in appearance to those on the West Highland. A North British three-coach train stands ready to depart for Spean Bridge on 20th July 1914, headed by West Highland Bogie 4-4-0 No.55. The through line to Loch Ness took the other face of the left-hand platform – note the stop signal partly hidden by the locomotive. By this time that platform was out of use.   (LGRP)

the 1914-8 War are also to be kept in mind. In 1905 Arthur Balfour's Unionist Government, weakened by internal squabbles over free trade versus protection, had chosen tactical retreat. After ten years in Opposition the Liberals had resumed office, overcoming for the moment their own deep-seated divisions, as a minority administration under Sir Henry Campbell-Bannerman. They were confirmed in power by a landslide victory in 1906, though Ellice met with defeat at St Andrews, against the nationwide swing. In 1909 the Liberal social reform programme and controversial budget were to bring on an epic parliamentary struggle in which Henry Asquith, prime minister from 1908, would face down the resistance of the Unionist-dominated House of Lords but sacrifice his House of Commons majority. Two almost deadlocked elections (January and then December of 1910) left the Government dependent on the Irish Nationalists and, in lesser degree, on the early Labour Party. In Asquith's sea of troubles, which included contentious naval expenditure, trade union militance and, above all, the latest drive for Irish Home Rule, the travail of the Invergarry & Fort Augustus Company was to count for little, though it engaged both the Board of Trade and the Scottish Office (below). While the Liberal Government were no more eager than their Unionist predecessors to frame a coherent transport policy, the etatists of both parties had come to favour a thorough review, and thus the future of Britain's railways promised to become a major topic in the general election due by 1915.* But the wartime electoral truce agreed in 1914 would supervene. In any case,

the fortunes of the Invergarry & Fort Augustus Company were already irretrievable.

* * *

Fresh discussions began in October 1910, when Dalkeith, Watson and North British general manager William Jackson met with the Invergarry & Fort Augustus directors in Edinburgh. Cunninghame and Reid were joined by George Malcolm, G.W. Robertson (above) and William Walters who spoke for Lord Burton's heirs. John Ferguson of Formans & McCall attended, as did Sir John Stirling-Maxwell, who had joined the North British board in 1906. By virtue of his Corrour and Morar properties, he was identified with the transport needs of Inverness-shire and had assumed something of a mediator's role.[34] The Burton Trustees had contributed nothing to the mounting deficit after 1908.** They were determined to make an end, and so too was Robertson, on behalf of the Forman family. Dalkeith stated that the North British could not propose more lenient terms. Moreover, the 1907 Agreement, though concluded without opposition, was just as much a statutory instrument as the contested Highland–Invergarry & Fort Augustus Agreement which Parliament had sanctioned in 1903; it could not be casually modified. Aid in any other guise was inadmissible – sure to be seized on by those who wanted expensive improvements at Mallaig, to which his shareholders were unshakeably averse. Nevertheless the North British would continue to work the Spean Bridge–Fort Augustus line

---

* Under the Reform Act of 1911, which reduced the maximum parliamentary term from seven years to five.

** The 65% share which Lord Burton had agreed in 1905 (see Chapter 9) was eventually paid.

for the time being. It lay with Cunninghame and his colleagues to terminate the arrangement if they so chose.[35]

Among the options scouted was an appeal to the Liberal Government for short term assistance until the Spean Bridge–Fort Augustus line could be refashioned as a light railway or tramway, and Ferguson was ready to estimate the costs involved. If help were forthcoming, a bill might be framed for parliamentary session 1911-12.[36] But other considerations arose. Legislation over three-quarters of a century had not disposed of all the ambiguities in the railway industry's relations with the state, and legal-cum-constitutional complications would arise if the situation were presented as a stark choice between conversion and abandonment. How far must a railway company persevere, as a public duty, in operating a loss-making line? Was it in law a larger question than the obligations of a private-enterprise corporation to their shareholders? Among several national newspapers which pondered these questions, the *Manchester Guardian* noted how the Invergarry & Fort Augustus served *"a notable shooting area"*, so that the patronage of seasonal sportsmen had propped up an otherwise unsustainable service – and one on which the public had come to rely. There was *"growing use of the motor car in the Highlands"*, with a consequent falling off in railway travel at first-class fares, and, before long, the Great Glen conundrum would be repeated in other disadvantaged districts.[37] The *Railway News*, taking the industry's side, warned that directors and managers must henceforth be doubly wary of "public interest" arguments. Working agreements would become hazardous,

for owning companies and operating companies alike, unless a distinct government policy emerged, with the conditions of any subsidy for deserving cases fully laid out.[38]

Not all would admit that Glasgow–Inverness and Oban–Inverness rail routes via the Great Glen had passed beyond recall. An *Oban Times* editorial held that state funds, if available, should be allocated to construction of the missing miles of conventional railway separating Ballachulish from Fort William and Fort Augustus from Inverness.[39] In various letters to the press, the Highland Company were urged to purchase the Invergarry & Fort Augustus and add the vital link along Loch Ness, as they might have done years before. One writer suggested that, until a through railway came into being, an economical steam railcar might be introduced between Spean Bridge and Fort Augustus.[40] Petrol bus and petrol lorry were not universally recognised as competitors in waiting. By stimulating local traffic to the point where a railway became viable, they might encourage the promotion of light lines – or so the argument ran. By similar reasoning, passenger and parcel traffic on the Invergarry & Fort Augustus could be given over temporarily to a "motor car" while conversion was carried out – and with every expectation that travellers would have increased in numbers by the time reopening came.

Reporting "surprise and alarm" in Lochaber, *The Scotsman* commented that the situation might have been predicted. A conventional railway in the Great Glen would never pay unless extended to Inverness, and closure or downgrading of the Invergarry & Fort Augustus could not be wished away:

Fort Augustus looking south in 1914, with the through line on the right and the normal modest train at its usual bay platform. In the distance is the signal box, very similar to those on the West Highland Mallaig Extension.   (Courtesy Science Museum Group)

[If] an understanding cannot be arrived at whereby the system will be worked on the full gauge (sic), as hitherto, it may be necessary to work the line…light*… [41]

That Fort Augustus had experienced a "rude awakening" was the *Inverness Courier's* theme. Over just half-a-dozen years, the railway had stimulated house building and brought many other obvious benefits, while local opinion held that their line had *"as much claim as others"* to state assistance. The newspaper predicted that the North British would hasten the transition to light operation once the requisite powers had been obtained. [42] By contrast, the *Northern Chronicle* looked gloomily (and presciently) ahead:

If they once admitted…that because a railway did not pay it must be closed, it might end in all the railways in the Highlands being shut up, except those portions from which the shareholders reaped big dividends. [43]

* * *

Another Donald Cameron, the twenty-fifth Lochiel, had succeeded as clan chief in 1905. An Inverness-shire county councillor and a campaigner for the expansion of Mallaig harbour, he took up the cause of the Invergarry & Fort Augustus – the North British must accept some responsibility and could not simply step aside. General manager Jackson's first reply (27th October 1910), subsequently quoted in full by the *Railway News*, was strictly factual:

We are working the line in virtue of…a statutory agreement… and have no power to work except in terms of that agreement [which] the Invergarry Company [can] terminate…at 31st January in any year on giving six months notice. Such notice we received in July last…I [have informed] the public and… other railway companies that the North British…would cease

to work the railway at 31st January next…[The] matter… should be taken up with the Invergarry & Fort Augustus Company, any proposal from whom will be carefully considered… [44]

Lochiel chaired a special meeting of Lochaber District Council. He called for an emergency county council committee and pressed the town councillors of Inverness and Fort William to act together against the threat of closure. [45] It proved part advantage, part complication that the Earl of Dalkeith and the Cameron chief were cousins,** whose recorded dealings over the next three years are interspersed with intimate family news. Could landlordly "networking" find a way out? Lord Lovat, once neutral towards any Great Glen line, was roused to defend what had become a local asset. He too served on the County Council, and he joined the emergency committee – as did The Mackintosh, Grant of Glenmoriston and Captain Edward Ellice. The five proprietors consulted with Inverness-shire's Liberal MP, Sir John Dewar (a baronet since 1907), who had already called for the Government's intervention. Sydney Buxton, President of the Board of Trade, declined to act, citing the advice of his permanent officials: the Railway Department had no power to forbid the closure of a failing enterprise; arbitration between the Invergarry & Fort Augustus and the North British was his only ready option; and, without new legislation, the Light Railways Act of 1896 could not be made applicable to a line already in existence. Dewar promised to apply more pressure. Meanwhile, despite Buxton's dusty answer, Lochiel and his allies should proceed as if seeking a Light Railway Order for an entirely new scheme; they must obtain positive statements from all the "principal residents and traders" that the railway, once reprieved, would be used to the utmost. [46]

---

*   That "light" also meant "narrow gauge" was a not infrequent misapprehension.

**   The late Lochiel, promoter-director of the West Highland Railway and a prominent figure in earlier Chapters, had made a Buccleuch marriage.

(Opposite and above) A selection of tickets from the Fort Augustus line, courtesy David Jones. Printed tickets were issued for a huge range of destinations and often remained in stock for many years. The Third Class Invergarry & Fort Augustus Railway single from Spean Bridge to Aberchalder (middle row, page 112) is overprinted with LNER, as is the First Class return (also Spean Bridge–Aberchalder) shown here. On the right, a Newspaper Label, courtesy Scottish Railway Preservation Society. Same-day delivery of newspapers was an important function of the railways in rural areas.

In late November 1910 a "conference" took place at Fort Augustus, grandiloquently reported in the Scottish press. The "delegates" included provost Young of Fort William, Angelo of Culachy, Bailey of Invergloy, MacDonald of Blarour (Spean Bridge), several members of the Inverness chamber of commerce and representatives of the Lochaber merchants' association. Both George Malcolm and David Reid attended.[47] Afterwards, Lochiel, Lovat and Ellice, by Dalkeith's invitation, joined in another North British–Invergarry & Fort Augustus meeting. Though no better strategy emerged, an understanding was reached that neither company would take precipitate action before every possibility of aid from public resources had been explored.[48] During the first fortnight of 1911 open meetings took place at Fort Augustus, Invergarry, Gairlochy* and Spean Bridge, to assess the progress of the rescue campaign. Lord Burton's self-sacrifice was everywhere invoked. ("*The loss had been principally borne by [him]. It would be gross ingratitude…if we were to allow [his] monument to crumble away.*") Lochiel's message was bleak: the Invergarry & Fort Augustus directors could not continue; the North British remained firmly of opinion that the line's working costs would always outweigh any "indirect benefits" for the West Highland; and conversion to a light railway was

---

*   By some accounts the Gairlochy district meeting was held at Lochiel's own Achnacarry.

Railings have been added to this concrete bridge, where the Great Glen Way follows the railway trackbed north from Invergarry station. It is typical of lesser Invergarry & Fort Augustus structures along Loch Lochy and Loch Oich. (A cycle way shared with walkers uses the Callander & Oban trackbed through Glen Ogle, where the old viaducts have been similarly treated.)
(Keith Fenwick)

impossible without the Liberal Government's assistance.[49]

At the eleventh hour, the Invergarry & Fort Augustus board consented to continue the 1907 Agreement for a limited time. The North British acquiesced. On Ellice's initiative, this stop-gap compromise was underpinned by a fund to which "large landowners and responsible residenters" would all subscribe. But in default of a lasting solution by 31st July 1911, closure at one month's notice must follow.[50]

* * *

Lochiel continued to besiege the Board of Trade on behalf of *"this wretched Invergarry Railway"*, making sure that the North British were kept informed. He continued to pursue an outer breakwater at Mallaig, on which any ambitious harbour improvement depended, and this drew a testy reminder from Dalkeith, somewhat in the tones of Wieland, that the North British had their own troubles. Whatever happened, the southern half of the Great Glen would retain a railhead at Spean Bridge – and the entire population along the West Highland route, landowners like his cousin included, would do well to remember what they owed to his company. Rail facilities brought higher sporting rents, and the loss-making West Highland had cushioned proprietors against the general fall in land values. As for the Government, they had better finance

the Mallaig breakwater and not indulge in "pauperising" social legislation.[51] Nevertheless, Dalkeith made a new proposal – the North British might buy out the Invergarry & Fort Augustus Company (though for a mere £22,500); and he stretched the temporary working arrangement past the July deadline, until all stop-gap finance was exhausted. On 31st October 1911, train services ceased. Cunninghame and his fellow-directors had insisted that the sum on offer be increased by at least £5,000.[52]

In answer to a formal question in the House of Commons, tabled by Dewar, Buxton's Parliamentary Secretary stated that the good offices of the Board of Trade were exhausted; legislative intervention was "extremely unlikely". To give statutory shape to any conversion plan seemed impossible and the Invergarry & Fort Augustus Company, refusing to sell to the North British at so ruinous a figure, indicated that they would dispose of their railway for scrap.[53] One opportunity remained – if Inverness-shire County Council, on the recommendation of their emergency committee, were to have all the salvageable materials along the Spean Bridge–Fort Augustus line valued by an independent arbiter, the resultant sum might be measured against whatever the North British board could be persuaded to offer. This idea, it seems, was Dalkeith's, propounded at a an "off the record" meeting with Lochiel in a London club several months before; and in late December the latter wrote that he

An up train at Invergarry in North British days. The roofboard on the nearer coach, a bogie vehicle with lavatory access, reads "Fort Augustus and Spean Bridge". The stacked boxes suggest a useful traffic in rabbits besides seasonal game.   (Highland Railway Society collection)

At the very peak of the pre-1914 holiday season, an overnight East Coast train arrives into Inverness, where the connecting Far North service waits. There was an equivalent West Coast train, and through coaches by the Midland Route too. Summer and autumn traffic made Inverness a tempting goal for those who thought to challenge the Highland Company's monopoly. The reality, during eight months of the year, was otherwise, when combined trains north of Perth catered sufficiently for the Highland's English business.

Highland Railway Society collection)

had put it forward:

> I enclose my report [to the Council]. In my remarks moving [its] adoption I extolled the NBR, eulogised...Lord Burton and concluded by abusing the Board of Trade for their apathy. It was agreed...to write to both Companies to ascertain if they were willing to submit [the matter] to arbitration...[54]

Dalkeith instructed Jackson to take note, but his private response was guarded, prompting a reproachful second letter from Lochiel:

> Surely...reference [to an arbiter], to value the line at the scrap [figure] of the rails and bridges after allowing for transport to Glasgow...should be satisfactory? The buildings to be valued according to the present demand for houses in the area, the goodwill at its commercial value to the North British after allowing for working expenses...I do not think [the total] will even equal your...offer.[55]

As the year turned, the possibility of a favourable outcome became more widely known, and in February 1912 a lengthy article in the *Glasgow Herald* urged the Scottish Office into action. North British take-over of the railway as it stood appeared much the simplest course, preferable to the protracted business of conversion to light operation; and the Invergarry & Fort Augustus must be persuaded to accept the "half loaf"* which Dalkeith had proffered:

> It is a question of saving the Invergarry Railway to the public (sic) on terms...which one party is prepared to offer and which...the other party can only persist in rejecting

at irreparable loss to themselves and injury to the district. [The] Secretary for Scotland can, we believe, advantageously interpose...[56]

The writer, harking back to the Crofters' Act of 1886 and the Treasury Guarantee for the Mallaig Extension, argued that the clear trend of policy, ever since the Napier Report in 1884, had been towards "*recognising that the Highlands and Islands are not... an economic proposition (sic)*". The railways already in existence ought to be preserved, but it was high time to consider what motor transport might contribute.

In March 1912 the District Councils of Lochaber and Aird-Loch Ness, together with the Ellice Trustees and Bailey of Invergloy, sought and obtained an interim injunction to prevent the dismantling of the Invergarry & Fort Augustus Railway. Their status as complainants was questionable, until Captain Edward Ellice's intervention made certain – holding shares and debentures in the floundering company, though he had quit the board, he had a sure title to object. Several scrap-value tenders for the "rails, ironwork and other plant" had already been received, and the directors argued that these assets would deteriorate unless quickly removed. Nonetheless the Court of Session dismissed their plea and upheld the interdict. ("*Once a railway had been established it was to a certain extent an asset of the public.*") Though nothing more than a feeder to the West Highland and *de facto* a North British branch since 1907, the line was legally a distinct entity and its total abandonment inadmissible.[57] Because the Invergarry & Fort Augustus had preserved in form a now meaningless independence, the directors found their hands tied.

---

* The North British figure, measured against the first cost of the Invergarry & Fort Augustus, fell far short of even half-a-loaf.

The engine shed at Fort Augustus, glaringly over-generous for a two-locomotive branch line but appropriate to an intermediate depot on the might-have-been through line to Inverness. The goods shed was likewise much larger than local traffic ever required.

(LGRP)

Cunninghame and his colleagues had the right, as a last resort, to appeal to the House of Lords. However, the end was near. They returned to negotiations, concluding "an out-and-out sale" to the North British, on the basis that the "£5,000 difference" would be raised from local sources – i.e. Inverness-shire County Council and the two District Councils immediately concerned (though public subscription had been mooted). It took some time to regularise the local authorities' borrowing powers (and technically this made sure that the Scottish Office could not impose inhibiting conditions). The formal Agreement, drafted in July 1913, was subscribed by Lord Lovat and Ellice on behalf of the County Council – whereupon the rolling stock and other equipment, removed eighteen months earlier, came back to Fort Augustus. On 1st August trains ran again. In its final form the Agreement (scheduled

to the Provisional Order which the North British lodged for Parliament's approval in session 1913-14) would take full effect the following year. It specified the purchase of all Invergarry & Fort Augustus property, including the Lovat Arms Hotel; the option of conversion to light operation; and the possibility of relief from local rates, together with some relaxation of Board of Trade rules at the Railway Department's discretion.[58]

Also included were powers of abandonment "beyond Fort Augustus station, in the direction of Inverness". The North British board minutes contain a sadly emphatic postscript. It was resolved to lift the track between out-of-use Fort Augustus swing bridge and Loch Ness pier, crediting the Invergarry & Fort Augustus Company account with a token sum for such materials as could be re-used.[59]

The abandoned station building at Invergarry, unlike those at Gairlochy, Aberchalder and Fort Augustus, long remained visible from the A82 trunk road. Eventually the entire station area became an untidy forestry base.

(J L Stevenson, courtesy Hamish Stevenson)

References

NRS/BR/LNE/8/764 – because the Treasury's Mallaig Guarantee ran till 1931, the North British general manager's files relating to the West Highland Extension were reclassified "LNE" from 1923.

Note 12 – the Cameron of Lochiel Papers (Lochaber Archive) include the Glenquoich estate Letter Books, which contain much of George Malcolm's correspondence.

1. NRS/BR/IFA/4/8, David Reid to Railway Department, Board of Trade, 3 July 1903.
2. NRS/BR/IFA/4/8, Reid to Lord Burton, 4 July 1903.
3. NRS/BR/IFA/4/8, Reid to Burton, 7, 9 and 15 July 1903. NRS/BR/IFA/1/3, Invergarry & Fort Augustus Railway minutes, 10 October 1903.
4. NRS/BR/IFA/4/8, Reid to Burton, 9 July 1903, and to Thomas Wilson, 9 July and 15 July (telegram) 1903.
5. NRS/BR/IFA/1/3, Invergarry & Fort Augustus Railway minutes, 10 October 1903.
6. *Railway Magazine*, Vol. XIII, July-December, 1903.
7. *Railway Times*, 30 May 1903.
8. *Railway Magazine*, Vol. XIII, July-December, 1903.
9. NRS/BR/IFA/1/3, Invergarry & Fort Augustus Railway minutes, 20 January, 20 February, 21 April and 14 October 1904.
10. NRS/BR/IFA/1/3, Invergarry & Fort Augustus Railway minutes, 20 January, 20 February and 21 April 1904.
11. NRS/BR/IFA/1/3, Invergarry & Fort Augustus Railway minutes, 21 April 1904 and 17 October 1906.
12. Lochiel Papers, Lochaber Archive, CL/1/12/1/Glenquoich letter books, George Malcolm to William Walters, 8 August 1905.
13. 13. NRS/BR/IFA/1/3, Invergarry & Fort Augustus Railway minutes, 10 October 1903 and 20 February and 21 April 1904. Railway News Supplement, July 1904.
14. NRS/BR/IFA/1/3, Invergarry & Fort Augustus Railway minutes, 10 October 1903, 21 April and 14 October 1904, 20 October 1905 and 17 October 1906.
15. NRS/BR/IFA/1/3, Invergarry & Fort Augustus Railway minutes, 10 October 1903, 20 February, 21 April and 14 October 1904, 11 April and 20 October 1905, 12 April and 17 October 1906 and 21 March 1907.
16. NRS/BR/IFA/1/3, Invergarry & Fort Augustus Railway minutes, 20 February, 21 April and 14 October 1904 and 20 October 1905.
17. NRS/BR/IFA/1/3, Invergarry & Fort Augustus Railway minutes, 14 October 1904.
18. D. Ross, *The Highland Railway*, Stenlake Publishing, 2010, p.90.
19. NRS/BR/IFA/1/3, Invergarry & Fort Augustus Railway minutes, 10 October 1903, 20 January and 21 April 1904, 20 October 1905, 12 April 1906 and 12 October 1907. NRS/BR/NBR/8/1198, North British Railway, files relating to Invergarry & Fort Augustus Railway, 1906-19, Reid to William Jackson, 9 April 1907.
20. Information provided (2017) by Edward Ellice, Invergarry & Fort Augustus Railway Museum.
21. NRS/BR/IFA/1/3, 20 February 1904 and 11 April 1905.
22. NRS/BR/IFA/1/3, 11 April 1905 and 12 April 1906.
23. D. Ross, op. cit., pp.91-2.
24. Aberdeen University, O'Dell Collection, OD.f.Kf.Hig, North British Railway petition against Provisional Order for amalgamation of Highland Railway and Great North of Scotland Railway (with additional notes). NRS/BR/IFA/1/3, Invergarry & Fort Augustus Railway minutes, 12 April 1906.
25. *Railway News*, 6 April 1907. See also NRS/BR/HR/1/17, Highland Railway minutes, 27 March 1907.
26. NRS/BR/NBR/8/1198, Burton to Earl of Dalkeith, 30 November 1906.
27. NRS/BR/NBR/8/1198, Reid to Jackson, 6 December 1906.
28. NRS/BR/NBR/8/1198, William Whitelaw to Dalkeith, 1 January 1907
29. NRS/BR/NBR/8/1198, James Bell to Jackson, 11 December 1906 and Simpson & Wilson to Jackson, 16 March 1907.
30. NRS/BR/NBR/8/56, North British Railway minutes, 7 March 1907. NRS/BR/NBR/8/1198, Bell to Jackson, 13 March 1907, Board of Trade to Jackson, 25 March 1907, James Watson to Jackson, 28 March 1907 and Wilson to Jackson, 16 April 1907; also minutes of Highland Railway-North British meeting, Perth, 2 April 1907, and David Deuchars to Jackson 22 April and 15 June 1907. NRS/BR/IFA/1/3, Invergarry & Fort Augustus Railway minutes, 21 March and 29 April 1907
31. NRS/BR/NBR/8/1198, Agreement, Working of Invergarry & Fort Augustus Railway.
32. NRS/BR/IFA/1/3, Invergarry & Fort Augustus Railway minutes, 29 April and 12 October 1907, 30 April and 19 September 1908 and 20 April 1909.
33. NRS/BR/IFA/4/13, Invergarry & Fort Augustus Railway minutes, 29 October 1909 and 28 April 1910
34. NRS/BR/IFA/4/13, Invergarry & Fort Augustus Railway, papers relating to relations with North British Railway, 1907-13, memorandum of Edinburgh meeting, 20 October 1910.
35. Ibid.
36. Ibid.
37. *Manchester Guardian*, 25 October 1910.
38. Railway News, 29 October 1910.
39. *Oban Times*, 19 November 1910.
40. *Inverness Courier*, 15 November 1910.
41. *The Scotsman*, 26 October 1910.
42. *Inverness Courier*, 1 November 1910.
43. *Northern Chronicle*, 2 November 1910.
44. *Railway News*, 12 November 1910.
45. NRS/BR/IFA/4/13, press cuttings, November and December 1910.
46. Ibid.
47. *Oban Times*, 26 November 1910.
48. NRS/BR/IFA/4/13, press cuttings, November and December 1910.
49. *Inverness Courier*, 13 January 1911, *Oban Times*, 14 January 1911 and *Railway Times* 14 January 1911.
50. *Railway News*, 4 February 1911. NRS/BR/IFA/4/13, Lochiel's report to Inverness-shire County Council on the work of their emergency committee, 20 November 1911.
51. NRS/BR/LNE/8/764/Box 6, North British Railway, general manager's files relating to West Highland Railway Mallaig Extension. Donald Cameron of Lochiel to Dalkeith, 25 May and 29 May 1911, and Dalkeith to Lochiel, 28 May 1911.
52. *Railway Times*, 4 November 1911.
53. *Railway Times*, 18 and 25 November 1911. NRS/BR/IFA/4/13, Invergarry & Fort Augustus Railway, papers relating to relations with North British Railway, 1907-13, Lochiel's report to Inverness-shire County Council on the work of their emergency committee, 20 November 1911.
54. NRS/BR/IFA/4/13, Lochiel to Dalkeith, 21 December 1911.
55. NRS/BR/IFA/4/13, Lochiel to Dalkeith, 25 December 1911.
56. *Glasgow Herald*, 26 February 1912.
57. *Railway Times*, 29 March 1913.
58. NRS/BR/IFA/4/13, Agreement, Transfer of the Invergarry Railway Undertaking.
59. NRS/BR/NBR/1/64, North British Railway minutes, 30 September 1914.

LNER, ex-North British, C15 4-4-2T No. 9155, assigned to Fort Augustus duties, with a typical train of the mid-1920s (van, brake-composite coach and horsebox) into Spean Bridge. Parcels and small goods traffic may have been sufficient for a van to be regularly employed – passenger numbers are another matter. Though the "Junction" signal cabin has gone, the double junction is still in situ. By comparison with North British provision in 1914, with day-to-day variations catering for local needs, the LNER timetable was simple: there were two trains each way daily in winter and three in summer – these included one through working to and from Fort William and gave at least one connection into and out of the principal West Highland services. Side-platform Spean Bridge lacks a footbridge or subway; the overbridge seen in both photographs which carries a minor road has always sufficed. It was modified during the alterations to accommodate the Invergarry & Fort Augustus Railway.   (Colour-Rail)

From 1933 Spean Bridge station would display successive bus connection signs (see also p.121). This example, in the style of British Railways Scottish Region, was erected c.1950. Facing the filled-in bay is the very modest Invergarry & Fort Augustus station building of 1903, which by 1970 when this photograph was taken, had become a Post Office. Entirely out of use by the late 1980s, it has since been demolished. The signal box at the far end of the up platform replaced that shown on p.79, which had suffered severe fire damage.
(G. L. Pring/Railway Record of the British Isles)

CHAPTER ELEVEN

POSTSCRIPT

The promotion of the Invergarry & Fort Augustus Railway reopened the question of a new westerly rail route to the North – unresolved in 1895. But that is to put matters very simply. Great Glen conflict, postponed in 1889, had entangled the Highland Company, the North British and the Caledonian from 1894 – a conflict which was bound up with the protracted politics of the West Highland Mallaig Extension and the possibility of a through line from Oban to Fort William and Inverness. On a longer view, the whole story spans four decades – beginning in the 1870s when doubt hung over the half-finished Callander & Oban Railway. This study charts these 40 odd years and lingers where other histories have passed lightly. It pays special attention to the Glasgow & North Western project in 1882-3, as the West Highland's precursor; to the events of 1893-4 from which, two years later, the Invergarry & Fort Augustus scheme developed; and to the wait-and-see interlude of 1897-1901 during which the Spean Bridge-Fort Augustus line was completed and a prospectively amicable arrangement with the North British took shape only to disappear.

By 1903 the opening of a minor branch, as the Invergarry & Fort Augustus had become, no longer warranted wide attention. Nevertheless, the occasion was celebrated in classic fashion, and the company minutes show how seven guineas went to purchase a ceremonial gold whistle. [1] As with so many local lines of earlier date, "quality of life" immediately improved: the trains might turn a meagre profit (in the Great Glen, no profit at all); coal and livestock traffic, and tourist traffic too, might fall short of over-optimistic projections; but same-day newspapers, a brisker postal service and better-stocked shops brought wider horizons, while local enterprise found encouragement – witness the hopeful vendor of "Highland walking sticks" for summer visitors who was accommodated at Fort Augustus station.[2] Railwaymen and their families were quickly absorbed into the community – witness the two "social occasions" which marked the departure of the Highland Company's Fort Augustus staff in 1907. The stationmaster and his clerk were each presented with "a silver-mounted tobacco pipe and pouch", and the former received in addition a "well filled purse of sovereigns"; for the permanent-way inspector – active in the village pipe band and in the shinty, football and cricket clubs – there was "an inscribed marble clock and meerschaum tobacco pipe".[3] And there can be no doubt that interest in the 1911-2 campaign to preserve the Invergarry & Fort Augustus ran deep. The weekly *People's Journal*, which circulated across the North of Scotland and cultivated a populist tone, stood a world away from the principal daily papers and the lugubrious railway press, but it too praised Cameron of Lochiel and his landed associates and

carried a cartoon publicising their endeavours.[4]

The moneyed men whom Charles Forman persuaded into Great Glen speculation had misjudged the situation, following the drawn battle of 1897. Though any "peace" between Highland and North British (like the more formal "peace" between Caledonian and North British after 1891) remained at best uneasy into the new century, the Invergarry & Fort Augustus directors scarcely held a winning hand in playing company against company. From 1901 they found themselves the owners of a finished but idle railway, their bargaining power sadly diminished. With ultimately dire consequences, they had failed to recognise that so-called contractors' lines, on whatever scale, belonged to the past. So says hindsight. Yet, taking Scotland as a whole, those elaborate speculative schemes of the 1880s, the Glasgow & North Western and the Strathdee, Strathdon & Speyside, were not the last of their kind. After the parliamentary bouts of 1889-91, when Caledonian and North British were alike prevented from absorbing the Glasgow & South Western Railway, there had been attempts to promote a line linking upper Clydesdale with Nithsdale, in the expectation that all three companies were potential purchasers – this despite the New Lines Agreement which Caledonian and North British had concluded.[5] Moreover, if the West Highland Railway and the Glasgow Central Railway were Charles Forman's greatest works, his ultimate speculative venture was a fully surveyed and late-in-the day cross-Border route by Tweed and Clyde, duplicating the secondary lines already in existence between Kelso and Symington. Prompted by a quarrel between the North Eastern Company and the North British (1897-8), Forman's last project implied a general reordering of Anglo-Scottish partnerships. The East Coast alliance was soon repaired, but board room rumbles and talk of precautions against the scheme's revival would continue well beyond the engineer's death in 1901.[6]

Because faith in free enterprise and suspicion of monopoly died hard, so too did the era of contractors' lines. Reality prevailed, however, in the report of the Parliamentary Committee on Railway Agreements (1911):

Such competition as still exists is not necessarily in the public interest and the cost of such competition tends to fall on the public in the end. Parliament can forbid amalgamations and outlaw certain agreements but it is virtually impossible to legislate against understandings or against abstaining from competition. Informal agreements are less useful...than formal union...and have other disadvantages...The future points to more, and better, agreements and, in many cases, outright amalgamation.[7]

* * *

Well before the sale of the Invergarry & Fort Augustus was finally settled, as described in Chapter 10, William Whitelaw had become a director and then the vice-chairman of the North British.* In 1912 he succeeded the Earl of Dalkeith as chairman, demitting his Highland chairmanship. At the Grouping in 1923 he would be elected to head the London & North Eastern Railway, which absorbed the North British. As he himself observed later, he had seen traffic on the Invergarry & Fort Augustus begin and was to see it all but cease in 1933.

The re-established timetable of 1913-4 comprised passenger and mixed workings, operated by a lone locomotive outshedded from Fort William. There was connection with the principal West Highland trains throughout the week, but the pattern varied from day to day, meeting other local needs. (See panel on right) In sum, this compared not unfavourably with provision on the Mallaig Extension – until the 1920s the evening service north from Glasgow went no further than Banavie. The Spean Bridge–Fort Augustus line does not greatly feature in the North British record during the 1914-8 War; but preparations for the anti-submarine Northern Barrage seems to have required special trains to and from Corpach and Fort Augustus, a journey with two reversals. (American materials, unloaded at Corpach, were taken through the Caledonian Canal. Other trans-Atlantic consignments, landed at Kyle of Lochalsh, went on to Invergordon by rail.) When the Lloyd George Coalition Government aired their short-lived plans for post-war Reconstruction and invited proposals for new light railway schemes, neither a Fort Augustus–Inverness line nor "conversion" between Spean Bridge and Fort Augustus received serious attention, but revival of the might-have-been link between West Highland Tulloch and Highland Kingussie (or Newtonmore) was eagerly canvassed. Previously suggested (in 1914) but now dismissed was a light line to Ardnamurchan, from Kinlochiel on the West Highland Mallaig Extension, via Ardgour and Strontian – which recalled the shadowy Kentra scheme of the early 1890s.[8]

From 1919, the Spean Bridge–Fort Augustus timetable resembled that of 1914; and from 1923, under London & North Eastern ownership, the norm became one or two coaches – in the winter months, sometimes a solitary brake-composite – with vans or cattle trucks added at need, behind an ex-North British tank engine. Among other legacies of wartime Control, the railwayman's eight-hour day made savings imperative. The junction at Spean Bridge was simplified, eliminating the supplementary signal box necessitated by Forman's layout.

North British Railway
Invergarry & Fort Augustus

Train Service, May 1914

Trains called at all stations, although they only stopped at Invergloy Platform when a request was made to the guard at the previous stopping station or when passengers were on the platform to be taken up. Trains also stopped there to attach or detach wagons.

The 8.30am passenger from Fort Augustus reached Spean Bridge at 9.25am. The return working - 'passenger' on Tuesdays, Wednesdays and Fridays and 'mixed' on Mondays, Thursdays and Saturdays - left at 10.25am. This gave connection with the 5.50am Glasgow-Fort William which called at Spean Bridge at 9.35am and with the 7.50am Mallaig-Fort William-Glasgow due at Spean Bridge at 10.18am. Arrival back at Fort Augustus was at 11.20am on Tuesdays, Wednesdays and Fridays and at 11.40am on other days.

Save on Thursdays, there was a 'mixed' to Fort William, reversing at Spean Bridge. On Tuesdays and Fridays it left Fort Augustus at 11.45am and reached Fort William at 1.25pm; on Mondays, Wednesdays and Saturdays, departure was at 2.30pm (Fort William 4.30pm). The latter gave a good connection into the 1.40pm Mallaig-Fort William-Glasgow train due at Spean Bridge at 4.03pm. On Thursdays the up 'mixed' left Fort Augustus at 5.55pm to reach Spean Bridge at 7.10pm. Fort William passengers changed into the 3.20pm service from Glasgow due at Spean Bridge at 7.22pm, which at this period did not go forward to Mallaig.

Tuesdays, Wednesdays and Fridays saw a later afternoon 'mixed' from Spean Bridge at 4.15pm for a 5.30pm arrival into Fort Augustus. Fort William passengers took the 1.40pm Mallaig-Glasgow (Fort William 3.45pm) changing at Spean Bridge. Mondays, Thursdays and Saturdays offered instead an evening departure from Fort William at 7.05pm, with reversal at Spean Bridge (7.25 - 7.30pm) and arrival into Fort Augustus at 8.25pm; this working connected with the 3.20pm from Glasgow.

Weekly Coal Train, from 1933, Saturdays only

From Fort William					
Spean Bridge	dep	10.30am	Fort Augustus	dep	12.45pm
Gairlochy		10.47	Invergarry		1.25
Invergarry		11.35	Gairlochy		2.15
Fort Augustus	arr	12.00 noon	Spean Bridge	arr	2.30

Shunt at Invergloy and Aberchalder as required.

---

line to Ardnamurchan, from Kinlochiel on the West Highland Mallaig Extension, via Ardgour and Strontian – which recalled the shadowy Kentra scheme of the early 1890s.[8]

Along the West Highland, the North British contemplated long-section working and sought trades-union agreement on split shifts at intermediate stations; but the board, who preferred to postpone any drastic cost-cutting measures until the Grouping had been fully negotiated, bequeathed these unpalatable decisions to the successor-company.[9] In August 1924 came a derailment at Gairlochy, serving notice that, without track renewal on a generous scale, passenger business on the Invergarry & Fort Augustus must soon cease. What had caused the accident was debatable, but the ensuing investigation exposed the poor condition of the original point work, which did not meet the latest standards of the Ministry of Transport (successor to the Board of Trade).[10] Ten years later, with plans afoot to refashion the redundant station buildings into holiday homes, the expense of preliminary repairs would

---

* Not only a growing reputation but also connection with the Baird family, industrialists strongly represented on the North British board, smoothed Whitelaw's path.

The semi-derelict station building at Aberchalder, still in use after a fashion, stands forlorn on the former side-platform c.1955. Compare with the photograph on page 98.

(LGRP)

prove discouraging – which implies that general upkeep had been skimped too. (They were let as more spartan "camping apartments".)[11] Nevertheless, the London & North Eastern's tranche of proposed closures in 1933, which included their little Great Glen branch, had some positive features. It was recommended that the loading banks at Gairlochy, Invergloy, Invergarry, Aberchalder and Fort Augustus remain in use, served by a railway-owned lorry based at Spean Bridge and all under the care of the Spean Bridge stationmaster (who would be given a motorcycle for his extra duties); thereby goods and mineral traffic could be retained. But the outcome was a surely short-term expedient: with the line left to deteriorate, a weekly coal train continued to work out and back from Fort William.[12]

In the 20th century the MacBrayne Company, in part railway-owned from 1928, would establish a road transport network for passengers, mail and goods throughout the western Highlands and Islands. An experimental service between North Ballachulish and Fort William, touching the Corran–Ardgour Ferry and connecting (at Ballachulish Ferry station) with Callander & Oban trains, had shown its worth before 1914[13] – which confirmed once and for all that the West Highland Ballachulish Extension was not to be resurrected. During 1911-

Sign at Spean Bridge after 1933; 'Railway' has been overwritten with 'Coach', i.e. the MacBrayne mail bus.

(J L Stevenson, courtesy Hamish Stevenson)

3, with all Invergarry & Fort Augustus trains suspended, motor transport had proved adequate, if second-best, while in 1914 the North British had thought to employ a "motor car" between Fort William and Banavie, for passengers on the evening train from Glasgow (above).[14] Introduced in the mid-1920s, the Fort William–Fort Augustus–Inverness bus service was hampered by the limitations of the then highway along the Great Glen, which crossed and re-crossed the Caledonian Canal by weight-restricted bridges;* but completion of the modern A82 in the early 1930s both strengthened the case for closure of the Spean Bridge-Fort Augustus line and put in question the future of the Loch Ness mail steamers. Contradictions persisted, however – Inverness-shire County Council, fearful for their pristine main road, were hostile to the London & North Eastern plan for lorry traffic to and from Spean Bridge and endorsed the precarious weekly coal train.

History is "what happened, in the context of what might have happened", and two what-ifs suggest themselves. Until the general election of 1918 returned a House of Commons intent on scaling down wartime collectivism, there was every chance that emergency Control would evolve into post-war state-ownership. When De-Control and Grouped amalgamations became the preferred prescription, an all-Scotland Group was assessed, though in the end rejected. It does not follow in either case that the Invergarry & Fort Augustus would have survived, but the chances of a coherent national transport policy would have been greater. The West Highland and with it the Invergarry & Fort Augustus, different in character from the rest of the North British system, became distinctly anomalous as "London & North Eastern", though this was offset by the devolved management which Whitelaw favoured. In any case, he and his directors upheld the policy

---

* There is anecdotal evidence that passengers were requested to alight and cross on foot.

Fort Augustus station and yard in 1937, some four years after the withdrawal of passenger services. One platform has been obliterated but track can still be seen outside the other – which would facilitate the dismantling of the Caledonian Canal swing bridge and the Oich viaduct during the 1939-45 War.
(Graham Maxtone collection)

to which the North British had clung after 1901. There would be no large expenditure on the West Highland, least of all at Mallaig, without a commensurate Treasury input. The Mallaig Extension Guarantee had been devalued by the terms of De-Control and the London & North Eastern yardstick was road spending – government ought to assist railway improvements in corresponding measure.[15]

The War of 1939-45 brought a last reprieve of sorts. Though the swing bridge at Fort Augustus and the River Oich viaduct were dismantled for their scrap steel, the line, shorn of its "extension", was sufficiently refurbished to provide a relief route if circumstances demanded. One visitor during this time of greatly restricted travel noted how part of the track to the abandoned Loch Ness pier remained in place – lifting had been postponed during the previous hostilities. With road traffic strictly regulated, coal loadings increased and other bulky goods returned temporarily to rail. But this ceased forever in 1947.

*   *   *

The route of the Invergarry & Fort Augustus is today traceable for much of its length. A sign-posted path by the right bank of the river leads to the hidden but still sturdy piers of the Spean viaduct and the remains of General Wade's High Bridge. (Unfortunately the present information board at the former mistakenly describes the West Highland Mallaig Extension.) The explorer who penetrates beyond Mucomir will encounter hazards near Invergloy; here the bridge under the busy A82 has been removed and the viaduct demolished, though its piers remain. Beyond is Letterfinlay summit, where a passing place (see panel on page 107) obtained the Board of Trade's approval in 1901; by the time of Major Pringle's reinspection in 1903 the loop points had been removed – the Highland Company presumably saw no need to break the longish section between Gairlochy and Invergarry. Altrua viaduct (a concrete arch) is intact as are many lesser bridges and culverts on the exposed stretch above Loch Lochy. North from Invergarry station (partially restored as an information centre and budding museum) the former trackbed has been incorporated into the Great Glen Way – walkers and cyclists pass through the Loch Oich tunnel and over the Calder Burn

From the mid-1920s a number of operators, including the MacBrayne Company, essayed a regular coach service through the Great Glen. After 1933 "MacBraynes" inherited the postal contract for Glen Garry and Glen Quoich and their buses connected with West Highland trains at Spean Bridge, where mail sacks were exchanged.
(John Sinclair collection)

The West Highland Railway makes an easy climb out of Glen Spean to the minor summit at Achindaul; before swinging away on a falling gradient to cross the River Spean, the Invergarry & Fort Augustus ran parallel. Between the two lines stood the latter company's scarcely necessary engine shed (see also p.76). It still stood in 1950, the date of this photograph – and would remain some forty years more, put to this or that use. The last Invergarry & Fort Augustus metals at Spean Bridge amounted to a looped siding trailing in to the up side of the West Highland loop, together with the disused bay platform track.

(LGRP Roberts)

viaduct. At Fort Augustus the tall, strikingly castellated, piers of the Oich viaduct stand in plain view, provoking many an enquiry as to their origins.

How far do the present pages address these enquiries? On the operation of the Invergarry & Fort Augustus, other historians are more knowledgeable, and a full investigation of working timetables and traffic notices would bring to light much to enthuse any reader with a general railway interest. It appears, for example, that terminating all the trains at Fort Augustus station after 1907 was not just a matter of economy; the decision satisfied complaints that occupation of the section onwards to Loch Ness, with the swing bridge locked against Caledonian Canal shipping, had too often delayed passing vessels. The first arrival (1903) and final departure (1907) of the Highland Company's locomotives, with North British conductors between Crianlarich and Spean Bridge, is well documented. But what transfers took place during the intervening years? Even as a political history, my Great Glen study is far from exhaustive; and for more information on board-room machinations and on several actors in the drama, the books of David Ross, who has treated all five of the Scottish pre-Grouping companies, are a sure standby.

During the sixteen years since the publication of *Plans, Politics and People*, I have refined but not fundamentally altered my interpretation of the West Highland Railway's origins. Nevertheless, questions remain – and one in particular lacks a clear answer. At some point in 1888 it was decided that the line presented to Parliament, already less than "direct" though arguably "optimum", should wander by Rannoch and Loch Treig into Brae Lochaber. Set aside the widespread assumption

that the North British aimed at Inverness, set aside all the special pleading in which the North British subsequently indulged – were the consequences of this decision dispassionately considered at the time? A through railway by the Great Glen, built on West Highland foundations, could wound but not quickly or decisively defeat the established Highland Company – and therein lies a tale of much wasted enterprise.

References
1. NRS/BR/IFA/1/3, Invergarry & Fort Augustus Railway minutes, 10 October 1903
2. NRS/BR/IFA/1/3, Invergarry & Fort Augustus Railway minutes, 10 October 1903, 21 April 1904 and 17 October 1906
3. *Inverness Courier*, 14 May 1907
4. *People's Journal*, 11 February 1911
5. *Engineering*, LXVI, 9 December 1898
6. NRS/BR/NBR/8/1209, proposed Manchester, Newcastle & Glasgow Railway, 1893-1900.
7. Parliamentary Papers, C.5631.
8. *Oban Times*, June and November 1914, and January-February 1918
9. NRS/BR/NBR/8/1055, January, May, August and November 1921, March and September 1922 and January 1923.
10. NRS.BR/LNE/8/739, Gairlochy Accident, 5 August 1924.
11. NRS/BR/LNE/8/339, May 1935
12. NRS/BR/LNE/1/216, London & North Eastern Railway minutes, 28 September and 30 November 1933
13. David MacBrayne centenary history, 1951.
14. NRS/BR/NBR/1/64, North British Railway minutes, 14 May 1913 and 25 February 1914.
15. For example, NRS/BR/LNE/8/764/Box 7, general manager's files relating to West Highland Railway Mallaig Extension (continued from North British period), William Whitelaw to Sir Murdoch MacDonald, MP for Inverness-shire, 6 November 1923.

INDEX

Who Was Who

A guide to the main personalities who appear in this book.

Abinger, 3rd	William Scarlett, 3rd Lord Abinger, promoter-director and first chairman (1894-5), West Highland Railway
Abinger, 4th	James Scarlett, 4th Lord Abinger, promoter-director (1896-1903), Invergarry & Fort Augustus Railway
Anderson	John Anderson, secretary-manager (1865-1907), Callander & Oban Railway
Baillie	James Baillie of Dochfour, director, Highland Railway; promoter, Lochend Light Railway; MP for Inverness-shire (1895-1900)
Burton	Michael, Lord Burton, previously Sir Arthur Bass, long-term lessee of Glenquoich estate; promoter-director, subsequently chairman (1899-1909), Invergarry & Fort Augustus Railway
Cameron, 24th chief	Donald Cameron of Lochiel, 24th chief of Clan Cameron, promoter-director, West Highland Railway; MP for Inverness-shire (1868-85)
Cameron, 25th chief	Donald Cameron of Lochiel, 25th chief of Clan Cameron, principal campaigner on behalf of the threatened Invergarry & Fort Augustus Railway, 1910-3
Conacher	John Conacher, general manager (1891-99), North British Railway
Cunninghame	John Cunninghame of Craigends and Foyers, promoter-director, subsequently chairman (1909-14), Invergarry & Fort Augustus Railway
Dalkeith	John Scott, Earl of Dalkeith, chairman (1905-12), North British Railway
Dougall	Andrew Dougall, secretary-manager (1865-1896), Highland Railway
Ellice, Edward	Captain Edward Ellice, of Invergarry (Glengarry estate), promoter-director (1896-1905), Invergarry & Fort Augustus Railway
Ellice, Mrs	Mrs Eliza Ellice of Invergarry, widow of Edward Ellice (d.1880)
Forman	Charles Forman (Formans & McCall), engineer, West Highland Railway and Invergarry & Fort Augustus Railway
Hall-Blyth	Benjamin Hall-Blyth (Blyth & Westland), consulting engineer, Great North of Scotland Railway and North British Railway
Innes	Charles Innes (Innes & MacKay), solicitor and political campaigner
Jackson	William Jackson, general manager (1899-1918), North British Railway
Linse	Leo Linse, Abbot of the Benedictine Abbey at Fort Augustus
Lovat	Simon Fraser, Lord Lovat, at first neutral towards the Invergarry & Fort Augustus Railway, latterly a campaigner on the company's behalf (1910-3)
MacBrayne	David MacBrayne, proprietor of western Highlands and Islands steamers
Mackintosh	Aeneas Mackintosh of Raigmore, chairman (1892-6), Highland Railway,
MacPherson-Grant	Sir George MacPherson-Grant of Ballindalloch, chairman (1897-1900), Highland Railway
Malcolm	George Malcolm, Invergarry, factor, Glengarry and Glenquoich estates

Matheson	Sir Donald Matheson, promoter-director and first chairman (1896-8), Invergarry & Fort Augustus Railway
Millar	Robert Millar, general manager (1901-8), Caledonian Railway
Moffatt	William Moffatt, general manager (1880-1906), Great North of Scotland Railway
Neilson	John Neilson, promoter-director, subsequently chairman (1898-1906), Invergarry & Fort Augustus Railway
Paterson	Murdoch Paterson, company engineer (1875-97), Highland Railway
Pringle	Major John Pringle RE, Railway Department, Board of Trade
Reid	David Reid (Keyden, Strang & Girvan), agent-cum-secretary (1898-1914), Invergarry & Fort Augustus Railway
Ristori	Emmanuel Ristori (British Aluminium Company), promoter, Invergarry & Fort Augustus Railway
Roberts	William Roberts, company engineer (1898-1913), Highland Railway
Steel	Charles Steel, general manager (1896-8), Highland Railway
Stirling-Maxwell	Sir John Stirling-Maxwell of Pollok and Corrour; at odds with the North British Railway but ultimately (1908) a North British director
Strang-Watkins	G. Strang-Watkins (Keyden, Strang & Girvan), agent-cum-secretary (1896-8), Invergarry & Fort Augustus Railway
Thompson	James Thompson (Sir James from 1897), general manager (1882-99), subsequently chairman (1901-6), Caledonian Railway
Tweeddale	William Hay, Marquess of Tweeddale, chairman (1887-99), North British Railway
Waldron-Smith	Thomas Waldron-Smith, engineer, proposed Glasgow & North Western Railway
Walker	John Walker, general manager (1874-91), North British Railway
Watson	James Watson, company solicitor (1892-1922), North British Railway
Whitelaw	William Whitelaw, chairman (1902-12), Highland Railway; chairman (1912-22), North British Railway; chairman (1923-38), London & North Eastern Railway
Wieland	George Wieland, secretary (1873-92) North British Railway and (1895-1901) West Highland Railway; chairman (1901-5), North British Railway
Wilson	Thomas Wilson, general manager (1899-1910), Highland Railway
Young	James Young, contractor, Invergarry & Fort Augustus Railway

BIBLIOGRAPHY

M Barclay-Harvey, *A History of the Great North of Scotland Railway*, Locomotive Publishing Company, 1949

D Cattanach, *G B Wieland of the North British Railway* (unpublished monograph)

G Dow, *The Story of the West Highland*, LNER, 1944/1947

K Fenwick & N T Sinclair, *The Perth & Dunkeld Railway*, Highland Railway Society, 2006

P Fletcher, *Directors, Dilemmas and Debt*, Great North of Scotland Railway Association and Highland Railway Society, 2010; Caledonian Conundrums in the Highlands, *Highland Railway Journal* 88, Early 2009; Inverness and the Railway Mania of 1845, *Highland Railway Journal* 90, Summer 2009; McBean's Proposed New Highland Railway, 1874-76, *Highland Railway Journal* 94, Summer 2010; A Shareholders' Revolution: The Highland Board at the Turn of the Century, *Highland Railway Journal* 96, Early 2011

C E J Fryer, *The Callander & Oban Railway*, Oakwood, 1989

C Hamilton Ellis, *The North British Railway*, Ian Allan, 1955

J Kernahan, *The Black Isle Railway*, Highland Railway Society, 2013

J McGregor, *The West Highland Railway: Plans, Politics and People*, Birlinn (John Donald), 2005

C McKean, *Battle for the North*, Granta, 2006

A Perchard, *Aluminiumville*, Crucible, 2012

C J A Robertson, *The Origins of the Scottish Railway System*, John Donald, 1983

D Ross, *The Highland Railway*, Tempus, 2005; *The Caledonian, Scotland's Imperial Railway*, Stenlake, 2013; *The North British Railway – a History*, Stenlake, 2014

J Thomas, *The West Highland Railway*, D&C, 1965; *The Callander & Oban Railway*, D&C, 1966; *The North British Railway*, Vol. I, D&C, 1969, and Vol. II, D&C 1975; *The Skye Railway*, D&C, 1977; *Forgotten Railways, Scotland*, D&C, 1982

H A Vallance, *The Highland Railway*, revised edition D&C, 1963; *The Great North of Scotland Railway*, D&C, 1965

D Watts, Thomas Walrond-Smith, civil engineer, 1843-1919, *Joint Line* (M&GNR Society Magazine), Summer, 2021

Note that the books by Thomas (except *North British Railway* and *Forgotten Railways*) and Vallance are currently in print from House of Lochar.

Highland Railway Society

The Highland Railway Society caters for all those interested in the varied aspects of the railway, including its predecessors and its successors to the present day.

The illustrated quarterly *Highland Railway Journal* is distributed to members and contains a wide variety of articles and information. Members queries are a regular feature and details of new books, videos and models of interest are reported. The Society's publications include a series of books commemorating the 150th anniversaries of the opening of various sections of the system.

Meetings are held regularly in both Scotland and England. An annual gathering is held each September and includes a full day of talks, films, etc., as well as an opportunity to meet fellow members.

The Society has Library, Photographic and Drawing collections which are available to members. Copies of drawings are available for purchase. Modellers are well catered for. Complete kits are produced in limited runs. Specially commissioned modelling components such as axle boxes, buffers and springs are available, plus a comprehensive set of transfers to enable any Highland loco to be named.

Membership details can be found on the Society's website at www.hrsoc.org.uk.

Over recent years local volunteers have begun to restore the former Invergarry station as a working museum. It has become a place of interest on the Great Glen Way. This photograph shows what had been achieved by 2018. Further progress has been made, and the track is now extended. More details at www.invergarrystation.org.uk.

(Keith Fenwick)